EXPLODING
STAR

EXPLODING STAR

A Young Austrian Against
Hitler

FRITZ MOLDEN

Translated by Peter and Betty Ross

WILLIAM MORROW & COMPANY, INC.
NEW YORK 1979

For Hannerl

Translation copyright © Weidenfeld and Nicolson 1978

First published in Great Britain by
Weidenfeld and Nicolson

11 St John's Hill, London SW11
Originally published in Austria under the title
Fepolinski & Waschlapski, copyright © 1976 by
Verlag Fritz Molden, Wien-München-Zurich

ISBN 0–688–03381–4

Library of Congress Catalog Card Number 78–69727

Printed in Great Britain by
Willmer Brothers Limited, Rock Ferry, Merseyside

2   3   4   5   6   7   8   9   10

Contents

Foreword

The events recorded in this book are based on my own experiences and observations. Since they took place more than thirty years ago and I possess little in the way of diaries or notes dating back to that time, I have had to rely largely on memory and on the documentary evidence, much of which has fortunately been preserved. In some instances I have also had to have recourse to the accounts of my comrades and acquaintances of those days. While I have conscientiously endeavoured to adhere as closely as possible to the facts as I know them, faults of memory cannot be excluded. In respect of any such lapses I would crave the reader's indulgence.

I have not, as a rule, changed the names of individuals. In some cases, however, only their *noms de guerre* were known to me. In others, their true identity has been withheld, either in deference to the wishes of those concerned, or out of regard for their present circumstances. Nor have I used the real names of certain persons who appear in a negative light, since in writing this book it was very far from my intention to exact vengeance for events that had taken place a whole generation before.

FRITZ MOLDEN
Vienna, May 1976

1
Jacob the Elephant

'Fepolinski and Waschlapski – where's your hand gone? This is the third time I've had to speak to you about it during lunch today. It bodes ill for Jacob the Elephant!' My father's voice had risen slightly, for he was gradually losing patience with me. Already, even before we had finished our soup, I had several times broken one of the elementary rules of the luncheon table, namely that the proper place for hands was on top of, not underneath, it. I began to fear the impending punishment, for today was the day on which Jacob the Elephant's letter arrived. I had already seen it peeping out of father's coat pocket – some fifteen or twenty typewritten pages which appeared regularly at the beginning of each month. The letter came from India, for that is where Jacob the Elephant lived, and it had travelled a long way, by ship through the Suez Canal, probably via Trieste to Vienna and the Döbling post office to us at 7, Oster-leitengasse. Letters from Jacob the Elephant were an event of some magnitude in my life, and the alarming possibility that father might not be able to read me this one seemed to hang like a dark cloud over the Osterleitengasse and the springlike atmosphere pervading it.

My mother plucked at my sleeve: 'What's the matter with you today, Fepolinski? You've gone and put your hands under the table again!' Father looked grave. 'Yes,' he said, 'unfortunately Waschlapski would seem to be getting the upper hand again; I'd dearly like to know who's going to win in the end. If it's Waschlapski, then you, my lad, will simply have to spend the summer in Vienna. There's only six weeks to go now. After that we'll all be off to Lans and you'll be left behind. We shall

have to hand over Waschlapski and Fepolinski to Erna or
Mitzi; they can look after the pair of you.'

Father did not seem to be joking – far from it. And, in fact, at
this particular time things always seemed to be going wrong.
Like, for instance, the affair of the scripture teacher which, as I
remember it, ushered in a whole string of mishaps.

The teacher, a Carmelite father from the monastery in the
Silbergasse, a very nice, kindly man, was always at pains to give
his lessons a more personal slant. During one of his classes a
few days before, a girl had mentioned a young uncle of hers
who had celebrated his first mass. The good father then asked
if anyone else had relatives in the Church, a priest, or chaplain,
a monk or a sister of mercy. Two children put up their hands.
One was the proud possessor of an aunt in the Ursuline Order.
The other had a sister who attended the same class as an assistant priest's brother. As for me, I could scarcely contain myself,
having, after all, something of far greater import to announce.
All agog, I put up my hand. On being asked by the Carmelite
what it was I was in such a hurry to say, I blurted out a sensational piece of intelligence: 'My great-grandfather was pope!'

The scripture teacher instantly ceased to be nice and kind.
He boxed my ears and wrote my mother a note. Apart from
two precocious fellow pupils who had laughed fit to burst, no
one in the class appreciated the enormity of my remark. Nor
did it dawn on me until much later exactly what it was I had
come out with.

At first I was utterly confused. For had not my mother often
told me about my beautiful great-grandmother Pave, whose
portrait hung in our drawing-room and whose father or grandfather had been pope? What could there be about something
I had always thought so marvellous that suddenly made it
shameful enough to deserve a box on the ears?

It was not without truculence that I handed my mother
the scripture teacher's note when I went home at lunchtime.
Stifling her laughter, she affectionately enlightened me. Beneath
the portraits of the lovely Pave and her husband, the dashing
Pero – my great-grandfather – I was given some coaching in
family history. I now learnt that the pope I had claimed as my
great-grandfather was the celebrated Pius IX, 'Pio Nono'. This
supreme head of Christendom had come from Senigallia; in
secular life he had been Count Giovanni Mastai Ferretti and

had possessed a sister who had married a de Ponte. The fruit of that marriage had been the beautiful Pave. And it might, incidentally, my mother said, be a good thing if I were in future to give his reverence the Carmelite – not to mention other people – a more accurate account of the family's genealogy.

The mishaps which imperilled the reading of Jacob the Elephant's letter were soon followed by another which came hard on the heels of the Carmelite affair. It was springtime, already almost hot, and the chestnut trees in our garden were in full bloom. At the bottom of the large garden, my brother Otto and several other bigger boys were engaged in building a hut. I was eight at the time, Otto some six years older, and he and his friends knew how to keep me at a respectful distance. For instance, I was not allowed to play any part in the actual construction of the aforesaid hut, being called on at most to perform auxiliary tasks. I looked up admiringly to the fourteen- or fifteen-year-olds and, for a short while, numbered amongst my heroes not only Otto, but also his friend Hansi Gries, who lived in the house next to the Idealkino. This proximity to the cinema lent him a touch of raffishness. And heroic status was also accorded to Rupert Sacken, whose home was just round the corner from the Kasino Zögernitz, the local suburban dance hall.

Well, that afternoon – I remember it as though it were yesterday – Hansi Gries remarked carelessly to Otto: 'By the way, you know, I'm a Nazi now,' and, taking a swastika badge out of his coat pocket, he fastened it to his lapel.

This scene took place in May 1932.

Sacken was not very impressed. 'Nothing wonderful about that. I belong to the Young Fatherland*; they actually let you in at fourteen now.' Otto, however, was greatly agitated by Hansi Gries's statement, and embarked on a furious argument with him: 'How can you become a Nazi? It's quite impossible! You, a Schotten Grammar School† boy, become a Nazi? It's

*Young Fatherland (Jung Vaterland) was the youth division of the Heimwehr (or Heimatschutz), the ultra-right (fascist) private army of Prince Ernst Ruediger Starhemberg.

†Schottengymnasium was a famous grammar school founded in 1175 by Irish monks, erroneously called 'Scots' by the Viennese. For the past 160 years it has been run by Benedictine monks.

beyond belief! Any idea what sort of people the Nazis are?
They're the dregs – revolting! Why not join the Heimatschutz?' Hansi laughed deprecatingly: 'The Heimatschutz!
That's nothing. But being a Nazi's fine. You've no idea what
super things they've got. Even at sixteen they let you have a
motorbike. And you can go to Germany free! Anyhow, just
you wait until Hitler comes to power!'

Hansi Gries's line of reasoning seemed plausible to me. 'Hey,
Otto,' I said, 'I'm a Nazi too!' Wham, came a clout on the side
of my head, and another and another. Hansi tried to hold Otto
back and then they set about each other furiously until parted
by Rupert Sacken.

For me, the affair was not to remain without a sequel. At
suppertime Otto, who never otherwise squealed on me, told
father about my decision to become a Nazi. It was father's
evening off and might, in my view, have been far better employed than on a discussion of that afternoon's incident. For
instance, father might have told us a story. But I had a vague
premonition that nothing would come of that just now. Father
looked up, finished chewing what he had in his mouth and then
said: 'Well, Fepolinski, and why have you become a Nazi all
of a sudden – can you tell me that?' After hum-ing and ha-ing
for while, I finally admitted that the chief reason was the motor-
bikes; as for the others, I would have to get Hansi Gries to repeat them for me. Father finally expressed his relief; Hitler's
dogma, he said, had not yet taken an ineradicable hold on
Feppchen's innermost being and it woulld be possible to bring
him back onto the right course. Everyone was laughing at me.
I felt rather sheepish. Not until I was in bed with mother standing beside me, did things come right again. Every night, mother
sang me a lullaby:

> Clean and clad in white pyjamas,
> Cosy in your bed you lie,
> Envied by tigers, bears and llamas
> And also by little Hare Mandili.

The whole emphasis fell on the words 'Hare Mandili' and, as
she pronounced them, my mother gave a little jump while I
bounced up in bed. And only Hare Mandili connoisseurs can
know how securely and dreamlessly a child sleeps after that.

In those days, ticklish situations used generally to have a happy ending. And, of course, on the day of the oft-repeated reprimand, 'Where's your hand?', I did after all get to hear Jacob the Elephant's missive. 'Come into the drawing-room, Fepolinski,' said my father, 'and I'll read you the letter.' Those were magic words, the key to a whole, secret father-Fepolinski world.

When father was young and had completed his studies, he went to the University of Budapest as Reader in modern history. He was a bit lonely in Budapest, because he did not feel at all at home there. One day his wanderings took him to the Zoological Gardens and there, as is proper in a Zoological garden, he came upon an elephant – the selfsame Jacob. Father took a liking to Jacob the Elephant and in return Jacob the Elephant held father in high esteem, which was understandable, seeing that both were foreigners. These companions in misfortune struck up a close friendship beside which all the Hungarians were as nothing. In 1914 war broke out, father had to join the army, and for Jacob the Elephant life also took on a more melancholy tinge. There was not enough for an Indian elephant to eat so that the unfortunate creature grew frightfully thin. Then came 1918, the Central Powers lost the war; in Hungary, too, belts had to be tightened still further, and Jacob the Elephant, who was, after all, one of His Majesty's civil servants, was allowed to retire. He was given a small pension paid in pengös, whereupon he decided to return to his home in India where he could live quite comfortably on this income.

Loyal as always, Jacob the Elephant was reluctant to lose all contact with his friend, my father, yet could not write letters because he had no fingers, while all attempts to write with his trunk came to nothing. The problem was solved with the help of Yaromir the Monkey. Yaromir was a relation, young, agreeable and gifted, the scion of an impoverished line. Jacob the Elephant first sent him to a typewriting school in Bombay. When he had become proficient, they acquired a typewriter and once a month Jacob the Elephant dictated to Yaromir the monkey the letters he sent to father.

I have myself seen those letters, for my father read them aloud to me each month. They invariably consisted of exciting stories about Jacob the Elephant and his adventures in the jungle. About his frightful contest with the rattlesnake which was only brought to a successful conclusion by the courageous, last-minute intervention of Yaromir the Monkey. Or about the Crocodile family, its patriarch, Crocomax and his five sons, Crocodale, Crocodele, Crocodile, Crocodole and Crocodule. Not till later was a daughter, Crocodella, born to him, an occasion the happy family proposed to celebrate by eating Yaromir the Monkey for dessert. Again, the danger was narrowly averted, this time by Jacob the Elephant.

Jacob the Elephant wrote every month and only once did a letter fail to arrive. On arriving home, father said: 'Well, there's no letter from Jacob the Elephant, I'm afraid, but he's sent me a telegram.' And taking a piece of paper out of his pocket, he read: 'Yaromir the Monkey has sprained left hand stop Hence regret no letter this month stop Love from Jacob the Elephant stop.' I was relieved but at the same time sorry not to be hearing the latest story from India.

It was not till years afterwards that I realized that the 'Letters from Jacob the Elephant' were father's manuscripts for monthly talks on the Austrian radio – *A Month of World Events*. And on that one occasion, when he had read us a telegram instead of a letter, there had been no manuscript for the broadcast. It must have been early in 1934, for this was when the German Ambassador in Vienna made representations to the Austrian government, asking that father's talks be given a less anti-Nazi slant. Thereupon my father had told the Minister of Education, whose responsibility it was, that, if he could not give his talks as he saw fit, he would rather not give them at all. One broadcast was omitted as a result. At this juncture Dollfuss*, then Federal Chancellor, intervened and asked father to go on with his talks, since one could not allow a foreign power to tell one how to run one's own broadcasting system. The series was resumed and the correspondence of Jacob the Elephant went back to normal.

Jacob the Elephant and 'Fepolinski and Waschlapski from furthest Walachia' were contemporaries. They are intimately bound up with my early boyhood. To trace the genesis of my double name, denoting those 'two souls that dwell in each

*Dr Engelbert Dollfuss, leader of the Christian Social Party, was Chancellor of Austria from 1932. He was murdered by Nazi agents in the Federal Chancellery on 25 July 1934.

man's breast', is inevitably somewhat complicated. In its original form, it was the beginning of a poem by Heinrich Heine. There is no denying that I disliked the name at first but, like the rest of the family, eventually got used to it. Nor is there any doubt that Fepo, Peppchen or Fepoliski was formed by contracting my two Christian names, Fritz and Peter. In due course it was joined by Waschlapski, which, deriving as it does directly from *Waschlappen* or face-cloth, can without difficulty be traced back to the less heroic phases of my early childhood. 'From furthest Walachia', however, was my 'style'. For it was from there, after all, that the Moldens had come. However, to explain the provenance of my generation, it is necessary to mention several other parts of the far-flung Austro-Hungarian Empire. For my mother's ancestors on her father's side came from Croatia, Dalmatia and Venetia and, on her mother's, from Hungary and Carniola. My father's family stems on the distaff side from Tyrol, the Gastein Valley and Upper Austria, while his father came from Austrian Silesia, that tongue of land in the Bielitz region which remained Austrian after the Seven Years' War, when Maria Theresa was forced to cede the rest of Silesia to Prussia. This partly explains why, in our house, old Fritz was never referred to save as 'Frederick of Prussia, wrongly called the Great'. However, before settling in Bielitz, the Moldens had lived in Walachia.

I knew little about the country of my forebears; it lay far away to the east, somewhere on the Black Sea, beyond Bukovina, where there was a river called the Pruth on whose banks lay a part of Walachia known as Moldavia. It was from here that the Moldens came and they had originally been called Moldauer, that is Moldavians. Walachia was the country of my most secret dreams. There I owned wild horses, performed heroic deeds, dwelt in well-nigh impenetrable forests and, until well into secondary school, I would sometimes drop the Fepolinski and Waschlapski and style myself 'he of Walachia'.

Gradually the name Fepolinski and Waschlapski fell into disuse. Only my parents went on using it, sometimes in severe and disapproving, sometimes in tender and rather wistful, tones. And it was used on two more occasions after the war. The first was in May 1951, when my mother was in private nursing home and nearing her end. She had already undergone two operations and was growing steadily frailer and weaker. She was extraordinarily loving and affectionate. Sometimes she would ask us to read aloud to her: Rilke, whom she loved and admired and whom she had known well, or Hans Carossa. And sometimes father – and only he – would read her some of her own poetry. On this occasion we were alone together and she congratulated me on a leading article that had appeared that day in the *Presse**. She asked me to read it to her again, smiled at me very tenderly and said: 'Fepolinski and Waschlapski, how proud I am of you. Now you're writing leaders yourself. From furthest Walachia to the editorial offices of the *Presse*!' A week later she was dead.

The last time the name Fepolinski and Waschlapski was used, and by one who was entitled and authorized to do so, was two years later, at my brother Otto's wedding in the Burgkapelle in Vienna. His bride Laurence and he were married by an old family friend; throughout the ceremony father stood in the front pew, his face grave and composed. Afterwards he took me by the arm, together we went down the steps of the Hofburg-kapelle to the Schweizer Hof, and father said in his deliberate way, slightly raising his voice: 'Fepolinski and Waschlapski, you're grown-up now. It's time you began to pay heed to others. It's not something you can delegate to anyone else, nor must you delegate it to anyone else – promise me that.' He took my hand and shook it, something which he, who detested porten-tous words and gestures, never used to do. I did not quite under-stand him and nodded, somewhat confused. 'You can count on me,' I said. 'I promise.'

A bare two months later, father was also laid to rest along-side my mother in the beautiful grave the city of Vienna had provided for her in the Zentralfriedhof.

And with my parents, Fepolinski and Waschlapski also dis-appeared for, apart from the dead couple, no one had really known the Siamese twins from furthest Walachia. In their stead there was now only one grown man who, like so many other people, had to battle his way through life.

---

*Die Presse, a liberal newspaper founded in 1848, became known as the *Neue Freie Presse* after 1886. It was published by Ernst Molden from 1930-38 and again from 1945-53, after Austria's liberation from the Nazis. Fritz Molden joined the staff in 1946, became managing editor in 1950 and, after his father's death, became editor and publisher.

2
Osterleitengasse

Boyhood in Döbling, a middle-class suburb west of the city of Vienna and scattered over the slopes of the Vienna woods, during the late twenties was an exciting affair. The school in the Vormosergasse was a single-storied building and had four classrooms all told, for the four-class primary school. The building went back to the time when Döbling was still a village. A small office for the headmaster, a staff room, two wcs, one for boys and one for girls – wcs that smelt of the special brand of disinfectant, black and oily, that was used for cleaning them. The whole school reeked of it as, I believe, all Austrian schools, from Galicia to Venetia, had always reeked since the days of the old monarchy. It says much for the quality of the product manufactured by the firm of Beetz in Vienna that it continued to enjoy such popularity several decades after the collapse of imperial Austria. The Beetzian smell of the lavatories, the high classroom walls adorned with a crucifix, the catechist from the Silbergasse, all these belong to the memories of my early boyhood.

Döbling was a world in itself; there was the semi-urban central part between the Gürtel and, roughly, the Hofzeile; the proletarian quarter with its great new block of workers' flats, the Karl-Marx-Hof in Heiligenstadt, proud symbol of the red Vienna of the twenties, and, finally, the villages on the terraced vineyards of the Wienerwald, between them, orchards, vineries, vineyards and still, here and there, even cornfields.

Today, almost fifty years later, it seems scarcely conceivable that, at the end of the twenties, more horse-drawn vehicles used to pass through Döbling than motor cars. True, there were already two or three taxi ranks. One of these I knew well for, once a year, it was the starting-point of a journey. When we went to the country for the summer, we used to get into a taxi and drive to the Westbahnhof or perhaps the Südbahnhof. There were two kinds of taxi, those with a basic fare of fifty groschen and very superior ones, usually Austro-Daimlers, whose basic fare was eighty groschen. But goods vehicles were for the most part still horse-drawn. I still remember the drivers of horse-coaches who, with imprecations and much brandishing of whips, drove long files of two-wheeled carts heavily laden with flag-stones from the Mauthausen quarries, as they rumbled into town from Heiligenstadt and the landing stages of the broad-beamed, wooden barges on the Danube Canal.

I began my Döbling career – it must have been round about the autumn of 1927 – in 'Professor' Matura's famous kinder-garten in the Hohe Warte. It was an extremely cheerful and, for those days, exceptionally progressive kindergarten, run in accordance with Swiss pedagogic principles of some sort; it alarmed my grandmama's many sisters, my mother's numerous aunts, who were eternally nagging her about it. I enjoyed being there very much, not least because we had weekly puppet shows. Our Frau Matura's husband, a real professor, was not only the author of all the plays, but also the puppeteer and a maestro of extempore theatre. Everything the puppets did was to us palpable reality, until the moment when, at the edge of that reality, Professor Matura's enormous feet impinged on our field of vision.

Every day I walked home holding the hand of our kind but strict nursemaid, Erna. Holding Erna's other hand was my friend Monika of the black tresses. The first rumpus that im-printed itself on my mind happened outside the entrance of Stumpf's, the venerable bakery in Döbling High Street. At that time Monika was already a very independent young lady who resented having to be taken home. But unluckily for her she lived opposite us at No. 10, Osterleitengasse, and was unable to shake off the conscientious Erna. She would display endless ingenuity; this particular day, for instance, she said she had just got to nip round the corner and see her grandparents in the Pokornygasse. Monika's grandfather was a famous anatomist. He had a long white beard, always wore a big, round, black bowler hat, a black bow tie, a black suit and a snowy white shirt, and carried a beautiful cane. He was sometimes accompanied on his daily walks by my grandfather, who likewise had a long white beard and wore a black suit, but never a hard hat. Grandfather's hat, also black, had a soft brim, and recalled the hats worn in Bismarck's day.

Erna was adamant; Monika had got to accompany us to the Osterleitengasse. Increasingly stubborn, Monika said no; she was going to see her grandparents; the argument grew more heated, Monkia's struggles to get away more desperate, Erna's grip more inflexible. Then, plaits flying, Monika darted down her head and furiously sank her teeth into poor Erna's thumb, blood began to flow and, with the last of our strength, we tottered into Frau Schlegel's toyshop, where first aid was administered to Erna.

Monika was boxed on the ears several times, first by Erna and then by her mother, dear Aunt Miez, a very beautiful woman whose hair had been white for as long as I could remember.

But sometimes going to kindergarten, when I was taken or fetched by my mother, would be an experience of a special kind. A wonderful world would open up before me, for mother would tell me stories – though whether they were true or not, I cannot say. Probably they were born of the mood of the moment. Whatever the case, I was happy and content, holding her hand and listening to her voice as we walked through the big market gardens that lay between the Hohe Warte and the line of the old suburbs, or made our way home to the Osterleitengasse through the Werthheimstein-park.

At home there was Mia. Even if she happened not to be in, her presence there was real, as indeed it still is. Mia, the joy of all Molden children, had already looked after Uncle Richard, father's younger brother, as she was then looking after Otto and me. She also took care of my daughters Gabriella, Sascha and Andrea and my brother's children, Peter and Paula, while today I still have the happiness of hearing my small sons, Ernst and Berthold, shout with glee when the garden gate opens and Mia, only a little bowed, comes in with short, rapid steps.

In my day, Mia lived in a strange, ornate, wonderful cornucopia of a house in the midst of vineyards half way up the Kahlenberg. There was only one other house in the vicinity, Herr Neunteufel's diminutive inn, *Zur schönen Aussicht*, complete with dogs, cats, goats, and rabbits. The delight of us children at having the run of such a paradise when permitted to spend the weekend at Mia's, or even go there after school, was almost indescribable.

Mia also had a husband who, for simplicity's sake, had always been known to all the Molden children as 'Mias Mann', 'Mia's husband'. He had been boilerman at the Nussdorf brewery and, when this closed down as a result of the great crisis in the late twenties, he had bought a second-hand 'autotrike', thus making himself more or less independent. Autotrikes are no longer obtainable. They were curious vehicles, like a motorcycle with two seats at the back and, in front, two wheels side by side, over which a large box was suspended. It was a kind of miniature van and was used by Mia's husband for business purposes.

At weekends the autotrike became of paramount importance to us children. The moment would come when Mia's husband would pick up each of us boys in turn and dump him in the box on the autotrike, Mia would seat herself behind him and thus we would travel through Nussdorf and Klosterneuburg to Weidling and then up a little side valley where Mia's brother-in-law had a cottage on an allotment in the middle of the woods. There weren't just rabbits there, but real live deer as well; the water had to be pumped from a well, we ate Schnitzel and potato salad out of little glass dishes. Lying tired in bed on Sunday night in the Osterleitengasse, I would try and decide what I'd enjoyed most until this exercise sent me to sleep.

Today the house of my childhood – still almost unchanged – is lived in by my brother and his family. Hence I cannot say with certainty which were the impressions I obtained in early childhood and which have simply accumulated with the passage of time. My parents went to live at 7, Osterleitengasse in 1924, the year of my birth. The date of the house is about 1740. It was originally a single-storied building which was reconstructed in about 1800 and further added to in 1835. Since then the large, two-storied house in its Viennese suburb has remained virtually unaltered, lived in by respectable merchants' or craftsmen's families.

Next to it there is still a small wine merchant's business, while on the other side there used to be large stables; beyond

this, and on the other side of the road, are other decent, bur-
ghers' houses with gardens such as befitted the wholesome
world of the early nineteenth century. Behind our house, too,
there was a big garden, somewhat unkempt, with lots of lilac
bushes, little paths and the remains of a once magnificent
avenue of trees. At one time that avenue used to lead up from
the Danube to Maria Theresa's little chateau, and the Empress
herself is said to have used it when, having left the city by boat,
she rode up there from Heiligenstadt. In our imagination, the
ten magnificent chestnut trees lent imperial glamour to our wild
garden. Not that this prevented us from using the drive, still
recognizable between the trees, as a football ground or a centre
for our Red Indian battles.

We occupied nearly all the first floor of the old house. Even
today when, on a warm summer evening, I lean out of the windows hung with white spotted muslin, I seem to see the warm,
peaceful glow of the seven or eight gas lamps that used to
illuminate the secure world of the Osterleitengasse. One day –
it must have been in 1934 or 1935 – the gas lamps were up-
rooted and replaced by big, electric arc lamps. So outraged
was my mother that she wrote about it the following poem, of
which I am very fond.

> Time was when, with the fall of night,
> My room in darkness lay,
> Save only for the star-dust light
> Of the distant Milky Way.
>
> But arc lamps now invade our street,
> And batter our window bars,
> Putting the night into retreat
> And driving away my stars.
>
> Round the sleeping house they blare
> In strident fanfaronade.
> Nothing keeps out their lurid glare,
> Not curtains or shutters or shade.
>
> Cast these idols down, O Lord,
> Give heed unto our cry;
> Let blessed darkness be restored
> And with it our starry sky.

The largest and grandest house in the Osterleitengasse belonged to the imposing Herr Schlesinger, general manager of the Phoenix, an insurance company which, in the aftermath of the great economic crisis of May 1931 when even the Creditanstalt Bank felt the wind, was to become the centre of a scandal. I still recall my parents' converations on the subject, not that we boys understood very much. Every day at lunchime father came home from the editorial offices of the *Neue Freie Presse*, bringing with him news of the outside world. My mother would listen attentively and ask questions, and I believe that father secretly enjoyed having to initiate her into practical matters such as cabinet crises, political changes and the intricacies of railway time tables. These were things about which mother, the family's great fount of wisdom, knew little or nothing.

Her great influence upon us was her deeply-held religious faith, which she had at one time lost, but which she recovered at some time during my kindergarten days, and was able to pass on with a sure touch to her sons. Father told me later that she had had to wrestle with herself before arriving at the modern, uncomplicated form of Catholicism from which she derived so much assurance and which she was able to pass on, not only to her children, but also to her husband. For my father, with his liberal background, this confrontation with metaphysics was a momentous step. His father had been an atheist who, in many of his books, had disputed the existence of God.

My grandfather, incidentally, had a heart of gold. Nevertheless, to us children he always remained somewhat alien and aloof. He was, I think, severe without knowing it and, although he loved me, I always stood in great awe of him. Years later, in 1942, I came upon him lying dead in the street. He had fallen from the second floor of his house in Döbling High Street, and we never knew whether Hofrat Berthold Molden, then ninety years old, had leant out too far to observe the weather, or whether he had voluntarily taken leave of life. When I saw my grandfather lying there, small and frail, with no external injuries, childlike despite his age and white beard, I experienced for the first time a profound tenderness towards him such as I had never really dared to feel while he was alive.

Peaceful though the world of the Osterleitengasse was during the days of my early childhood, the world outside had already ceased to be so, and sometimes the glare of its flames reached as far as Döbling. It was in 1927 that buxom Julie, our cook, suddenly seized me by the hand, hurried me up to the attic and made me poke my little head out of the skylight. Above and beyond the roof of the Krünes' house, we saw flames and a great deal of smoke. Later I was told by Frau Maceovich, our smartly turned out costerwoman, that what I had then seen – in the summer of 1927 – had been the burning of the Palace of Justice*. The first premonition of civil war and of the future terrible course of events was written in the flames that flickered above Vienna from the burning Palace of Justice.

When we went away for our summer holiday, the spectre was forgotten and we children heard nothing more about the gravity of the political situation. Sometimes father stayed behind or else had to leave earlier or come back later, but we never stopped to wonder why.

That year our parents had taken a villa in Prein, a small summer resort some eighty kilometres south of Vienna, on the southern fringe of the Alps not far from the Semmering and next to the proud, lofty Rax, the mountain which the Viennese call their own. At that time Prein was a small village; our villa was close to the church and possessed a wonderful asset in the shape of a flat roof, a flat roof, moreover, upon which one could walk about, since it had trelliswork all round it – closely meshed trelliswork, so that even I, a small boy, could be left alone up there.

There were plenty of children to play with at Prein. Otto was there, of course, and our cousin, Niki Preradović, the son of Uncle Ivo, mother's eldest brother. At Prein, Otto and Niki started the Nikotto Circus, whose only initial adjuncts were an unusually attractive name and a poster which the two of them had pinned to the parish notice board: 'Tonight the Nikotto Circus will put on a grand performance. Entrance 20 groschen, commences 7 o'clock.' Punctually at the hour a number of summer visitors appeared in our garden genuinely expecting some kind of circus, whereupon its two surprised managers, Niki and Otto, set about giving an extempore performance. I was the only available star and was employed in multiple roles; they wanted me to be the lion as well as the horse upon which they

---

*The Palace of Justice was set on fire by revolutionary social-democratic demonstrators in July 1927.

rode, but I objected and was thrashed for my pains, a fate I frequently suffered at that time. At the end of the performance I had to pass the hat round.

At Prein my whipping boy's existence was shared by a tubby little girl called Lori Possanner. Some years later, slim, beautiful and every inch a lady, she was to queen it over Milan. But in the summer of 1927 she was horribly teased by Otto and Niki because of her puppy fat and subjected to appalling practical jokes. Lori suffered the climax of martyrdom in the raspberry thicket above the village. Otto, Niki and I hauled her halfway up the steep slope, whereupon we all ran off home, leaving Lori behind, unable to move because of her girth. For hours the poor little creature sat crying amongst the raspberry bushes which scratched her skin and tore her clothes. Only towards evening was she missed by her mother and mine, and eventually found after a long search. This time it was Otto and Niki who were thrashed.

Later, there were summer holidays on the Adriatic. Mother had grown up at Pola, the daughter of Dušan von Preradović, an officer in the Imperial and Royal Navy – the daughter of pirates, as she once called herself in *Buccaneers*, one of her finest poems. She adored Dalmatia, Istria, the *macchia* of the Adriatic landscape. Her childhood by the sea had been one of the happiest chapters in her life, so much so that one cycle of her poems is entitled *Childhood by the Sea*. She intended to write a big trilogy of novels devoted to this subject, but was fated never to do so. And she wished her sons to enjoy a childhood by the sea and, in some small measure at any rate, the bliss she had herself experienced.

Almost every year mother used to go to far-off Dalmatia, or else to Istria. She had many relations and friends in those parts – her beloved brother, Ivo, or her brother Peter, who lived at Zagreb, the capital of Croatia. At Solitudo near Ragusa, or at Divulje, or staying with Ivo at Sette Castelli, she would sit by the sea and go for walks along the beach or through the *macchia*, able to think, dream and, above all, write. Sometimes father accompanied her, and later on we boys would go too. An unforgettable summer was the one we spent in Castel Stari between Spalato and Trogir. At nearby Divulje, the air base of the Royal Yugoslav Navy, Uncle Ivo was commander. It was altogether very grand; Ivo had a motor-boat at his personal disposal, also a chauffeur and a secretary, and wore a magnificent, gleaming white uniform. At that time Uncle Ivo was to me a hero beyond compare; I worshipped him madly.

Once he let me spend two days on board his ship. He commanded the *Dalmatia*, the only cruiser the Yugoslavs had. A summer or two later we were at Yelsa on Hvar Island when dashing, incomparable Uncle Ivo actually landed a seaplane in the bay where we used to bathe. For days we were the centre of interest. Who can describe my pride when my Uncle Ivo settled me in the amphibian and, instead of taking it up as if it were any old aircraft, proceeded to race it across the bay on its floats?

So intense was the quality of those Dalmatian summers that they are almost palpable to me even now – the heat, the cicadas, mother's serene, happy face, the little bottles we used to fill with sea water to take back to Vienna, the violent thunder storms, Uncle Ivo, the fishermen who sometimes took me mackerel fishing.

Again, it was during those southern summers in the thirties that the scales fell from my eyes where girls were concerned. Up till then there had been a uniform category of sisterly or cousinly Monikas, Justines or Loris whose company was neither particularly desirable nor particularly to be shunned. One's attitude to them was one of indifference – they were a fact of life – with a single exception, Lucie Hahn. We were both pupils at the primary school in the Vormosergasse, and so besotted was I that I once actually bought her an ice lolly out of my pocket money. I believe that ice lolly cost ten groschen. She had promised me a kiss in return and kept her promise, if very fleetingly. At all events, I walked away bursting with pride – and barely five minutes later I saw Lucie presenting my ice lolly to another boy.

The rumblings that heralded the approach of a more evil world had already been audible even in my nursery. In the winter of 1933–34 I went to the Neuland School; my mother had taken me away from the primary school in the Vormosergasse, mainly because she thought I was acquiring too much of an accent there. In that respect, her choice of the Neuland School in the Kaasgraben turned out to be a mistake, for whereas the pupils in the Vormosergasse consisted principally of middle class and Jewish children from the residential parts of Döbling, the markedly Catholic Neuland School was attended mainly by poor children from the working-class district. There were no fees, needy children could stay as part-boarders and were given their lunch for nothing. Such relief did those free lunches afford many families in the thirties that even good Social Democrats forgot their principles and registered their children at Catholic schools.

On 12 February 1934, I was sitting on the school bench next to my friend Karli Speta, son of a builders' foreman from the Barawitzkagasse, and behind my other chum, Richard Jicha, when suddenly the lights went out. It must have been during the second lesson. Shortly afterwards Anna Ehm, the headmistress, appeared and told the teacher to send us home at once as there was a general strike. Karli Speta and I, delighted at the unexpected holiday, left school and made for the big tram depot in the Grinzinger Allee. The trams were not running, their drivers were standing outside the gates: general strike. On we went, the day was beginning to clear up a little, the grey February weather to become a bit more clement, and Karli and I decided to go to the sports ground in the Hohe Warte.

The Hohe Warte sports ground was the home of the Vienna Football Club and the scene of its glorious victories. It was a club my father had supported as a student, and among whose ardent fans I too was numbered. In those days the interest of Austrians, or at any rate of the majority of Viennese, was centred almost solely on football, as it now is on skiing. Feelings ran high, for every club boasted tens of thousands of supporters. Quite ordinary games drew gates of thirty or forty thousand. Those were the bitter days of unemployment; even on weekdays, when I would sometimes go to the Hohe Warte to watch a championship match after school, ten or twelve thousand unemployed workers' tickets might be sold at that ground alone. In Austria, football was the sport of the little man who, even if unemployed, would rather go without a meal than miss a big match.

On that February morning, then, Karli Speta and I hurried to the Hohe Warte to kick a ball about on the training ground there. The boys' trainer of the 'Vienna' knew us, of course, as we were shortly due for admission to the schoolboys' team, and he would sometimes let us practise. Today he and a bunch of players were standing beside a small doorway that led into the training ground. On seeing us approach, he yelled: 'Clear off, lads. High time you were at home. There'll be shooting here any moment now.'

We didn't understand what it was he was trying to tell us. Then suddenly, up above us, next to the meteorological station, we saw uniformed figures – soldiers and Heimwehr men. One of the latter, a friend of my brother's, recognized me and called out telling me to go home at once; I'd no business to be out in the streets today.

But first we decided to go back to the Barawitzkagasse where Karli Speta lived. We still hadn't grasped what was really going on. Suddenly we heard shots from the direction of the Karl-Marx-Hof* a little way below us. Startled, we ran home to Karli's, a big, grey tenement dating from the turn of the century which had always attracted me because of its sink and w.c. in the passageway, not to mention kindly Frau Speta herself, a memorable cook. Karli's mother, as agitated as we were, packed me off home. My mother would be in an awful state, she said.

I ran down to the Heiligenstädter Strasse, past the Wertheimsteinpark, with the intention of climbing the steps leading up to the Weilgasse, but I had no luck – fighting was already in progress there. A few Heimwehr men were posted down below, while at the top shots were coming from the Social Democratic workers' flats in which the Schutzbund† men had barricaded themselves.

'Buzz off home, yer little bastard!' a Heimwehr man snarled. I ran off, my heart pounding, to the Radlmayergasse and from there was at last able to reach home unscathed via Döbling High Street. Mother welcomed me with floods of tears. In imagination she had already seen me bloody and dying amidst the street fighting of the civil war.

For those who lived in the Osterleitengasse, the shots and

*The Karl-Marx-Hof was a very large municipal apartment building, built in 1929 by Vienna's socialist county council.

†The Schutzbund was a leftish private army founded by the Social Democratic Party after the First World War. It was the left-wing counterpart to the right-wing fascist Heimwehr units.

gunfire of the February rising soon became a part of their every-day existence. At no great distance from us the Karl-Marx-Hof was being shelled, further off we could hear artillery fire from the Danube, where there was heavy fighting round another block of workers' flats, the Goethehof. The shooting in the Weilgasse went on for two more nights, until the workers' centre had finally been taken. Four days later the civil war was over. The Federal Chancellor, Dollfuss, whom we boys had until then regarded merely as a target for jokes about his diminutive size, had won the civil war against the workers. But it was a Pyrrhic victory, as soon became apparent. Dollfuss had des-troyed democracy to save Austria from National Socialism; the means he employed were inept and the methods wrong. Five months later Dollfuss himself was killed by the bullets of Otto Planetta and his Nazi terrorists. The entire western world had condemned Dollfuss for his bloody repression of the workers' rising in February 1934. It was considerably less perturbed when the little Chancellor himself fell victim to assassins five months later.

I remember how fond my father used to be of going to Klosterneuberg to see his cousin and close friend, Dr Karl Straubinger, then a youthful head of department in the Ministry of Agriculture. We boys were sometimes allowed to go too, to play with our cousin Herta. In the drawing-room a party of men would sit discussing politics; next to the master of the house would be father with, on his other side, the then Minister of Agriculture and future Chancellor, Dr Engelbert Dollfuss.

I was with mother in the Tyrol when Dollfuss was murdered. Together with some of my parents' friends we were staying at Emperor Maxmilian's beautiful hunting lodge at Kühtai, al-most two thousand metres up between Sellraintal and Ötztal. I was already old enough to be allowed to sit and listen to the conversation of this group of remarkable men and women, and found it highly stimulating. But I also used to go marmot hunt-ing or bathing in the ice-cold glacier lakes with my friends, the sons of Graf Stolberg, to whom the hunting lodge belonged.

My father was in Vienna at the time of the assassination. After having tried for hours to ring us up at Kühtai, he eventu-ally got through. He would not be coming to the Tyrol, he told mother, for the murder of Dollfuss would plunge the country in to civil war again; a German invasion was anticipated.

Otto was staying with friends at Zell am See and, immediately after the outrage, volunteered for service with the local Heimatschutz, which meant that he would now be standing guard outside some barracks or other to prevent the Nazis seizing power in the Salzburg district.

Hitler's shadow fell across Austria. At that time I did not, of course, know all the political ins and outs of the situation. One thing, however, I did know, and that was that the Nazis were bad.

On 1 May 1934, before an audience of forty or fifty thousand boys and girls in the Vienna stadium, Dollfuss had most impressively proclaimed Austria's determination to resist National Socialism. He had never meant very much to me or to thousands of other children, but the little man of almost dwarflike stature, who had the courage to defy the remote and powerful Hitler, made a profound impression on us. And three months later he was killed by the Nazis.

Nevertheless, National Socialism had suffered its first serious setback. The seizure of power in Austria had gone awry.

Some time before, in the autumn of 1933, father had taken Otto and me to Am Hof in the Inner City where a modern building housed the headquarters of a new organization calling itself the Fatherland Front. Father had for a long time been vice-chairman of the Austro-German People's League, a supraparty association to which Social Democrats like Renner, Christian Socials like Seipel, and Liberals like the Federal President, Hainisch, had belonged. In the summer of 1933 my father, who had been deeply upset by Hitler's accession to power in Germany, had resigned from his post of vice-chairman of this pan-German association and decided to join the Fatherland Front. While he considered it imperative to rally all forces against Hitler, he most emphatically rejected the means employed in repressing the workers' rising. This brought him into some conflict with Dollfuss despite the fact that he was on friendly terms with him, as he was later to be with his successor, Schuschnigg*. Dollfuss had founded the Fatherland Front as a militant organization for the defence of Austria's independence.

*Dr Kurt von Schuschnigg was a Christian Social politician, who became Austrian Federal Chancellor from 1934-38. He was arrested by Hitler when he tried to resist him.

Inside the Fatherland Front building father took us to the office of the then general secretary, who handed me a triangular red, white and red badge, adorned with oak leaves and bearing the inscription 'Be united'. Deeply though this impressed me, I was still no wiser about current events than I had previously been. But through listening to conversations between my father and his friends, and hearing the news brought home by Otto, I became convinced while I was still very young that there was something fundamentally wrong about the Nazis, a conviction that was to help me weather the years between 1938 and 1945.

Austria was then a country utterly divided against itself. Today the extent to which people had become politically motivated can no longer be conceived. So much was this the case that not even the everyday existence of us children was immune. Ten-year-old boys would bloody each other's noses for differences of political opinion. In our class, the second form of a primary school, scarcely a week went by without there being an ugly set-to between Nazis and Blacks, as the followers of Dollfuss and Schuschnigg were called. At other schools there were brawls between Nazis and Sozis (Social Democrats) or between Sozis and Blacks. This intense political consciousness permeated all social levels and all age groups. Everyone in Austria had to profess a political opinion, whether he wanted to or not, which made it all the harder for people to hold their tongues in 1938, as many had in fact been forced to do since 1934.

The political fanaticism which disrupted the country following the defeat of the First World War is readily explicable. For six hundred years Austria had been a great power, only to find herself in 1918 suddenly left an unviable, rumplike extension, a mere remnant. 'Austria is what remains,' Clemenceau had said when the peace treaty was signed at St Germain in 1919. What remained of the second largest empire in Europe, the old Austro-Hungarian monarchy, was a little sausage-shaped country between Lake Constance and the Neusiedlersee, nor did its barely six million inhabitants know why they were suddenly supposed to constitute a nation. No less than fifty million subjects of the former Dual Monarchy now found themselves in the latter's successor states and it was they who got the best of the bargain; little, newborn Austria was left with the debts, the burdens, and all the aftermath of a lost war. Small wonder that Austrians were discontented with their lot and failed to come to terms with it. It was a fate the full implications of which were beyond the comprehension and competence of those who had grown up in the old Austria.

The First World War gave rise to a polarization of forces such as could never before have occurred in Austria, notwithstanding all the fanaticism generated by different ideologies, religions and the various national camps. The common bond that held all these together, the ruling dynasty, had disappeared. The old army, in whose keeping Austria had been, was no more.

What remained was hundreds upon thousands of civil servants whose employer, the erstwhile Empire, had disappeared but whose pensions and wages had to be paid by the new Austria. What remained was tens upon thousands of officers and NCOs accustomed to defending a world empire and fighting for the monarchy on the battlefields of Europe and who suddenly found themselves roaming the streets, workless, despised and reviled. What remained was chaos; political antagonism between the various camps, hatred between Reds and Blacks, between Clericals and anti-Clericals. And there still lingered the dreams of a Ritter von Schönerer, dreams of a pan-German fatherland. How much more logical it must have seemed to people in 1919 to integrate with Germany what was clearly an unviable Austria than to leave the hopeless 'rumplike extension' to struggle on its own.

We were fortunate in having a father who kept aloof from political passions. His guiding principles were liberalism, justice and, in the second half of his life, religious faith. He had never belonged to a political party and had preserved the gift of looking at things objectively. In the thirties this was a rare quality and one not held in high esteem. 'Be my brother, mate, else I'll smash your pate' was the political order of the day, and not in Austria alone. Father could not and would not accept it and always tried to bring up his sons to see the world through his eyes.

One of the advantages of our parental home was that, to Otto and me, political terms such as National Socialism, Fatherland Front, Austrian corporate state, Little Entente, Western powers, Abyssinia, the Duce, the Führer, became as familiar as the twice times table. All these things were talked about daily by my parents, and this was fortunate, for later on it was to help us understand the world when it seemed to be falling apart.

Again, at school, there was constant talk of politics. Indeed, everywhere people were always talking politics, no doubt precisely because of its having been forbidden since 1933. Public houses sported notices such as 'Drink and eat here at your ease, but leave out politics if you please!' or again, 'If a scoundrel you would meet, A copper's nark is hard to beat.'

The political joke enjoyed a happy revival. Today political jokes are rare, as a result, no doubt, of parliamentary democracy. When political events take place in public, their every detail being ventilated in parliament, in the press and in the mass media, jokes do not thrive so well. A more favourable breeding ground for jokes is provided by a dictatorship where they are, after all, the only vehicle for the free and irrepressible expression of opinion. From 1933 onwards, therefore, when the authoritarian state was coming into being under Dollfuss and Schuschnigg, the political joke was bound to experience a renaissance such as had not been seen in Austria since the strict censorship of the years before 1848. Even during the First World War, in what was known as the 'four nations' prison' of Austria-Hungary, it was possible for a newspaper like the *Fackel* to appear, while prior to 1914 there had been no censorship of the press in Austria. Now, however, there was – first during the regime of that miniature Metternich, Dr Engelbert Dollfuss, and afterwards under the well-meaning but then quite humourless Dr Kurt von Schuschnigg, the difficulty of whose task in the thirties caused him to take a gloomy view of the world. Not until after the *Anschluss* did suffering enable him to attain true greatness and acquire that invaluable gift, a sense of humour, which he possessed to such a high degree.

In 1935 I joined the 'Neuland' youth movement. The Neuland was a Catholic organization founded by two young Viennese clerics, Dr Michael Pfliegler and Dr Karl Rudolf, with a view to liturgical reform, which evolved into a modern Catholic movement with a strong ideological slant. Founded in the twenties, its first real breakthrough came when the Neuland School was built thanks to the efforts of the movement's mentor Dr Karl Rudolf, as also to those of Anna Ehm and a number of other friends.

The school was a modern building, designed by Professor Clemens Holzmeister. The pupils, teachers and instructors called one another by their Christian names and addressed each other familiarly as '*du*' (thou). There were regular excursions, memorable expeditions into the countryside that often lasted several days.

We went in for a great deal of sport and every morning we all attended mass together; the services were read simultaneously in German and Latin, which was regarded as an altogether revolutionary innovation. The altar in the Neuland School chapel was, even then, in a central position and the priest said mass facing the congregation. This new trend inevitably attracted young people to whom the much ossified clericalism of the Dual Monarchy and of the established church had nothing fundamental to offer. During the first ten years the Neuland group was quantitatively small but qualitatively of a high standard. Then the number of Neuland groups began to grow rapidly and, in the early thirties, the Neuland youth movement was forging ahead at a pace scarcely conceivable in the seventies when young people are totally uninterested in youth groups of whatever description.

The prerequisites for the commitment of young people to ideas of all kinds were, it is true, incomparably better in those days. Our energy was not expended on watching television. No one was rich enough to travel about the world by motor car or aeroplane. Even skiing was beyond the means of most people, primarily because it involved travelling to the mountains by train. Young people in 1930 played football or, at most, went swimming in one of the free municipal pools. Much that is taken for granted today had not been discovered, and much was taken for granted that is wholly unknown today.

My experience of the cinema goes back to the early days of the silent film. But soon 'My brother makes the noises for the talkies' was all the rage and commonly heard in cafés. I still recall the small orchestra, usually consisting of two or three musicians, which, in the days of my youth, was posted beneath the screen of the Idealkino in Döbling and underlined in music what was happening in the film.

The wireless of those days consisted of a small black box with a knob enabling one to regulate the volume, and headphones through which one could only obtain Ravag, the

Austrian broadcasting company which remained in existence until 1938. Thanks to the contraption known as a crystal set, the scarlatina I caught at the age of five was, for me, an unforgettable experience, even if the strict quarantine it involved was a sore trial to my mother's patience. With breathless excitement, I listened to transmissions punctuated by crackles and squeaks, and became completely infatuated with the new medium.

Not till much later, in 1937, did father give the family a wireless for Christmas, a proper receiver with a loudspeaker, on which several stations could be obtained and to which more than one person could listen at a time. This present did not occupy any great place in our lives. Only after Hitler's invasion of Austria was it released from the corner of the drawing-room, where it had spent its loveless days, to become the centre of our day-to-day existence. For then it became our gateway to the world – Radio Beromünster*, initially also Bratislava and Budapest, then London, Paris, for a while, and, finally, the 'Voice of America'. To these stations people would tune in day after day, despite the heavy sentences imposed for listening to enemy broadcasts, and in this way the radio became the secret hub of thousands of households.

Daily newspapers had always played an important role in the Osterleitengasse. Quantities of them would lie strewn about all over the house. In the late twenties and early thirties there were sometimes as many as thirty dailies appearing in Vienna – morning papers, midday papers, afternoon papers, evening papers and late night editions. There were also sporting papers that appeared two or three times a day. The *Sporttagblatt* and the *Sporttelegraph*, printed on green paper, satisfied the tremendous thirst for information of young football fans like myself.

There were besides a number of children's coloured comics; one, called the *Papagei*, was sold by a disabled soldier at the number 38 tramstop by the Schottentor. 'Comics, ten groschen, the *Papagei*, ten groschen, comics, ten groschen!' His hoarse voice still rings in my ears each time I pass that spot.

Another of the marvels that have vanished from children's lives is the magic lantern, a large contraption with which father

*The Swiss German-language radio station.

sometimes gave shows on Sunday afternoons, when he would project slides onto a white screen. All agog, we would sit watching in the darkened room, tensely awaiting the inevitable moment when, to father's annoyance, the thing would overheat and cease to function. He was never on easy terms with anything the least technical. In the early thirties someone presented him with a film projector. Since he did not own a ciné camera. he borrowed one from a friend so as to film the family in the minutest detail. At last the day came when we were to see the film, but after a minute or two the projector blew up, the film caught fire and the house in the Osterleitengasse was within an ace of being reduced to ashes. With a shrug and the words 'I never could cope with these modern gadgets,' father renounced his function as a producer of home-made films.

Since the availability of spare-time pursuits for the young was limited by comparison with today, the most obvious thing to do was to expand one's intellectual interests and, since politics was such a dominant factor in everyday life, join a political group at a comparatively early age. We considered it quite normal to be politically committed by the age of fifteen if not before, whether to Social Democracy or to National Socialism. Or alternatively to the Heimatschutz, Sturmscharen or the Freiheitsbund, all of whose followers were also known, in the political jargon of the thirties, as 'Blacks' or 'Fatherlanders', although they did, of course, differ and from time to time fight each other. The Heimatschutz was the strongest and most militant of these organizations, with a distinct tendency towards the Italian brand of fascism; the 'Ostmärkische Sturmscharen' were set up as it were in competition by the authoritarian wing of the Christian Socials, while the Freiheitsbund was the uniformed organization of the Christian trade unions who rejected Fascism outright. There were also other groups such as the Communists, who, however, were never of any importance in Austria, or again the numerically strong Zionists.

In Vienna at this time there were 200,000 Jews, almost all of whom could be said to belong to the section of the population that comprised the intellectuals, the culturally active and those primarily interested in politics and commerce. The Viennese Jews were split into two distinct and violently opposing schools of thought – Zionists and assimilationists. Some of the latter were believing, orthodox Jews, some were Catholics or even Protestants, many were liberal agnostics, but common to all was the idea of assimilation; in other words, they consciously desired to be Austrians or Germans – and nothing else. For almost two generations their conflict with the Zionists had formed part of the political and cultural scene in Vienna.

At my school there were several Jewish boys, two of whom were Zionists; in 1938 they and their parents promptly emigrated to Palestine. Two others belonged to families that had long been assimilated and had lived in Vienna for generations, so that the thought of vegetating in the deserts of Palestine dressed up as peasants seemed to them ludicrous. The fathers of these schoolmates of mine had served at the front as officers during the First World War and one, in fact, had been killed. Even later on, after the *Anschluss,* these families could not bring themselves to leave, and all died in Auschwitz or Theresienstadt. One of my friends did succeed in escaping and reaching Italy; he was liberated at the eleventh hour by the Americans and survived. Today he lives in the United States.

But because their roots in Austria went so deep, many felt a blithe confidence which was to prove their undoing. Unlike the Zionists, who in the early thirties had already begun to regard Austria simply as a place of transit, many of the assimilated Jews were actually unaware of their Jewish origin. Up till 1938 it had been something that had not mattered in the least.

Nor did my brother Otto and I learn that we had Jews amongst our forebears until obligatory certificates of Aryanism were introduced in the Third Reich. Our great-grandfather Wilhelm Molden of Bielitz was a furrier. Every winter he would travel by horse-drawn sledge from Bielitz to the fur market in St Petersburg. When his son, Berthold Molden, matriculated, he gave him a magnificent beaver coat which was still worn by my father and which, despite its venerable age of over a century, I myself reverently wear in cold winters. We had, of course, heard stories of this kind about our great-grandfather but that, although baptised, he was of Jewish origin, was something we did not know. Father undoubtedly knew about it, but it was of no concern to him. Anyone familiar with the world in which Ernst Molden lived would understand why it took a Hitler to make my father pay any heed to questions of race.

Shortly after the First World War my father joined the editorial staff of the *Neue Freie Presse*. He had originally studied
history and, after obtaining his doctorate, had worked at the
Institute for Austrian Historical Research. In 1912 he was appointed Reader in history at Eötvös College, Budapest University, where he remained until war broke out. At this juncture
his father, Berthold Molden, was appointed *Hofrat* in charge of
the Press Division in the Foreign Ministry.

Berthold Molden was one of a group of advisers brought
together as a kind of shadow cabinet at the Belvedere Palace in
Vienna by Archduke Franz Ferdinand, heir-apparent to the
throne of Austria-Hungary, who was assassinated with his wife
at Sarajevo on 28 June 1914. There is still in existence an old
document handed by my grandfather to the Austrian Foreign
Minister Count Berchthold, on 7 July 1914, which formed the
basis of the Austrian ultimatum to Serbia and which, in its way,
was a contribution to the outbreak of the First World War.
During that war, my grandfather was concerned with journal-
istic and, to some extent, political matters at the Ballhausplatz,
and this resulted in his being arraigned as a 'war criminal' in
the propaganda put out by the victorious allies.

When the First World War broke out, father enlisted in the
4th Imperial and Royal Infantry Regiment, the Hoch-und
Deutschmeister, which was traditionally linked with Vienna.
He was sent for training to Kiralyhida near Bruck on the
Leitha. From there he was soon transferred to Vienna University Hospital, which is how he happened to meet my mother
who had volunteered as a nurse. Early in 1915 father was on
the point of being sent to the front in Galicia with a replace-
ment battalion of his regiment when his younger brother
Richard, law student and an officer cadet in the Imperial Army,
was killed during one of the big Russian offensives in the Car-
pathians. According to a law then in force, a family's only sur-
viving son was not required to serve at the front. Not long
afterwards, father was appointed to a post in the Foreign
Ministry and, in 1916, became an attaché at the Austrian Embassy in Copenhagen. While there he took part in the negotiations that paved the way for the Peace of Brest-Litovsk between
Russia and the Central Powers. Before leaving for Copenhagen,
he had married my mother, Paula von Preradović, and it was
in March 1918 that my brother Otto was born.

At the end of the war, father was transferred to the Hague in neutral Holland, only to be recalled to Vienna by Otto Bauer, then Minister of State for Foreign Affairs, so that he could join the Austrian delegation to the peace negotiations at St Germain. Differences of opinion arose between him and Otto Bauer and my father left the foreign service. Evidently the Moldens never stuck it for very long at the Foreign Ministry; twenty-five years later I myself was to quit the Ballhausplatz after a brief spell there. My father was offered the chair of modern European history at the University of Peking and would have been happy to accept. However, not only had the war been lost, but the family fortunes also. Both my grandfathers, Berthold Molden, *Hofrat* and journalist, and Dušan Preradović, officer in the Imperial Navy and scientist, had put their life's savings into War Loan and had now lost the whole lot.

No one had any money and there were two families to feed. A year was to elapse before Berthold Molden, dubbed a war criminal, could once more establish himself in Vienna as leader-writer on the *Volkszeitung*. Much to his chagrin father had to turn down the appointment in Peking. His dream of making a career in the academic world was quickly over, and throughout his life he was to feel a twinge of regret whenever China was mentioned.

It was at this juncture that Moriz Benedikt appeared on the scene – the legendary Moriz Benedikt, brilliant self-made man, whose family had come to Vienna from somewhere in Moravia or Galicia and who, with his colleague Eduard Bacher, had reigned as uncrowned king over Austro-Hungarian public opinion since the nineties. The name of Moriz Benedikt was synonymous with that of the *Neue Freie Presse*.

The paper owed its existence to the theft of the subscription lists of the old *Presse*, that child of the revolution of 1848 which, under the rubric 'Equal Rights for All', had been well on the way to capturing a substantial proportion of the country's readers. Victim and thieves' accomplices remained at daggers drawn for twenty years, until the death in the mid-eighties of August Zang, the founder of the *Presse*, when the rival papers were finally amalgamated.

During the nineties and the first decade of the twentieth century not only was the *Neue Freie Presse* the most considerable newspaper in Austria, it was also one of the most important in the world. No matter what the event, whether the Russo-Japanese War or a meeting between the French president and the Tsar in St Petersburg Bay, the correspondents of the *Neue Freie Presse* would be on the spot reporting back to Vienna from their private Pullman car on the Trans-Siberian Railway, or their private yacht in the Gulf of Finland. The legend used to run – and it would seem to have been true – that a prime minister would first go to Schönbrunn to receive his appointment at the hands of the Emperor, and then at once proceed to the Fichtegasse to present himself to the editor-in-chief of the *Neue Freie Presse*.

Moriz Benedikt was the undoing of many a man, from prime minister to editor. One of the latter was Theodor Herzl, whose conflict with Benedikt has been admirably described by Amos Elon in his book *The Pride and the Pity*. Without reference to the *Neue Freie Presse* no account of the fortunes of Herzl, founder of the Jewish state, would be complete.

Benedikt, then, had heard of my father. He invited him to come for an interview and offered him a post on the paper, initially as a leader writer. To the *Neue Freie Presse* father brought a new spirit that had enjoyed little currency there hitherto, namely the spirit of Austrian patriotism unqualified by the reservations of the upper middle class, liberal Jewish world. While not upper middle class, the Moldens had always been fervent Austrians. Our grandfather Berthold had by chance watched the Battle of Königgrätz in progress. When war broke out between Prussia and Austria in 1866 he was not yet sixteen and his parents had sent him away from what seemed the danger zone of Bielitz to friends in Königgrätz, well behind the lines and apparently completely safe. There, from the roof of a barn, he witnessed the course of the battle and the Austrian defeat. That event must very early have awakened in him a great love of his country. His unquestioning loyalty to Austria was something he succeeded in passing on to his son.

My father lacked the intellectual effervescence that was the hallmark of the editors of the *Neue Freie Presse*. He came from the world of those who carefully weighed their words, the world of those who were the silent guardians of Austria. Hence things cannot have been easy for him to begin with amongst that fastidious, brilliant band of editors. But so much had his influence grown by the end of the twenties that, as deputy editor-in-chief, he was to all intents and purposes head of the editorial board. For by this time Moriz Benedikt was dead and his son, Ernst, had taken over the paper.

Ernst Benedikt had been forced by his father to join the staff, though he had never really wanted to be a journalist. He was a biologist, botanist, and musician, in short a polymath, but he could never put his whole heart into being a journalist and newspaper editor. When, in the early thirties, he was eventually compelled to sell his shares in the *Neue Freie Presse* and relinquish his editorship, he was very far from heart-broken. He was succeeded by Dr Stephen von Müller, who committed suicide in 1938 when the Nazis marched in. Father was in charge of the editorial board from 1930 to 1938. It was an important period of his life; the *Neue Freie Presse,* though already in economic straits, was still the country's main political organ, and his leaders and commentaries enabled him to influence the course of events.

The danger that was hanging over Austria had been obvious to him since 1933, the more so because, like so many other Austrian patriots, he had been a pan-German and had seen in the Austro-German People's League a suitable means whereby he and like-minded friends from the Reich might create a common and viable basis for a German Central Europe. Hitler's accession to power put an end to this dream, the Austro-German People's League was dissolved and my father became a fervent advocate of Austrian survival. The series of talks, 'A Month of World Events', which he gave every month on Ravag, as the Austrian broadcasting company was then called, was one of the most popular programmes in Austria, as it was to be in Germany after the 'co-ordination' of German Press and radio. Small wonder that my father figured on the Nazis' black list.

The years immediately preceding the *Anschluss* were spent by us boys in much the same way, no doubt, as Russian adolescents had spent those immediately before the great revolution of 1917, that is to say heedlessly, as yet unaware of the writing on the wall. That there was a sort of civil war going on round us we knew; we heard shots and saw telephone boxes being blown up; there were assassination attempts, railway installations were dynamited, while the pressure from the north, the pressure of big Germany on little Austria, increased. We shook off these impressions like so many raindrops, and went on with our ordinary everyday existence. It may have seemed normal to us because we had known nothing else.

Our life at home was still that of a middle class, intellectually inclined Austrian family; things had probably been going on in just the same way since 1910. We had a cook and a housemaid and also, while we were still very small, a nursemaid. We lived in large, high-ceilinged rooms of a kind not built today because it would be regarded as a waste of space. In the summer we would all go, bag and baggage, to spend two months in the country. But we did not own a motorcar. Father had an office car at his disposal which came to fetch him in the morning, brought him home at lunchtime, and took him back to the office in the afternoon. At night he came home by late-night bus. I cannot remember the office car ever being used for private purposes. In the first place, my father would have considered it indefensible, in the second, the idea would never have occurred to him. If necessary, we used a taxi, but travelled as a rule exclusively by tram or late-night bus, longer journeys being made by train or ship. The first time my father travelled by air was during the Second World War, and not until after the war did he acquire a car of his own.

Our way of life could not exactly be described as comfortable. The daily round was so arranged as to suit the master of the house. Owing to the *Neue Freie Presse*'s method of publication, father would arrive home late for lunch. The evening paper came out at about 2 pm and he would not be home until half past, so that was the time the family ate. At five he and mother, but not us children, would have tea. At six he would return to the office and stay there until midnight. On weekdays he would not normally be home again until one o'clock in the morning, though there was, of course, the famous and much-cherished evening off, usually on a Tuesday or a Wednesday. Father's Sunday evenings belonged exclusively to his family, for the paper did not appear on Monday morning.

My mother's working day was also subject to a strict routine but, as she wrote only at home, she was always accessible to us. Though there were, of course, certain hours at which she must not be disturbed, we never had the feeling that her time was limited, her daily programme too full for her to tell us a story,

or her duties so onerous that she could not recite Little Hare
Mandili at bedtime. It was to our mother, and her exceptionally
happy relationship with her husband to whom she formed such
a good counterpart, that we owed the gay, serene world that
completed our parental home.

It was in the Mediterranean that my mother felt most at ease.
To her, home meant the islands of Dalmatia, the Istrian coast,
sailors and the sea, the elegant society of Venetia. The de Pontes
came from that blessed and fertile strip of land between the
Alps and the Adriatic, and their family connections extended
to Bergamo and Milan in Lombardy. It was a family which,
for centuries past, had produced doctors, lawyers and merchants. While staying at the family's holiday house on the island
of Lukoran, the entrancing Pave de Ponte had fallen head over
heels in love with a young officer of the Imperial Army, Petar
von Preradović. Petar was the son of one of those border
families, by turns armed farmers, soldiers, officers and again
armed farmers, who for generations had guarded the old imperial military frontiers that once ran right across Croatia,
Slavonia and Western Serbia to the Danube and Transylvania.
Petar von Preradović was thus the product of a centuries-old
tradition of a hard world indissolubly linked with the land, with
death and with the Imperial Army. His parents had died young
and he was educated at a military school and later at the old
Maria-Theresa Military Academy in Wiener Neustadt. As a
young man he had almost forgotten Croatian, but on first being
garrisoned somewhere in the neighbourhood of Gospić and
Karlovac he had rediscovered his mother-tongue and come to
love it. Within a few years he had become the most eminent poet
of the Illyrian movement and is still revered today as the Croatian national bard. Every town in Croatia has its Preradović
Street, and there is a memorial to him in the capital, Zagreb. I
first went to see it with my mother when I was ten years old, at a
time when Zagreb was still called Agram; with awe I looked
up at the bronze statue of the old gentleman who, clad in the
high-collared officer's uniform of the old Austrian army, stood
there bare-headed in the midst of the flower market.

Years later in 1951, returning to Croatia for the first time
after the war, I went to Zagreb and paid my respects to my
great-grandfather in the market-place. To my alarm, I found
that the political upheavals had not left even the Croatian

national bard unscathed. Poor great-grandpapa's high collar with the insignia of a general of the Imperial Army had been removed, leaving the elegant, close-fitting tunic and the fine head but, in between, a thin iron rod which had previously supported the collar. Petar von Preradović presented a truly lamentable spectacle, with his bare, scrawny vulture's neck.

I was on my way to Belgrade at the time to interview Marshal Tito. The latter, who was then at the height of his power, received me one afternoon at his official residence. The conversation was at first conducted through an interpreter but, with sudden affability, the Marshal began to talk to me in the lingua franca spoken by everybody in the old Imperial Army, from general to the lowliest soldier. It was an army consisting of twelve different nationalities, who had to agree on a common language of command, namely German, and had imposed upon that language variations so marked that it no longer had very much in common with the German of Goethe, Schiller or Grillparzer.

Tito asked about Vienna and Wiener Neustadt where he had served, evinced pro-Austrian sentiments and expressed the hope that relations between Austria and Yugoslavia would soon take a turn for the better. As the interview neared its end, he suddenly asked whether I was not the great-grandson of Petar Preradović. Upon my saying I was, he remarked: 'That almost makes you a fellow-countryman. Can I do anything for you, have you any particular wish?' I thought for a moment and then suddenly called to mind my collarless great-grandpapa. When I told Tito of the lamentable state of Petar Preradović in Zagreb market-place, he roared with laughter, recited a verse or two from Preradović's most famous poem, *Putnik* (The Traveller), and said: 'I shall have the matter put right. You can count on me.' I thanked him and took my leave.

On my way home I told my friends and relations at Zagreb about my conversation with Tito. They expressed their scepticism; nothing would be done, they said. The new Yugoslav regime's hatred of Austria was so intense that it would even extend to a statue. But when, a few months after my return, my cousin Neda came to see me in Vienna, the first thing she said was: 'Your great-grandpapa has got his collar back!' So Tito had granted my wish; the failure to restore the general's insignia along with his collar would no doubt be regarded by

General Preradović himself as a legitimate concession to the new socialist society.

But to return to Pave de Ponte and her Pero. They overcame the difficulties – in their case mainly financial – which at that time beset an officer in the Imperial Army when he wished to get married. In due course Pave bore three children of whom two survived, my grandfather Dušan and his sister Milica. Dušan grew up in his father's garrison town and, at an early age, entered the naval college in Pola. He devoted himself heart and soul to his career. For a man of that period he was widely travelled, having, in the course of his service, visited the Far East and Brazil; a tangible reminder of his time in Brazil remains in the family – it is still at 7, Osterleitengasse – in the shape of a wooden chair.

In the late eighties, the *Kronprinz Rudolf*, a ship of the line, entered a Brazilian port with my grandfather in command. The Emperor of Brazil, Dom Pedro, announced his intention of inspecting the vessel. During the hectic preparations that preceded the arrival of the eminent guest, it was suddenly discovered that there was no chair on board fit for an emperor. As a last resort, an unpretentious kind of deckchair was brought up from grandfather's cabin and lent imperial dignity with the aid of a decorative rug. The Emperor duly appeared, inspected the ship, seemed greatly impressed and graciously distributed decorations – not least to the captain. Upon being offered refreshment, he kindly condescended to sit down on the makeshift throne, which promptly collapsed beneath its august burden. Having been helped to his feet, the emperor showed no sign of annoyance but treated the whole thing as a joke. The 'Dom Pedro chair' has ever since held an honoured place in the Molden household.

Later on in his career a great misfortune was to befall Dušan Preradović. In 1906 he was about to be called to the Admiralty in Vienna and stood a good chance of some day being appointed Admiral of the Fleet. But on returning from a long cruise in foreign waters to the naval base at Pola, his ship – the only iron-clad the Imperial and Royal Navy possessed – ran on to a reef off the island of Krk. The previous day he had dropped anchor at another naval base where he and his cronies had celebrated his return. Now, as the night was fine and clear, and he needed to recuperate before the festivities that awaited him at Pola, he handed over the vessel to his first lieutenant and went below. An hour later the ship was aground.

No matter who was to blame, the ultimate responsibility lay with my grandfather, and the traditions of the Dual Monarchy demanded that he resign from the service. Thus, quite unexpectedly and much to his dismay, my grandfather found himself at the end of a career from which he had still had so much to expect.

There now happened one of those little miracles so typical of Austria. Held in high esteem both by the Admiralty and by Archduke Franz Ferdinand, Dušan was appointed head of the Imperial and Royal Navy's meteorological station at Pola which, though a civil post, in fact enabled him to continue his life along much the same lines as before. On the outbreak of the First World War he was recalled to active service with the rank, first of captain of a ship of the line and, eventually, of Admiral.

In his domestic life grandfather was not always a match for his robust wife, Helene Falke-Lilienstein, who was the eldest of seven children and had a strong personality. Coming as she did from a long line of civil servants and officers, her approach to life was energetic and practical. She had little understanding for the poetical vein which Dušan had inherited from Petar Preradović. Her job was to perpetuate the line and to do her best to see that it prospered and that the children were properly brought up. Their sentimental effusions met with total incomprehension on her part.

Grandmama's youngest sister was Aunt Gabriele and we all adored her. Heaven had endowed her with wit, infinite charm, and a strong personality; she was a small, dainty woman whose gentle strength and wise common sense made her the focal point of the family for many decades. At a very early age Aunt Gabriele had married a young man in good circumstances who answered to the ultra-Austrian name of Dr Oskar Negedly Edler von Savenegg. The things that befell Uncle Oskar would be difficult to credit if one did not know they had in fact happened.

He was a gay and dashing young man, who held an appointment under His Imperial and Royal Majesty's Ministry of the Interior. Relatively early he became District Governor of Prachatitz in the Böhmerwald, a little town at the end of a branch railway. There he lived in peace and comfort with his beloved

Gabriele. Until the day, that is, when he received the disturbing and momentous news that His Majesty the Emperor would be in the district on the occasion of the army's autumn manoeuvres and, such being the case, intended to honour the town of Prachatitz with a visit. 'No good can come of it,' he told Gabriele. 'It can only lead to trouble.' Nevertheless, he and the Burgomaster of Prachatitz set about preparing a reception worthy of their Imperial and Royal visitor.

A few weeks later the great moment came. The whole of Prachatitz was resplendent with a new glory, the railway station had been given a fresh coat of paint, there were garlands everywhere. Together with the band of the Landwehr* battalion, whose headquarters were at Prachatitz and who had been practising the national anthem for days past, all the notables in brand new suits or uniforms were assembled on the platform with, of course, the most high-ranking official – District Governor Dr Oskar Negedly Edler von Savenegg – at their head. And as such he was introduced to the Emperor when he stepped down from the saloon coach of the royal train. Uncle Oskar had been standing to attention for a long time. The Emperor held out his hand and said kindly: 'Tell me, my dear Negedly, haven't we met before?'

Uncle Oskar drew himself up even straighter. 'Yes, Your Majesty,' he replied, 'I had the honour of being attached to Your Majesty's staff during the occupation of Bosnia in 1878.' The Emperor Franz Josef looked at him and a glimmer of recognition crossed his face as he said: 'But of course, my dear Negedly, that's what it was. Well, well, my friend, we're growing old.' Still standing stiffly to attention, Uncle Oskar exclaimed deferentially: 'And foolish, Your Majesty!' There was a moment's silence before the Emperor passed on to the next in the line.

Supper that evening did not take its usual peaceful course. Aunt Gabriele took Uncle Oskar to task for not having adequately prepared what he was going to say. Uncle Oskar maintained that he had been carried away by the Emperor's condescension and had, of course, meant the 'foolish' to apply to himself, not to His Majesty, who must, in any case, have realized it was all a joke. Aunt Gabriele wasn't so sure.

*The Homeguard.

A week had gone by, life had returned to normal and the incident had been all but forgotten when, to Uncle Oskar's considerable alarm, an imperial messenger suddenly turned up with a letter summoning the District Governor to appear before the Lord Chamberlain at Schönbrunn. During the interview it was put to him gently but unequivocally that it might be best if he tendered his resignation. Thus terminated the career of District Governor Negedly Edler von Savenegg. The couple returned to Vienna where they lived for the remainder of their lives in a beautiful Renaissance building in the Bäckerstrasse. And there Aunt Gabriele died in 1961.

Uncle Oskar and Aunt Gabriele were part of my mother's world. In Pola mother had attended the naval school reserved for the families of sailors, after which she had gone to the *Institut der Englischen Fräulein*, an English foundation in St Pölten. It was at this time that she began to write. Although she herself always wrote in German and never in her mother tongue, of which she had a very good command, her first poems were published in 1912 in a Croatian edition. As far back as 1908 her poetry had begun to appear regularly in all kinds of Viennese newspapers; some were accepted by journals of high literary repute such as the *Neue Freie Presse* or the Munich *Simplizissimus*. When she had finished her schooling, she went – as many girls of good family then did – to be trained as a nurse at the famous Rudolfinerhaus in Vienna, run by that great man, Professor Billroth. On the outbreak of war she volunteered for duty as a Red Cross nurse.

It was then that she met father and, from that moment, a world began to take shape which only these two could have brought into being. On the basis of their inner resources, their particular modes of thought and their origins in two quite different regions of the old Empire, that still brilliant if already exploding star, they built up what was to become for us the world of the Osterleitengasse. It was a secure, wholesome world, yet always open to outside ideas, impressions and influences. Our parents were sociable people, although father's profession placed certain restrictions on their sociability.

From 1937 onwards politics played an increasingly important part in my life. At that time my brother Otto was already one of the leaders of the Freikorps, a 'Fatherland' organization for secondary schoolboys and students. Immediately before the

Anschluss it was placed under the command of the Sturmkorps, a militant body set up at Schuschnigg's instigation by his chief-of-staff, Alexander, for the purpose of combatting National Socialist underground and terrorist groups. Consequently, Otto and his friends were engaged almost daily in opposing some Nazi demonstration or outrage. I was still too young for any such militant activity; it was on a rather different plane that members of my age-group fought out their differences with National Socialism.

For instance, there was the battle for the ruined Castle of Hoheneck, which enabled us boys to give expression to our political antagonisms. For many years the ruins of Hoheneck in the Dunkelsteiner Wald had been the object of the Neuland movement's expeditions and rallies. In 1936 or thereabouts the movement split up into a National Socialist wing and the anti-Nazi First Regiment led by Fritz Hansen-Löwe. There was a third splinter group, also anti-Nazi, which joined forces with the Freikorps.

As a member of this latter group I, and some hundred and fifty boys led by Fritz Neeb, went to Hoheneck to prepare for the big Whitsun rally of 1937. However, the Nazi corps of Neulanders had also decided to assert its former rights to the ruin. Aboard the Danube steamer which left Vienna at 10 pm and arrived at Aggsbach in the early hours of the morning, and which both the contending armies had to take in order to reach that much coveted objective, Hoheneck, there was some preliminary skirmishing which, though violent, went off without any blood being shed. During the days that followed, however, a fierce battle raged round the ruins. Eventually the Freikorps succeeded in holding them, but not a few members of both youth groups spent the last days of their Whitsun holiday in the casualty department of St Pölten Hospital.

If feelings ran somewhat higher on this occasion it was, no doubt, mainly because of the romantic setting, though the event was by no means atypical of the political climate of 1937. 'Battles' of this description were the order of the day. In the autumn of that year, the headquarters of our 'Walter Flex' Frei-korps squad in Unter-Döbling was attacked on at least four occasions by Neuland groups of Nazi persuasion or by the Hitler Youth. We did not remain unavenged. That same autumn we in our turn carried out perhaps half a dozen raids on illegal meetings held by the Hitler Youth in a disused shed in the Wertheimsteinpark. In every case there was a splendid set-to. But as time went on it became dangerous to make one's way home at night wearing the uniform of our youth group.

As a rule, all the participants got away unscathed, for we were, in the final analysis, no more than a crowd of harmless young lads. On neither side did the adolescents who used to belabour each other in the streets of Vienna at that time harbour anything really sinister in their hearts. The evil lay with the wirepullers who were at work on the Nazis' behalf, as was soon to become all too apparent. There were bad times ahead for the peaceful world of No. 7, Osterleitengasse.

3

A Good Year for Nuts

The winter of 1937–38 was an exciting and, to begin with, very happy time. Even my youthful ears were receptive to the view expressed in conversation by the grown-ups – a view my own observations seemed to confirm – that the serious economic crisis was gradually abating and unemployment was on the wane. One could also detect a resurgence in the artistic and cultural fields, attributable not least to the stimulating influence of artists who had been expelled from Germany. At home we got many invitations; Otto was already at the university, numerous young people frequented the house, his first girl friends made their appearance and mother decided that the time had now come to step up the pace of our social life. I was sent to dancing classes, which filled me more with horror than anything else, for my thoughts were all with the youth movement, my one desire being to race through the streets in the obligatory shorts and stockings. However, the lessons proved to be not so frightful after all for, as everybody knows, one gets used to anything, even dancing. During the winter Otto went to the Arlberg, took a skiing instructor's test and, having said good-bye to the French and English girls he had met there, returned in high spirits to Vienna. There was a general feeling that the worst was over, indeed people actually believed that Hitler was beginning to acquire a sense of decorum.

This suddenly changed in February 1938. To the astonishment of us all we learnt that Schuschnigg had gone to see Hitler on the Obersalzberg. After 15 February we realized that crucial talks had been held there. For an amnesty was granted to all National Socialist offenders, while Arthur Seyss-Inquart, who belong to the National camp, was appointed Minister of the Interior. Throughout the country the Nazis resumed their activities and actually appeared in public without anything being done to stop them. Hitler made a speech, his first to be broadcast by the Austrian radio, in which he spoke of a 'German peace'. Four days later Schuschnigg replied with a speech in Parliament. This I shall never forget, for we boys marched to the Heldenplatz and the Ring to hear it, choosing as our battle-cry: 'Red, white and red, even unto death.' What I found surprising at this time was that fellow pupils of mine from avowedly Social Democratic families suddenly became enthusiastic supporters of Austria's cause. Not until later was I to discover that Schuschnigg had sought to make concessions in that quarter. None of us was in any doubt that, one way or another, things must come to a head.

At school we were learning virtually nothing. Everyone's attention was concentrated on the crucial negotiations that were to take place between the Ballhausplatz and the Reich Chancellery in Berlin. In the streets there were ferocious set-tos. The Nazis staged public demonstrations while the 'Fatherlanders' and even, on occasion, the 'Reds' counter-demonstrated in return.

On 9 March Schuschnigg announced that in four days' time, the 13th, a plebiscite would be held to determine the country's future; it was up to the Austrians to say whether or not they wanted a free and independent Austria. We all of us listened on the radio to this, the last, or rather last but one, speech by Schuschnigg. A mood of euphoria began to spread. Everyone felt that the plebiscite would turn out satisfactorily and that Hitler would have to leave Austria in peace; a great illusion, as we were to discover within a matter of days.

We handed out leaflets, marched in procession, exchanged blows with Nazi demonstrators, and so forth. This went on for no more than three days, but looking back they seem to me like months. At midday on Friday, 11 March – I had simply walked out of school – I gathered with my squad between Freyung and Hof to help defend the premises of the Fatherland Front and get ready to parade outside the office of the Federal Chancellor. There were some fifteen hundred of us, youngsters from the Freikorps and from the student groups in sympathy with it.

We had been singing patriotic songs and rehearsing chants

when all at once we were told that everyone under sixteen must return home forthwith as there might be bloody clashes; we were to leave the Inner City without delay. Those who, like my broher and his friends, were over sixteen were to be given weapons. Fighting was expected to break out and it was feared that at any moment there might be an invasion by German troops. With a heavy heart I took a number 38 to Döbling and was strolling in the direction of the Osterleitengasse when, to my utter astonishment, I suddenly saw outside the District Magistrate's Office in the Gatterbuggasse some two hundred SA men in full uniform; they were singing National Socialist songs and marching towards Döbling High Street and the Inner City. Several policemen were standing about on the pavement but they did nothing. I thought my eyes were deceiving me, for all of them wore swastika brassards. I ran home and informed my mother of what I had seen and of the fact that Otto had moved off with the armed SK* units.

Half an hour later, my father telephoned from the offices of the *Neue Freie Presse* in the Fichtegasse to say that the plebiscite had suddenly been called off; no one knew what was going to happen but he feared the worst. He believed that Schuschnigg's government would resign and that the National Socialists would seize power within a matter of hours. He would do his best to get home, he said. Father arrived back about an hour later. All of us, apart from Otto who was still with his unit, sat in the drawing-room waiting for Schuschnigg's speech, which was expected at any minute. At last it came. Schuschnigg said that he could no longer withstand either the pressure exerted by the German Reich or the ultimatum it had issued, and that under no circumstances did he wish to shed German blood. Accordingly he would offer no resistance to the German invasion. It was quite a short speech and it ended with the words: 'May God protect Austria.'

For the first time in my life I saw my father in tears. It did not last very long, a minute or two perhaps, by which time he had regained control of himself; then he kissed my mother and me and returned to his office. We must, he had said, stay indoors at all costs and, in the event of Otto's telephoning, we

---

SK—the Schutz-Korps, a well-armed, black-uniformed elite guard, was set up by Schnuschnigg to fight the Nazi terrorists.

should tell him not to come to the Osterleitengasse but to take
refuge with Aunt Gabriele in the Bäckerstrasse. That is precisely what happened. Otto telephoned two hours later. His unit
had been disbanded, though not before it had fought a number
of engagements. He and several friends of his from the students'
Freikorps had then sought shelter at No. 3 Bäckerstrasse, where
Aunt Gabriele and Uncle Oskar had taken them in. There they
remained in hiding for several days. Meanwhile, on the evening
of 11 March, a party of Hitler Youth arrived in the Osterleitengasse to arrest Otto. In our case the prelude to the Thousand
Year Reich was accompanied by the strains of that charming
air 'Give the Jews a pasting, put the parsons against a wall',
while our front door, which we had made no attempt whatever
to secure, was quite needlessly broken down. Angered by his
absence, the young heroes rampaged through Otto's room,
trampled on his possessions and left the battlefield victorious.

I was greatly struck by the attitude of many of our neighbours and fellow occupants in the Osterleitengasse who, only
a few days previously, had gone about wearing the badge of the
Fatherland Front and had greeted us punctiliously, whereas
now they cheered the Hitler Youth and looked away whenever
a member of the Molden family so much as showed his face at
a window. But such is clearly the way of the world. Since then
I must have met with at least a dozen cases of this kind, and
each time I have found it a very interesting experience.

Father did not come home that evening; he spent the night at
the editorial offices of the *Neue Freie Presse*, which had been
occupied by a squad of SA. On his return next morning he told
us that the entire editorial department of the *Neue Freie Press*
had been dismissed, with the exception of two editors who had
been members of the illegal Nazi Party. Two out of a total of
forty-four, though admittedly one must remember that out of
the forty-four editors on the *Neue Freie Presse* at the time, some
thirty-eight were Jews. Father had long been nicknamed the
'yiddischer goy'. A few hours later members of the 'Austrian
Legion' forced their way into our house. These legionaries were
Nazis who, in the years prior to the *Anschluss*, had fled to
Germany and there been put into SA uniform, accommodated
in barracks and given a military training. Now they had returned in the wake of the German troops and were terrorizing –
many in due course as Gestapo men – those who opposed

Hitler. The legionaries took father away for a long interrogation. So the second night after our liberation by 'our beloved Führer', Adolf Hitler, was again spent by mother and me on our own. Finally, in the early hours of the morning, father returned from his interrogation. That Sunday, 13 March, was my brother's birthday and, as was to happen so often in the years to come, we fell prey to false hopes. This time we were hoping that, after the failure to arrest him on 11 March, Otto might now be left in peace. We therefore decided in family council that Otto should return home that evening under cover of darkness, the assumption being that Vienna's Nazis would all have gone to the Ring to pay homage to 'their beloved Führer'. For just then Hitler was en route from Linz to Vienna, where he was to stay at the Hotel Imperial in the Ring. When Otto returned, the four of us celebrated his birthday, though we took care not to make too much noise; we sensed that before long there would be little left to celebrate. However we were happy to be all together again.

Towards midnight, by which time everyone had gone to bed, there was a ring at the doorbell followed by the entry of steel-helmeted legionaries who had come to take Otto away. For the first time in my thirteen years I discovered what it meant when someone was arrested, when a woman, my mother as it happened, was beaten up. One of the legionaries gave Otto a kick to make him hurry. Mother stepped between them in an attempt to stop him. The SA man lashed out and knocked her down. She fell across a chair, whereupon that gentlemanly individual seized his rubber truncheon and, with evident relish, brought it swishing down on to her back. Another legionary, presumably the leader, restrained him. 'Cut it out,' he said, 'our job is to arrest the son, not beat up the woman.' Astonished, the man with the truncheon replied: 'If you say so, but these democratic swine could do with a bashing.' Afterwards mother said she had hardly felt anything; her only reaction had been utter amazement that such conduct should have been possible in the first place.

As a thirteen-year-old I was in no danger at all, but we did not know what might become of Otto. As they took him away the legionaries grinned broadly when my mother asked about the probable time of his return. He was back relatively soon, having on this occasion been detained for only two and a half weeks

Not long afterwards my father was recalled to the *Neue Freie Presse*, for the SA men who had taken over the paper were incapable of coping with either the editorial or any other department, and recourse had therefore to be had to the former editors, in particular the few who were not Jewish. Even some of father's Jewish colleagues were employed up till the autumn of 1938 – roughly till the time of the *Kristallnacht,* when the persecution of the Jews began in real earnest. By then the *Neue Freie Presse* was approaching its inglorious end. At first the paper was the subject of a squabble between Ribbentrop, the Foreign Minister, and Funk, the Economics Minister, since both wished to acquire an organ that was read abroad and might be used as a vehicle for indirect Nazi propaganda in the world at large. This struggle between Ribbentrop and Funk gave the paper another year's lease of life. In the end Funk was victorious. The *Neue Freie Presse* was to continue as Germany's leading economic organ with its main sphere of influence in south-east Europe.

All went well until the end of January 1939, when Hitler visited Vienna and again stayed at the Hotel Imperial. Next morning he called for newspapers, whereat one of his SS aides went to the hall porter to fetch them. In those days, however, only the *Neue Freie Presse* was on sale at the Imperial and not, as it happened, the *Völkischer Beobachter,* the organ of the NSDAP. So the aide took a *Neue Freie Presse* and brought it to the Führer. Hitler flew into a rage when he saw that the paper was still appearing, a paper he had attacked most virulently at least a dozen times in *Mein Kampf,* depicting it as one of the chief means employed by the Jewish plutocracy to mislead the people. He ordered not only its immediate closure, but also the destruction of the paper's library – generally held to be the best of its kind in Central Europe – and, in addition, the sale of the printing machines outside Austria, or rather the 'Ostmark', as it was then so engagingly termed. The Führer's order was promptly carried out, the paper was closed, the machines were sold in Upper Silesia and, worst of all, the library was burnt. Thus, in February 1939, father found himself out of a job.

A number of his well-wishers, who had helped to make things a little less difficult for him since 1938, continued to protect and encourage him. One of these was Dr Rudolf Fischer, whom Funk had sent to Austria to bring the *Presse* into line. Fischer was an extraordinarily intelligent man, by no means a fanatical National Socialist at heart, who was glad to be assigned a task that enabled him to come to Vienna. He soon realized that the paper could not be run without a few experienced men and accordingly did his best to keep father on in the editorial department. This was by no means so simple, since my father's certificate of Aryanism revealed serious lacunae, and it would have been quite inconceivable in the Third Reich for a man encumbered with a Jewish grandfather to go about his business as editor of a daily newspaper. This same Jewish grandfather was also to present us with a number of problems in the days to come. Admittedly he brought us certain minor advantages; for example one did not have to join the Hitler Youth or any other Nazi organization, but there were also numerous disadvantages in that one could not become a member of, say, the Reich Chamber of Literature, which was de rigueur in my mother's case, or the Reich Press Chamber, to which my father ought to have belonged if he was to find work.

But with the help of Rudolf Fischer he was successfully installed as librarian, first to the *Neue Freie Presse,* then to an economic weekly called the *Südostecho* and, finally, after he had come under the Ostmark ban in 1940, and had been forbidden to work in Austria, to an economic newspaper in Holland entitled *Eurokapabel.*

Moreover, it is to the credit of the otherwise far from estimable Dr Seyss-Inquart that on 11 March 1938, at the start of his three days as Austrian Federal Chancellor, he at once telephoned my father, who had been a fellow student of his, and told him he would see to it that nothing happened to him and his family. Later on, as Reich Governor, he also kept his word within the limits of his competence, though by 1939 he had lost his post in Austria. Berlin thought him too weak, a spineless Ostmarker in fact. At the end of September he became Deputy Governor-General of Poland. Subsequently, after the occupation of Holland by German troops in 1940, he was appointed to the post of Reich Commissar in the Netherlands. Whatever evil things Seyss-Inquart may have done, he helped my father and probably made it possible for our family to survive. He not only tolerated father's appointment as librarian to the German-language *Eurokapabel* in Amsterdam, but actully helped to promote it. On several occasions he obtained Dutch entry permits for both my mother and me and, on top of that, when I was charged in Vienna and subsequently detained first at the District Court and then in Liesing prison in 1941-2, he intervened on my behalf and was, no doubt, partially responsible for my early transfer from gaol to the armed forces.

During those days in March and April 1938 we all had to take fresh stock – those of us, that is, who had grown up in what was a kind of prolongation of the old Austro-Hungarian monarchy, an intermediate state characterized by poverty, civil war and like phenomena but still reflecting the dying splendour of Austria as she once had been. Overnight we had suddenly been pitched out of this epoch into the Third Reich. It was some time before the Austrian people could even begin to grasp the fact that home was no longer their own country but Greater Germany.

At first we had believed – and naturally such things were frequently discussed at home – that there would not be an *Anschluss*, but rather a form of co-existence between two German states, possibly with Hitler as joint head of state. My father often declared that the 'National Catholic', Dr Seyss-Inquart, advocated such a solution.

In Seyss-Inquart's government there were two other friends of my father's. They, too, while certainly not fanatical National Socialists, were nevertheless 'outright Nationalists', as the die-hard pan-Germans were called at the time. The first was Dr Edmund Glaise-Horstenau, colonel on the Imperial and Royal General Staff, writer and historian, a minister under Schuschnigg (as representative of the 'Nationals') and Vice-Chancellor under Seyss-Inquart. During the Second World War he went on to play a minor role as 'German General with the Croatian Government' and eventually committed suicide at Nuremberg in 1946. The second was Dr Wilhelm Wolf, first and only Foreign Minister in Seyss-Inquart's Cabinet. In June 1939 Wolf met with a fatal accident, for which one can only be thankful, for he would have had a fearful struggle with his conscience, coming as he did from the Catholic camp and having already noted with horror in the first months after *Anschluss* what was beginning to become of Austria under Hitler.

There were many, among them persons as important as

Heinrich von Sbrik, the historian, and Neubacher, the Burgo-master of Vienna, who, as advocats of a pan-German State, were taken in by Hitler. Possibly it was much the same even in Seyss-Inquart's case. And once the bandwagon was in motion it must have been difficult to jump off.

Immediately after the *Anschluss* over 70,000 people were arrested. Every day more faces disappeared from our circle of relatives and acquaintances. Needless to say the Nazis herded the greater and lesser functionaries of the Schuschnigg regime into concentration camps. Many, however, were also affected who had played no part in politics, but had been prominent in the cultural, business and scientific worlds, or had simply been civil servants who had made themselves unpopular with the Nazis.

Feelings were confused; a great many Austrians regarded Hitler as a liberator, if not actually a Messiah. I remember only too well how women in particular seemed completely fascinated by the 'Führer', while certainly totally ignorant of what his politics involved. Later on, in prison, in the Wehrmacht and abroad, when I had become better acquainted with people from all walks of life, I also learnt that the members of the illegal Social Democratic Party had turned against the party leaders who had fled to other countries in February 1934. Otto Bauer, the party's undisputed ideologist, regarded the *Anschluss* as a positive, historically important event which ought not to be reversed. In Austria itself the Nazis at first showed themselves anxious to win over the Social Democrats. In the Vienna region, for example, they recruited hundreds of Schutzbund members who had been discharged after February 1934.

This explains the temporizing attitude initially adopted by the Social Democrats towards the Hitler regime, an attitude which may also be attributed to the fact that their programme had always accepted the principle of Greater Germany. Those who flatly rejected that regime belonged exclusively to the camp that had backed Schuschnigg: Christian Socials, Heimat-schutz, Ostermärkische Sturmscharen, Monarchists (in other words Conservatives) and, in addition, the adherents of the Christian trade unions. Indeed, these were also the groups – and with them young people like my brother Otto – which had up till 1938 borne the full brunt of the struggle against the more powerful National Socialists. Accordingly there were striking differences in people's attitude to the *Anschluss*.

Again, it had been by no means rare under the corporate state for National Socialists (the brown shirts) and Social Democrats to share the same cell in prison or the same hut in a detention camp, and from this had sprung a sense of comradeship which in many cases was to persist for decades.

These differences partially disappeared only when the war was no longer going so well for the Third Reich and ever harsher security measures had to be resorted to by the Gestapo. But this also meant a greater influx of illegal Revolutionary Socialists into the prisons and concentration camps. The immediate result was that a fresh sense of comradeship grew up, not this time between the red and brown victims of Schuschnigg's authoritarian system, but between the black and red victims of the Nazi regime.

In the weeks between 13 March and 10 April 1938, the day on which the Austrians and Reich Germans had been called upon by Hitler to vote retrospectively on an *Anschluss* that was by then a fait accompli, Austria witnessed an interesting botanical phenomenon. This was the flowering of the so-called March violets who overnight suddenly became conscious of their National Socialist convictions. It was fascinating to see how the caretaker's wife in the house opposite, a native of Bohemia whose views had hitherto been exclusively Social Democratic and proletarian, suddenly turned into a devout and ardent National Socialist who talked in broad Bohemian, overlaid with Viennese, of 'our beloved Fiehrer'. But it was just the same with more highly placed persons: well-known professors who lived in our street, lawyers, doctors, all of them became National Socialists overnight. One got the impression that everyone in Vienna who was not actually a Jew or had not been linked with the Schuschnigg regime had undergone a sudden transformation such as would have seemed inconceivable only a few weeks before. All at once everyone had been an 'illegal', everyone claimed that for years he had been a member of the NSDAP or one its affiliates. There began an unholy tussle for the newly created post of Gauleiter or for appointment as a Kreisleiter; everyone sought to acquire a party badge and, if that could not be done straight away, would at least place a swastika, more or less tastefully tricked out, in his buttonhole.

Those who were quickest to claim adherence to the Nazi movement were not necessarily the menfolk – they were in fact the Austrian women. How often in history – one merely has to recall the French Revolution – have women shown during the first weeks of enthusiasm and upheaval that they can change their spots far more quickly than the male of the species.

This miraculous transformation which people underwent showed how great was the ability of the Austrians, the Viennese in particular, to adjust themselves to the new circumstances and, in the twinkling of an eye, actually come to believe that they had always held the views they now professed with such conviction and enthusiasm. I noticed this at school; up till 11 March 1938 we had four boys in our class who with great honesty admitted being supporters of Hitler and whose fathers obviously belonged to the illegal NSDAP; we fought with them on occasion and as often made it up. On 14 March, when I returned to school, I could see that of the thirty-two boys in the fourth form, all but four now wore a swastika. So here again there had been an astonishingly rapid change that was almost reminiscent of a miracle in the Bible. Nor were the consequences of this miracle long in making themselves felt, for the four boys who did not wish to wear a swastika were ostracized.

During this first enthusiastic phase, the staff themselves made absolutely no attempt to intervene. Apart from the headmistress, Anna Ehm, not one of them tried to protect the non-Nazis, who had now become pariahs and enemies of the people. The upshot in my case was that, after a long talk with Anna Ehm, my mother decided to remove me from Neuland School and send me to Schotten Grammar School. The Schotten, one of the city's most venerable institutions, ranks among Austria's most exclusive schools. My brother had spent the greater part of his secondary schooldays there. In due course I made my first acquaintance with the Schotten boys and at once saw that hardly any of those in my group were National Socialists. If I remember rightly, there were only two or three loud-mouthed Nazis in the class; the others either had no interest in politics or were of the kind that greeted you with 'Heil Osterreich'.

The greeting 'Heil Osterreich' was one of those, as it happened, vain attempts by the Schuschnigg government to take the wind out of the Nazis' sails. It was, like the right hand raised in the act of affirmation, a concession to that spirit of totalitarian thinking which had also found expression in the fascist Italy of Mussolini. Dollfuss and Schuschnigg felt they had to adapt themselves, and doubtless also conciliate the Heimatschutz, if they were to bring over to their side the younger people who were becoming increasingly addicted to gestures of this kind. It was not only in Austria that such things were happening, but throughout almost the whole of Europe. For in those days the old Continent was passing through an authoritarian epoch. In Italy, Germany, Spain, Hungary, Yugoslavia, Poland, Roumania, Greece, Portugal – everywhere there was strong-arm rule – everywhere, parliamentary democracy had fallen into disrepute.

It was, of course, difficult for the Austrian authoritarian system of 1933–8 to demonstrate its independence. This was one reason why so many young people were taken in by Hitler. The country was in the throes of a serious economic crisis from which there seemed to be no escape. In the thirties six hundred thousand were unemployed, twenty-five per cent of the working population. Austria was evidently no longer viable. The great powers had abandoned her. By now she was simply a pawn in the politics of others. Veterans of the First World War who, in 1918, had seen the insignia and rank badges ripped off the uniforms of the officers, only to be solemnly informed not long afterwards that such First World War concepts as love of country, an officer's honour, gallantry, were sacred after all – people like these might well be utterly confused and, in the end, go running willy-nilly after false prophets.

The repercussions of the economic crisis of the thirties are barely imaginable today. I remember how twice a week we were joined at luncheon by the child of unemployed parents who was brought to the house by a welfare organization set up by Princess Fanny Starhemberg. I even remember a joke we boys used to snigger over, though we only partially understood it: Princess Fanny was the mother of Ernst Rüdiger Starhemberg, the Heimwehr leader, whose amorous adventures were much talked about. Her 'Winter Aid' was advertised with the slogan: 'Ask a starving child to share your meal.' Prince Ernst Rüdiger, or so the joke went, was launching a campaign with the watchword: 'Ask a freezing girl to share your bed.' I already knew a little about Prince Starhemberg, the 'Federal leader of the Austrian Heimatschutz'. My brother had belonged to its youth organization, the Young Fatherland. At the beginning of the twenties the prince had fought with the Oberland Freikorps in Upper Silesia, shoulder to shoulder with National Socialists, though in the years that followed he was to prove a convinced opponent of Hitler.

Starhemberg was a friend of Benito Mussolini's. Without him and his Heimatschutz Dollfuss's and Schuschnigg's governments would not have been possible at all. He became Vice-Chancellor, head of the Fatherland Front, head of sport; everyone was waiting for him and his Heimwehr to assume 'power within the state', but somehow his ambition never quite came up to scratch. Thus, in 1936 he meekly allowed himself to be elbowed out by Schuschnigg and contented himself with marrying, much below his station but with a dispensation from the Pope, an extremely beautiful Burgtheater actress named Nora Gregor.

By the middle of the thirties there were, if one includes the families of the unemployed, more than a million people in the most dire straits. Besides those receiving unemployment assistance were the so-called 'ineligibles', people who had been unemployed for more than a year and had therefore ceased to receive the dole. This poverty, which affected a substantial proportion of Austria's six million inhabitants, inevitably had repercussions throughout the country. Industry was largely at a standstill. Travelling from Vienna, say, towards the south, one could see dozens of silent and already dilapidated factories on either side of the Trieste road or the southern railway. In the industrial areas the situation was truly critical. The worst time was the winter, for logs and coal were beyond the means of the 'ineligibles'. People starved or froze to death. Tens of thousands were dependent on charity, soup kitchens run by nuns, alms from the winter aid organization and other emergency measures.

Most striking of all was the large number of beggars. At our house in the Osterleitengasse, a quiet street where there was hardly any through traffic, the door bell rang at least fifteen times a day. Outside, one or more beggars would be waiting. They always received something to eat – soup, bread or dumplings. My father had given mother money to distribute, thus enabling her to provide them with a little cash as well.

But even those not immediately affected by the crisis lived in modest circumstances. For example, I remember a restaurant in the 2nd District. On the door hung the menu card with the day's bill of fare: 'Rice and Liver Soup, Beef and two Vegetables, Stewed Dumplings with Vanilla Sauce.' Next came the information: 'The charge for the meal is one schilling' and then, in brackets: 'You may telephone in lieu of the soup.' Not many people had a telephone of their own and, if they did, it was often of the two or four party-line variety, which hung on the wall and was equipped with a timer. You could never converse for more than five minutes without being cut off. Moreover it was frequently engaged, since two or four people might be waiting to be connected.

Adolf Hitler had promised that everything would change abruptly after 13 March 1938. Initial proof of the ability of the Third Reich to cope with any problem was provided by the appearance in Vienna of the celebrated Bavarian Aid Column. This was a motorized unit belonging to the Bavarian branch of the National Socialist People's Welfare Organization and its role was to bring supplies to the population in distressed areas or in the event of some natural catastrophe. On reaching Vienna the aforesaid column patrolled the streets in order to provide nourishment for the allegedly starving population. In 1938 there were certainly still plenty of poor people who would gladly have accepted a free meal, but the fare served up appealed to no one, for it was *'Eintopf'*, a single dish consisting of whatever ingredients happened to be available. In the war years ahead, *Eintopf* was to feature daily on the menu of every eating-place, but at that time it was by no means to the taste of the finicky Viennese – and in the matter of food even Vienna's unemployed have always been finicky. Indeed, it was not long before the 'swill' was rejected, a circumstance that led to the first quarrels between German and Austrian National Socialists.

Business now began to pick up very quickly; large numbers of armaments contracts were awarded to Austrian firms; by the outbreak of war, work had already started on the Salzburg-Vienna autobahn and the spur in the direction of Villach, the Salzburg bypass, was actually completed during Hitler's day, and large railways projects were put in hand. Hitler's solicitude extended primarily to Linz, his adopted home town, where he intended to put up large edifices in his 'kitsch-palazzo' style. Vienna was treated much less kindly than Linz. Indeed Vienna was a city he hated, remembering as he did the the hard times of his youth. For he had been a failure in Vienna, having never got anywhere as either a painter or an architect. He had left the city profoundly disgruntled and depressed and his journey to Munich had been an escape, not just from military service, but in every other respect.

The Viennese very soon became aware of this, as did the functionaries of the NSDAP, though Hitler had once said that Vienna was 'a pearl for which he would provide the right setting'. The man he sent to Vienna to supervise the *Anschluss* was Gauleiter Bürckel, who had already proved himself in a similar capacity in the Saar. Needless to say, power was vested solely in Bürckel since the Reich Governor, Seyss-Inquart, was no more than a puppet. 'Bierleiter Gauckel', as the Reich Commissar was most aptly named by the Viennese, intended to bring 'the spineless Ostmarkers smartly into line', a task the Viennese certainly did not make easy for him.

Apart from the small territory of the Saar, Austria was the first region to be annexed by the Reich. Inevitably there were many changes, whose effect was bound to be felt in a great many quarters – in the most negative sense by those unlucky enough to be incarcerated by the new rulers, in the positive sense by the beneficiaries of those rulers. That is to say by the thousands of Germans from the Reich who, hard on the heels of the Wehrmacht, had moved into Vienna to take up leading positions there, and also by the host of Austrian 'illegals' who now felt that they could rest from their labours and await their reward for services rendered. Ample opportunities existed for rewarding a more or less deserving 'illegal', since there were in Vienna thousands of Jewish businesses, shops, factories and legal and medical posts available for distribution among the 'old fighters'.

Aryanization was going ahead on a wide front. Commissar managers were appointed to the various industries and most of them appropriated the attendant property in the shape of offices, houses and flats. There were undoubtedly numerous exceptions but, as always, these only go to prove the rule. Some people were extraordinarily fair and correct, especially those many employees of former Jewish firms who continued to run the business as if for the benefit of the old owners and who, after the war, duly handed it back as a going concern and, all things considered, in good order. One example of this was the Creditanstalt-Bankverein, the country's largest bank. Dr Franz Rotenberg, who headed it until 1938, was a Jew. His Austrian deputy, Dr Joseph Joham, and Dr Hermann Abs, a director of the Deutsche Bank who had been sent to Vienna from Germany, could not have treated him more fairly. A villa complete with park was placed at his disposal in Baden near Vienna, and there he spent the war, guarded by the ss. Their task however was not to keep him prisoner, but to make sure he was not inconvenienced in any way. After the war he was able to return to the Creditanstalt.

But in a large number of cases the position was unfortunately quite different and Aryanization proceeded apace. Indeed, on the strength of the slogan 'Out with the Jews', what more agreeable than to take immediate possession of a first-class business?

Finally, besides the Aryanizers, there was an influx from Germany of individuals whose sole aim was to buy up the contents of Austria's still well-stocked shops. In the streets of Vienna it was by no means rare to see Germans with enormous shopping bags buying ten pounds of butter in one emporium after another, or emerging from Meinl's with thirty tins of tea or, if they had any Reichsmarks left, purchasing yards and yards of cloth from the city's tailors. The Viennese soon began to regard them as figures of fun; overnight, 'Piefke'* became a nickname for German visitors to Austria, as did 'Like-me-not', because everyone disliked them. To others they were known as 'Preservems', for jam had soon taken the place of butter. The first Nazi jokes began to go the rounds at the same time as the nicknames; some may have been importations from the Reich, but others were genuine Viennese products.

To begin with, Hitler was called Schicklgruber, this being in fact the name of his father, who was illegitimate; subsequently he went by the description of *'Gröfaz'*†. Göring, on the other hand, was at first known as 'Iron Hermann' and then simply as 'Maier'. Maier dated from the early months of the Second World War when, in the course of a big speech at the Berlin Sports Palace, he declared: 'If an enemy aircraft ever succeeds

*A derogatory term for North Germans.

†An acronym for 'Grösster Feldherr aller Zeiten', or 'greatest captain of all time'.

in reaching the territory of the German Reich, then my name's Maier.'

Even at the age of fourteen I was struck by the grotesque, vulgar way in which people's enthusiasm, whether spontaneous or otherwise, would manifest itself. When Hitler stayed at the Hotel Imperial, thousands of fanatics stood outside for hours on end, bellowing until they were demented such messages as: 'Beloved Führer, Ostmark's son, out on to your balcony you must come.' Which the son of the Ostmark then proceeded to do.

A little later fat Hermann, Field-Marshal Göring, arrived in Vienna to see what he had set in motion, for it was he who had been in charge of 'Operation Otto', in other words the *Anschluss*. He too stayed at the Imperial. And at once the exultant choirs were on the scene with pleas of 'Hermann, dear Hermann, a welcome to you, come show yourself at your window do.' And Hermann, in one of his resplendent uniforms, obliged.

Finally, not long before the plebiscite of 10 April, Dr Joseph Goebbels, the Reich Propaganda Minister, also paid us a visit. I heard him speak in the Nordwestbahnhalle in Vienna; he was an outstanding speaker, extremely forceful and emotional. At all events he too was joyfully applauded by the National Socialist choirs who chanted: 'We're not moving, doctor, so don't go away, with you in this hall we'd rather stay.'

Hitler visited Vienna three or four times prior to 10 April and on two occasions I saw him at a distance of a few yards as he was entering or leaving the Hotel Imperial; at the time he seemed very alert and vigorous, and the only thing that struck me particularly was his penetrating glance, though most of the other Austrians in my vicinity almost fell to their knees when this 'greatest of all Ostermarkers', as the *Völkischer Beobachter* repeatedly described him, took a few steps along the Ringstrasse. What did not strike me at the time, but in retrospect suddenly seems highly remarkable, was the fact that Hitler was virtually unguarded. As he crossed the Ringstrasse in the direction of the Opera, accompanied by a few aides and a Third Reich panjandrum or two, he would have made an easy target for an assassin. This was one of the puzzles that were to give us much food for thought later on, during the war: Why was it, exactly, that neither the German resistance nor the various anti-National Socialist organizations in occupied Europe ever succeeded in doing away with him?

What preoccupied us now was, first, the magic power of attraction exerted by Hitler on millions of people and, second, the question of whether a decent, sensible man could also be a National Socialist. The famous joke then current seems to me an admirable illustration of this. God, so it went, had endowed man with three attributes, intelligence, decency and National Socialism. But, things being what they are, a German might only possess two of them. From this it followed that a German was either intelligent and decent, in which case he could not be a National Socialist, or he was decent and a National Socialist, in which case he could not be intelligent or, finally, he was intelligent and a National Socialist, in which case he could not possibly be decent. Generally speaking, virtually everyone in the Third Reich was classifiable under these three heads. For by the summer of 1939, at the latest, an intelligent and decent National Socialist had become an impossibility. By that time the scales should have fallen from the eyes even of the most naive. But the astonishing thing was that they never fell from the eyes of many thoroughly decent people, that not until 1945, and often much later, did these decent Austrians and Germans perceive how atrociously they had been duped by National Socialism and its representatives. And this is the more remarkable in that non-Nazis, though by no means more intelligent or decent than their Nazi fellow men, had nevertheless at once perceived that there was something terribly wrong about Hitler.

So far as we and many of our friends were concerned, it was an undoubted help to have come from a world and an environment that did not conform to National Socialism, to have grown up in a Catholic, decidedly Austrian family, to have had, in our own particular case, a father who happened to be editor-in-chief of a liberal newspaper. Put together, all these naturally tended to instil in us from the start an essentially sceptical frame of mind, and this attitude, which had begun to develop in the early days of the Third Reich, was in my case understandably completed when, in March 1938, father and Otto were arrested and my mother was beaten up by men of the Austrian Legion. No longer could be be fooled; and the same undoubtedly applied to many others besides ourselves.

The day of the plebiscite drew nearer and nearer. To judge from the newspapers and the all-pervading German radio, one might have believed that the 10th of April was to decide the future fate of Austria and of Greater Germany in general. It was of course obvious to anyone with a grain of sense that the whole thing was a farce. Since 12 March the entire country had been occupied by German troops, while the opponents of the Nazi regime were in gaol or in concentration camps. The *Anschluss* was a fait accompli. The minions charged with imposing the Nazi system, at their head the Security Service of the SS, the Gestapo and the SS proper, as well as officials from the German economic ministries and other economic organizations, had bound the country hand and foot to the Old Reich. Whatever its result, a plebiscite could do nothing to alter the facts. Moreover it was also perfectly obvious that, if only on psychological grounds and to win approval from the outside world, Hitler needed a plebiscite that would be ninety-nine per cent favourable. Accordingly the farce was played out to the bitter end, a performance which, with its lavish use of propaganda, might have provided a few tips for any of the political election campaigns in Central Europe during the sixties and seventies of this century. It was, of course, a relatively simple business, for the opposition, being in gaol, could easily be caricatured and presented in a negative light. Those theoretically still neutral, from Cardinal Innitzer to the former State Chancellor, Dr Renner, hastened to issue declarations of support. None of them remained aloof on this occasion, none of them dared refuse the friendly invitation from the rulers of the Third Reich to recommend that the electorate vote in favour.

Vienna was inundated with posters. Leaflets were handed out, all bearing the same message. 'Sieg Heil. One People, One Reich, One Führer. Vote for Adolf Hitler. Vote for the NSDAP. Vote for the Greater German Reich on 10 April.' They contained virtually nothing else; sometimes there would be an announcement of a plebiscite speech by Göring, Goebbels, Seyss-Inquart, or even the Führer himself. Gigantic posters went up with the same slogans, covering vast expanses of wall and bearing the signatures of Cardinal Innitzer or Dr Renner. We did not know at the time how Innitzer and Renner had been blackmailed, nor do we really know today to what extent blackmail was involved and to what extent the two men believed that they

were acting in the best interests of those who shared their convictions. Of one thing we may be certain, and that is that neither
Renner nor Innitzer was a Nazi. In the early months of 1938,
however, both overstepped the bounds of what might be termed
responsible behaviour and both committed serious blunders,
though undoubtedly with the best of intentions. For they made
it unconscionably difficult for hundreds of thousands of
people in Austria, Catholics and Social Democrats, to divine
what all this had to do with God and/or the Socialist credo.
Hence both Innitzer's initiative and Renner's endorsement were
a calamity for Austria, because they enabled the Nazis to sus-
tain their big lie for years on end. 'What exactly do you want?'
they could say. 'Here we have a Catholic Cardinal and a great
Social Democratic Chancellor and they both support the
Führer.' Not until many years after the war was it possible to
discover from contemporary publications that such had not
been the case.

In April 1938 their recommendations to the electorate came
as a heavy blow to those Austrians who were not National
Socialists; they undoubtedly contributed to the growing sense
of insecurity. But it is also true that they provided many with a
good excuse; if reproached for joining the NSDAP, they could
easily reply: 'Maybe, but didn't Renner and Innitzer also say at
the time that we ought to back Hitler?' But the despair of those
who had not the slightest intention of joining the NSDAP was
only increased by these two recommendations, which made
them feel more downhearted and forsaken than ever.

In any case the plebiscite of 10 April was itself patently
rigged. I still distinctly remember that my father and Otto voted
No. Yet the next day we were informed by the *Völkischer
Beobachter* that at the polling booth for the Upper Döbling
ward in the Pyrkergasse, the Yeas had amounted to one hundred
percent; no one had voted No. So something was evidently
amiss. Friends told us of similar results. In their own ward,
too, there were people who said they had voted No, but here
again it was officially reported that not one dissenting vote had
been recorded. According to the official version, the total number of votes cast in the Döbling district amounted to 38,416, of
which only 131 were Noes.

There is no doubt that even had there been a free poll on 10
April 1938, one month after the *Anschluss*, a majority of

Austrians would still have voted in favour of it. The scene had changed and unemployment was a thing of the past. Quite apart from pan-German sentiment, the mood was one of euphoria. A significant majority would certainly have come out in favour of Greater Germany, even if there had been no recourse to blackmail and fraud.

Why the Nazis had to put on this spectacle of a ninety-nine per cent favourable vote, thereby branding themselves, or so we thought, liars and buffoons, was a mystery to us at the time. But even today this same spectacle continues to be put on year after year in every Eastern European country. There, too, the Yeas amount to ninety-nine per cent, though eighty-five per cent would carry far more conviction. Dictatorial regimes are clearly incapable of tolerating even a small proportion of critical or dissenting votes. Those fifteen per cent could well form centres of intellectual opposition; they might be able to organize themselves and demand that they to be represented.

After the plebiscite life reverted to the old routine, albeit a routine now tinged with anxiety. I went to school. Otto, who had been released from prison early in April, was back at university, while father was busy seeing the *Neue Freie Presse* through its final vicissitudes prior to the paper's definitive interment by the Führer. Mother was reading the proofs of her novel *Pave und Pero*, which was to come out in the autumn of 1938. At first glance little else seemed to have changed. Or had it? Opposite us lived the Schlesingers. They were already talking of emigrating, as were the Hegners. In our own house, the occupant of the ground-floor was Dr Werber, a Jewish lawyer and for many years vice-president of the Viennese Football Association. He had resolved to quit the country while the going was still good. Other Jewish friends, however, said they had not the slightest intention of leaving. Herr Rappaport, for example, a high-ranking government official and an old friend of my grandfather's. After all, had he not been awarded a high decoration as an officer in the First World War and had not his family lived in Vienna for generations? It would never have occurred to him to leave.

Great-uncle Heinrich, a former director of a paper-mill in Upper Austria, now living in retirement in Linz, visited Vienna to consult my father and grandfather. He too had served as an officer in the First World War, he too had been awarded the

Gallantry Medal and he too had learnt only a few years before
that, according to the Nuremberg Laws, he was a Jew. What
ought he to do?

The father of Great-uncle Heinrich and my grandfather had
been of Jewish extraction. Nothing was definitely known about
his wife's origins, which only came to light after the war. When
we then discovered that grandfather's mother had been born
a Christian, the stigma of Jewish ancestry foisted on our family
by the Nazis was shown to be technically inaccurate anyway.
But since Uncle Heinrich was not married to a Christian – he
was a bachelor – he was designated a Jew and had to bear the
consequences. Evidently these caused him little concern, for all
his acquaintances in Upper Austria remained as friendly as
ever; he met them as usual in the same cafés and saw no
reason whatever to change his way of life. The silly juvenile
antics of the Hitler Youth, who roamed the streets chanting
anti-Semitic slogans at the tops of their voices, would surely
soon be a thing of the past. Even in Germany, in the 'old Reich',
it was felt, anti-Semitism had become a joke. After all, were not
a great many Jews still running businesses or working on their
own as artists, doctors or lawyers? So there was nothing to prevent you going back to your old way of life, unless you happened to be one of those cautious or far-sighted people who had
already heard the rumblings of the catastrophe to come and
were beating a timely retreat.

At Schotten Grammar School the *Anschluss* was little in
evidence. Most of the masters were in Holy Orders and thus by
definition non-Nazi, while the laymen, with one or two exceptions, were above suspicion in that respect. As I have already
said there were relatively few Nazis among the boys. We played
football, took an interest in everything imaginable, above all
in the civil war then raging in Spain, and, for the rest, looked
forward to the long summer holidays. For the *Anschluss* had
produced one advantage in that we could now at last visit
Germany and acquaint ourselves in person with the land that
was said to be so wonderful.

Father also favoured a visit to Germany, if possible by both
his sons. My mother thought Otto would do better to go to
Italy, since it was impossible to say for how much longer we
should still be able to travel abroad. In the end a compromise
was reached. I was to spend the summer with friends of the

family, Ferdinand and Jannerl Gatterburg, at their chateau in the Odenwald, having first accompanied my mother on a short visit to northern Italy, where she wished to wander round the scenes of the novel she had just finished. The book had been set in Venetia and Motta di Livenza, and also in Dalmatia. Otto, accompanied by friends from the youth movement and wholly in the spirit of that movement, was to hitch-hike to Italy; indeed, the ultimate gaol was Libya, at that time an Italian colony.

But first of all we boys intended to join up with friends who shared our opinions to find out what our chances were in the Third Reich of acting and behaving as we had always done, and for this purpose we wanted to find an Alpine hut that was as isolated as possible. One such, in a mountain pasture in the Montafon near Parthenen, was recommended to us by friends from the now, needless to say, disbanded Tyrolese Freikorps, an added advantage being that it was quite close to the Swiss frontier. We decided – there were about twenty of us in all – that at the beginning of July, when the holidays began, we would make our way to the Vorarlberg as unobtrusively as possible in small groups of two or three and rendezvous in Parthenen. Some wanted to proceed direct from Parthenen to Switzerland and the freedom of the West without bothering about such tiresome formalities as frontier posts and exit visas. By and large, not one of us had any idea that at this moment – a few months after the *Anschluss* – we were creating the first nucleus of an active resistance group. But it became apparent soon enough, thanks chiefly to the reaction of the Gestapo. All of us were very naive at the time and had no concept of the very real risks and dangers we were playing with.

Our first objective was Bludenz, where I met my brother Otto and friends from the Freikorps. From there we walked through the Montafon to Schruns and then along a small works' railway, used for conveying building materials to the Montafon power station then under construction, to Parthenen, a tiny village as yet quite unknown to tourists. Our route now followed the line of a funicular, but much to our dismay we were not permitted to ride on it, and instead had to make the climb on foot. Finally, after crossing extensive upland pastures, we reached our goal, a small Alpine hut. It was typical of its kind, fairly low, built of rough stone with a roof of wooden shingles and comprising a single room in which an open fire was burning; at the back was a stall where the sheep and cattle were housed in bad weather and where the milking was done.

Our ages ranged from fourteen to twenty-two; almost all of us came from the Freikorps, though some had belonged to the Neuland; many had belonged to both groups, originally to the Neuland and later to the Freikorps. We spent nearly a week up there. It was like the old youth movement days again, when we had gone on long hikes, cooked our own food and set ourselves endurance tests of the sort we used to take for granted in the Neuland. But now we were concerned with something different and of a more serious and more important nature than crossing a glacier barefoot, holding a hot plate in one's bare hands over an open fire, or getting up in time to run to morning mass in the village, three hours downhill followed by a three hour climb on the way back. None of that mattered any more.

We suddenly realized for the first time that what we were concerned with was politics, fundamental values which, though we were not yet able to formulate them clearly, confronted us with a reality that brooked no denial. Like my brother Otto, some of the older members of our circle had already been in prison; the Freikorps leader, Helmut Jörg, whom we all greatly revered, was in Dachau and no one knew whether he would ever come out again.

Young and optimistic as we were, we thought that one way or another we should be able to cope with any problem, even those presented by the all-powerful dictator Adolf Hitler and his Third Reich, of which by now we had had several months' experience. At this moment we felt impelled to face the enemy and go into action, to show that we, too, still had a place on this earth. Friends in Innsbruck told us of the first attempts to offer resistance to the Nazis in the Tyrol, where a particularly large number of young people and intellectuals had joined the National Socialists in the hope of being able to win back South Tyrol with Hitler's help. In the past the illegal NSDAP in Austria, and more especially in the Tyrol, had always made political capital out of the South Tyrol problem and cited the good relations with the Italian Fascists maintained by Dollfuss, and subsequently Schuschnigg, as an example of Austrian betrayal of the people of South Tyrol.

As early as the night of 11/12 March 1938, the first of the

big torchlight processions had been held by the Innsbruck National Socialists to the accompaniment of the South Tyrolese Andreas Hofer anthem. Immediately after the *Anschluss*, however, Hitler had to pay for Mussolini's tacit consent to the annexation of Austria, and this he did by acknowledging the Brenner line, at the same time declaring that the inhabitants of South Tyrol had two alternatives: either they emigrated to the Greater German Reich or they remained where they were, in which case they would have to reconcile themselves to outright Italianization. Hitler's action was wholly unexpected and came as a slap in the face for the National Socialists of the region. The non-Nazis in the Tyrol suddenly found themselves in possession of a truly splendid weapon that would enable them to demonstrate the hollowness and dishonesty of the entire National Socialist system. For did not that system claim that blood, nationhood and soil were matters of constant concern? In our view, therefore, we ought to strike while the iron was hot. We felt that it was up to us to do something about it, for our political leaders had all been arrested and were detained in prison or concentration camps. Those who had been released were under strict surveillance by the Gestapo. So we ought to bestir ourselves and show what we were worth.

Accordingly, at the end of our stay in Parthenen, we made our way in small groups down the Paznaun valley in the direction of Landeck and Innsbruck. Some reached the North Tyrolese capital on foot, while others cadged lifts. Once again I stayed with relatives and here, in company with the Parthenen group and friends from the Innsbruck Freikorps, I got the chance of participating in the first resistance operation. In the secretary's room at the Innsbruck city presbytery, which was also the office of Dr Paul Rusch, the newly appointed Suffragan Bishop of Innsbruck, there was a duplicating-machine. On this machine we were able to run off four thousand copies of a parody on the Horst Wessel song, the National Socialist anthem, sung to the tune of a Nazi song, the text deploring the fact that Hitler had sold out the former Austrian province of German-speaking South Tyrol to his friend Mussolini at the expense of the local Austrian population.

We worked for five or six hours, starting at nightfall, and by one or two in the morning had finished, full of pride at what we had done. The next morning each of us put a few hundred leaflets in his rucksack and spent the day by the Lanser See above Innsbruck. When darkness fell, we returned to Innsbruck to scatter leaflets in the streets. Some of us operated on foot, others from the open platform of the tram that used to run from Wilten to Hall. No one at this stage had expected a positive act of resistance either in Innsbruck or anywhere else in Austria, and the results were spectacular. The Tyrol Gestapo at once alerted the headquarters of the Reich Security Service, while Seyss-Inquart, the Reich Governor, who was then more or less still in office, promptly left Vienna for Innsbruck along with Himmler's representatives and those of other German government departments. There were raids on a vast scale, the assumption being that an active organization had been at work. What had certainly not entered into our calculations was the arrest of some four hundred Tyrolese on suspicion of having planned and executed the affair. Not one of us was included in the four hundred, for it didn't occur to anyone that such an operation could have been mounted by a few impudent fourteen to eighteen-year-olds, most of whom, in any case, hailed from other parts of the country.

I can no longer say for certain whether Bishop Rusch played an active part in the business. All I know is that, on the night we ran off the text, he suddenly appeared in the presbytery office and gave each of us a liturgical missal with a dedication in his own hand. I still possess my copy today. Psychologically, the whole operation had helped us in a quite unexpected way. We now felt we were putting up a fight and could do something. Initially we grossly overestimated our strength, though our first reaction was relatively sensible. My brother Otto, accompanied by those of his friends who wanted to join him on his grand expedition to North Africa in the summer of 1938, departed for Italy that same night via the Brenner and had long since vanished by the time the Gestapo became active. The younger members of the group – I believe I was in fact the youngest – stayed in Innsbruck for another two days as innocent summer visitors and then went their various ways.

By the time I got back to Vienna in September 1938, everything had again changed. Conditions had become noticeably more harsh, and in the meantime a considerable number of my parents' friends had been arrested. Three days after I got back, Otto returned from Africa and on the following day he was arrested by the Gestapo, who took him to the former Hotel Metropol, their prison in the Morzinplatz. He was accused of active opposition to the regime and of having participated in acts of resistance in Vienna and the Tyrol. So the Tyrolese affair had come out after all. How it had happened we do not know, for they released him again three weeks later, having left him in no doubt that he would be well-advised to join the Wehrmacht as soon as possible, for otherwise his days as a free man in Vienna would be numbered. Otto consulted with father and several of his friends and joined up. At the beginning of December 1938 he was posted to a motorcycle battalion of the 2nd Panzer Division. Initially he was stationed at Kritzendorf on the Danube, quite close to Klosterneuburg and Vienna.

After the autumn of 1938 I attended a new school, as the Schotten Grammar School had meanwhile been closed by the authorities of the Third Reich. Catholic schools and institutions were no longer permitted and the Fathers who taught at the Schotten had to turn to other activities. By entering Döbling Grammar School I was keeping up an old tradition, as father had gone there in the late nineties, although not for long, since his stay had been cut short by his lack of academic success. It was a fate both Otto and I were spared.

At Döbling I met a number of old friends from Freikorps days. New acquaintances included Harald Frederiksen, an American citizen of Danish origin who had remained behind after his father had left Vienna. He was later to play an important part in the resistance.

I had been there barely three weeks when we heard that the boys and girls of Vienna's parishes had been invited to attend a joint service in the Stephansplatz on the following evening. It was, I think, to celebrate the Feast of the Holy Rosary. Accordingly, on 7 October 1938, we all made our way there, proceeding in small groups, and congregated first in St Stephen's Cathedral. A surprise awaited us, for I had imagined that we should find perhaps three hundred young people there. The number – according to Gestapo estimates – was at least eight, if not ten, thousand. The church was full to overflowing and many people were actually standing in the Stephansplatz outside the great door. Cardinal Innitzer preached, then came prayers followed by hymn singing, after which everyone streamed out into the Stephansplatz. Suddenly there rang out, along with the hymns, the songs of the youth organizations and, finally, the patriotic songs of Austria. I thought my eyes and ears were deceiving me when all of a sudden thousands of young people, boys as well as girls, began singing, right hands upraised in the old Austrian salute, the 'Song of Youth' dedicated to the Federal Chancellor, Engelbert Dollfuss, who had been shot by the Nazis in July 1934:

> Come, youth of Austria, close your ranks,
> 'Tis you he still will lead.
> To him we owe eternal thanks,
> None better of his breed.
> The murderous shot that took his life
> Aroused our land from sleep and strife.
> With Dollfuss into the new age,
> The future and our heritage.

The Cardinal then reappeared on the balcony of the archiepiscopal palace and blessed the crowd. It was during this concluding phase that Hitler Youth patrols appeared from the direction of the Graben and the Schülerstrasse. Scuffles and brawls broke out at various points, especially outside the Heidentor of St Stephen's Church, where several Freikorps and Neuland groups had assembled and were battling shoulder to shoulder against the patrols. Parties from the Catholic Students' Associations had assembled on the far side of the cathedral and here, too, there was fightng. However the Hitler Youth were in the minority and had to withdraw relatively quickly. Four hundred people were said to have been arrested, but I do not know whether the number is correct. About a dozen of my friends were detained. At all events, we regarded that evening not only as a great victory, but as a turning-point. For the first time – after six months of National Socialist rule – thousands of young people in Vienna had publicly professed their allegiance to Catholicism, to Austria and to an outlook that ran counter to the system. We had staged a demonstration in the Stephansplatz; flushed with victory we marched singing through the streets before finally making our way home.

Next day at school we were told by one of the Hitler Youth

leaders in our class that it had already been agreed in the early hours of the morning to hold a big demonstration in the Stephansplatz that same evening to wipe out the 'disgrace' of the previous night, a disgrace consisting in the fact that thousands of young people had publicly met together and sung anti-National Socialist songs. There would, we were told, be a terrible retribution. My friends and I resolved to go to the Stephanspaltz to see what happened. It was about half past seven when we entered the square from the direction of the Graben. By that time, several thousand members of the Hitler Youth, all in uniform, had already assembled. The presence of SA troops, who were emerging from gigantic buses, plainly indicated that everything had been carefully pre-arranged, as did the blaring loudspeakers and their inflammatory exhortations. The evening began with the singing of anti-clerical songs, followed by chants such as 'We believe in Germany' and 'Dachau for Innitzer'. As a finale the archbishop's palace in the Stephansplatz was stormed by the Hitler Youth, the Cardinal's chapel desecrated and the palace furnishings smashed to pieces. Krawarik, the cathedral verger, was thrown from a first floor window and left lying in the street with both legs broken. The Cardinal himself had been concealed by his faithful followers in a small room in the attics of the palace.

For Innitzer, who only six months before had issued a statement that he would vote in favour of the *Anschluss* and had called on Hitler at the Hotel Imperial, that evening must have provided a particularly harsh demonstration of the true state of affairs. But at all events he had regained the confidence of the Catholics of Austria.

That night saw, not only the storming and gutting of the archbishop's premises, but the arrest in all parts of Vienna of at least five hundred young people who had taken part in the demonstration of 7 October.

My friends and I had kept in the background during the evening of 8 October but, while crossing the Kohlmarkt on our way home, we were stopped by a group of Hitler Youth and taken to the Rossauer Lände*. There the under-sixteens, of whom I was one, were interrogated for several hours and then sent home. The older ones were detained and handed over to the Gestapo

*Vienna's largest prison.

in the Hotel Metropol in the Morzinplatz. It was my first experience of the police and prison, but it only lasted for a few
hours and there were no immediate consequences either physical
or mental. So far as we were concerned, however, those two
October evenings in 1938 had been a victory. We felt we were
beng taken seriously, we were people the Gestapo and the Hitler
Youth had to reckon with, the SA's aura of absolute power had
suddenly been called in question, we had proved we were a
force that could not be ignored.

One consequence of the events of October 1938 was the salu-
tary lesson given to thousands of Austrian Catholics who had
thought that they could also be National Socialists. It was now
up to them to show their true colours: a man was either a
National Socialist or a Catholic; he couldn't be both. A bene-
ficial form of soul-searching was everywhere beginning to gain
ground. On balance the lesson was a good and timely one. But
in the autumn of 1938 there was no end to the run of sensational
events. In the sphere of foreign policy the Third Reich had
scored a further string of successes. Thanks to some tremendous bluffing and his conduct of the negotiations at Munich,
Hitler contrived to fool Chamberlain and Daladier and thus
inherit Czechoslovakia's Sudeten German territories from
Messrs Masaryk and Beneš without having to fire a shot. The
Czechs were compelled to give way. They would have been
prepared to fight, but had been told by France and Britain that
they could not count on their support. On his return to London,
Chamberlain exclaimed triumphantly: 'I believe it is peace for
our time.' In this case 'our time' was to last no more than
twelve months.

Obviously the successes scored by the Third Reich were not
without consequences at home, for Hitler's opponents felt disillusioned, whereas the euphoria of the National Socialists
knew no bounds. One of the first repercussions was the *Kristallnacht*: early in November 1938 a German diplomat was shot
dead in Paris by a Jewish émigré. This act was seen by the Third
Reich as a welcome excuse to have done with the Jews once
and for all. On the evening of 9 November the *Kristallnacht*
began. In all the larger German, Austrian and Sudeten German
towns, synagogues were destroyed, Jewish shops looted and
Jewish private houses attacked; wherever they could be found,
Jews were beaten up, reviled and arrested.

On the morning of 10 November I set off for school as usual. I had not gone far when I saw clouds of smoke rising from the nearby Döllinergasse where the Döbling synagogue was still in flames. In the lane stood a dozen or so SA men and Hitler Youth. Some elderly Jewish men and an old lady, who had presumably been trying to extinguish the fire, were being put aboard a truck. The old lady was bleeding from a head wound. With a laugh, one of the SA men exclaimed: 'Stop crying, you Jewish bitch, you'll be dead soon.' A Hitler Youth leader recognized me. 'Beat it, Molden,' he said, 'unless you want to go along too.' I turned round and continued on my way to school. The synagogue smouldered for most of that day. To add insult to injury the Jews were themselves compelled to clear up and repair the damage done to their homes and businesses by the Nazis. Notices sprang up at the entrances to parks and public places bearing the legend 'Jews not wanted' or 'Jew-free'. Jews were no longer allowed to engage in business and Jewish children were barred from school. Within a few days the Jewish community had been degraded to the status of sub-humans. And the time was not far off – the autumn of 1941 – when all Jews would be required to wear a yellow star on their clothing.

Even among those Jews who had hitherto believed they could still hold their own in the Third Reich, by virtue either of their services to the German cause or of their gallantry in the First World War, there was by now a growing awareness that they must take immediate steps to get away. At the same time, however, it was becoming increasingly difficult to leave Germany. There were, it is true, Jewish organizations and international groups, such as the Quakers, which sought to provide Jews with passports, tickets and entry visas to foreign countries, these being usually the basic requirements for a prospective émigré. But for two people who were intimately connected with us, help came too late. In 1941 Great-uncle Heinrich was deported to Theresienstadt and Herr Rappaport to Auschwitz. There they met their deaths, a belated consequence of the *Kristallnacht*.

At the time of which I am speaking, however, the idea of the 'final solution' already seemed to have entered the heads of those in charge of the Third Reich. For towards the end of 1938 the existing policy of encouraging, indeed often compelling, Jews to emigrate was brought to a halt. In the following year plans were put in hand for their deportation, not, however, to destinations abroad, but from Reich territory to the areas occupied by the Wehrmacht. Czechoslovakia became available for the purpose in March 1939, as did Poland in September. One of the first locations to be chosen was Theresienstadt, formerly a fortress of the old Austro-Hungarian empire. The start of this development coincided with the *Kristallnacht* and, in the months that followed, even a relative outsider could see that Vienna, for example, was becoming increasingly 'Jew-free'. Jews were expelled from their homes and resettled in the 2nd and parts of the 9th District, that is to say in mass accommodation in various hostels and old people's homes that had been evacuated for the purpose, such as those in the Seegasse near the Franz-Joseph station. As time went on, the area allotted to the Jews became progressively smaller, until finally the last of them had left Vienna. The residue consisted of so-called 'honorary Aryans' and Jews married to Christians, in all, probably no more than 1.5% of the city's former Jewish population. I find it hard to believe that there could have been people who never noticed that the Jews were being persecuted. Indeed, I was amazed to discover after the war that large sections of the population claimed never to have heard of anything untoward happening to Jews in the Third Reich. Here was another of those peculiar phenomena which kept occurring at the time and which are so extraordinarily difficult to explain.

A good twenty-five years later, I met at the Frankfurt Book Fair someone who had been shrewd enough to distrust the atmosphere of calm that preceded the *Kristallnacht*. Dr F. Hajek, a wise and most kindly man, who later worked in the Wiener Library in London, told me he had arrived in Basle in September 1938 to await a visa for an overseas country. One disaster had followed another and he was in despair. Barely six months previously he had been living peacefully in Prague, but now, after the integration of Austria and the Sudetenland, he was a homeless and harried refugee. A world war was imminent, and what would happen then? As he set out each morning to inquire of some arrogant consul whether his visa had arrived, Hajek would ponder on the vileness of the year 1938.

It was on one such gloomy morning in late autmn that his landlady told him in agitated tones that Radio Beromünster had just announced the looting, burning and destruction of synagogues and Jewish businesses and homes throughout Germany. The *Kristallnacht* had taken place. Hajek, distraught, hurried to the nearest newspaper kiosk and bought the first daily he saw in order to learn the details of this appalling event. As he picked up the *Basler Nachrichten*, his eye lighted on the front-page headline. '1938,' he read, 'A Good Year for Nuts.'

4

One People, One Reich,
One Führer

In the drawing-room the family had gathered about the round,
early nineteenth-century table covered with its crochet-work
cloth. A warm fire burned in the white majolica stove. Otto,
clad in the grey uniform of the German Wehrmacht, and home
on weekend leave, was telling us about his life in the army.
This was late in 1938, three months after he had enlisted.

It wasn't really too bad, Otto said; they had been issued with
superb modern motorcycles and most of the instructors were
nice fellows from the Reich who were already on friendly terms
with the Austrian recruits who, it seemed, were nearly all from
the Vienna area. As prescribed in the regulations, they were
being put through their paces and licked into shape in the woods
beside the Danube near Kritzendorf, where the company was
stationed. This was at any rate better, Otto thought, than being
in prison unable to do anything, or waiting for the Gestapo to
strike again. He had already made friends with some of his fellow recruits – for instance, Robbi Baier, in whose company he
was later to go through the whole of the campaign in France.
He was now wondering when his unit, which belonged to the
2nd Panzer Division, one of the crack divisions of the German
army, would receive orders to move towards the Czech border.

It was an open secret, discernible daily to all who chose to
read between the lines of the *Völkischer Beobachter* and elsewhere, that the Czechoslovakian question was soon to be settled.
Already the opening moves had been made in the war of nerves
that invariably preceded the annexation of a neighbouring
country by the Third Reich. Newspapers and the radio announced that distraught German citizens had been beaten up by
a disreputable Czech mob, that they had been forced to ask

for the protection of the Reich, and that mild protests on the part of the German leaders had been ignored by the arrogant Czech government with its 'judaeo-plutocratic affinities'. So what could the peace-loving German Reich do except intervene in order to protect its fellow countrymen?

No one doubted that within a few weeks or months Czechoslovakia would have ceased to exist. In view of the lamentable way the British and French had behaved at Munich in September 1938, there was small hope that they would behave differently in the spring of 1939 and yet another ally of the western powers would be swallowed up by Hitler. Nor had Czechoslovakia any hope of defending herself. Her fortifications and lines of concrete bunkers, which would have enabled the Bohemian-Moravian area to be effectively defended, had already been taken over by Germany when the Sudetenland was ceded to the Reich in the autumn of 1938. What remained of Czechoslovakia was a narrow strip of land which could in places be crossed by tanks in a matter of two or three hours.

Otto had some interesting and, to us, new things to say about his officers and NCOs. Most of them were by no means sympathetic to National Socialism. They were young men who would, of course, serve their victorious fatherland and who were at pains to carry out properly the duties that fell to them as German soldiers. But within this cadre of one of the crack divisions of the German Wehrmacht, Otto had sensed little of the National Socialist fanaticism which had been apparent among the young Nazis of Austria in 1938 and which he had expected to find as a matter of course in most young Germans. On the contrary, he had gained the impression that certain of his officers adopted a somewhat critical attitude towards National Socialism even if, understandably enough, they took care not to make this plain to recruits they did not know.

In Vienna, Germans from the Reich had become an everyday phenomenon and were scarcely distinguishable from Austrians, now styled Ostmarkers. In 1942, however, Hitler was to abolish the term Ostmark and substitute the words 'Donau und Alpengaue', 'Danubian and Alpine regions'; what had formerly been Austria disappeared as an administrative unit and all that now remained were the Reichsgaue of the Lower Danube, Vienna, Styria, Carinthia, Salzburg, the Upper Danube and, finally, the Tyrol-Vorarlberg. The Reichsgaue were immediately dependent on Berlin. Each was administered by a Gauleiter and Reich Governor. The only legacy from Austria's past that was appreciated and therefore retained was her military history. A modern cruiser was named *Prinz Eugen*, while time-honoured regimental names, such as Hoch- und Deutschmeister, were handed on to units of the German Wehrmacht.

In the schools, teachers were somewhat at a loss as to how history should be taught, and it therefore became the custom to finish with the end of the First World War, an engaging practice which was retained until well into the time of the Second Republic. For even after 1945 teachers never knew quite what view to take of the First Republic, the Schuschnigg era, the period between the *Anschluss* and 1945, or the various phases of occupation up till 1955, nor could they decide how all this should be presented. Since the habit of cocking a snook at authority has, as everyone knows, never really caught on in Austria, where circumspection has always been the rule, they thought it best not to teach the history of the past fifty years at all. In consequence, Austrian secondary schoolchildren learned materially more about the ancient Greeks and Celts than about what went on in Austria in the twenties and thirties of this century. This all started with the Nazis and their recasting of the history of the Austrian Empire; the Habsburgs, for instance, were dismissed in extremely negative terms, while the role of the Catholic church was likewise presented in a new and derogatory light. Needless to say, it was the Protestants who were now in favour and accorded a positive evaluation, whereas the Counter-Reformation was held to be the source of all evil.

At Döbling Grammar School I was fortunate in having a very sensible history teacher, who continued to teach his subject along the old lines. On the other hand, our German teacher, Dr Müller – after the war he was pounced on in the street and killed by men newly released from Nazi gaols – was determined to convert us to the faith of good old Wotan. When he went with us on school outings to the Wienerwald, he would seek out a suitable grove of oak trees and proceed to lecture us on the old Germanic pantheon, in the hope of converting us to neo-paganism. His success in our class was small, in fact I doubt if he made a single convert, and this grieved him. As a person,

Müller was quite a decent sort; thus, he never penalized me for my various inadequacies, always treated me very kindly and would even give me good marks.

The same could not be said of the headmaster; he did everything in his power to make it clear to non-Nazi or otherwise 'suspect' pupils that he was a convinced National Socialist who considered them sub-human, if nothing worse, nor did he ever cease to make life as difficult as possible for those of us who were not National Socialists. When, soon after the war, I chanced to meet this man in the street, he all but embraced me and was utterly dumbfounded by my failure to respond with equal enthusiasm to the happy reunion.

Never before had the country experienced such an outbreak of iconoclasm, and the situations to which it gave rise were often grotesque. For instance, the world of the theatre and the press in Vienna had largely been dominated by Jews. Indeed, the same could be said of medicine and the law, a fact that had materially contributed to the spread of anti-Semitism in Austria. To many non-Jews these sectors of cultural and economic life seemed difficult of access. This is not, of course, to suggest that some secret Jewish society – for example the 'Elders of Zion' so often cited by Hitler – had issued a decree whereby no one in Vienna but a Jew might become a doctor, dentist, lawyer, solicitor, theatrical producer or journalist. Rather, Jewish immigration from the east, from Poland, Roumania, Slovakia and Hungary, had given rise to a powerful concentration of gifted, ambitious and, above all, hard-working people who, since the last third of the nineteenth century, had made Vienna the goal of their professional and private dreams.

These people, coming as they did from the ghettos of Galicia and from every part of eastern Europe, were intent on one thing only – success. And in this their greatest rivals were none other than their fellow Jews, who, having been long settled in Vienna, where they had hitherto led a peaceful, undisturbed and respected existence, now saw themselves in danger, on the one hand of being placed in the same category as the newcomers from the east and, on the other, of being outstripped by them. Small wonder that the last three decades of the nineteenth century gave rise in Vienna to such figures as Schönerer and Lueger and, with them, that Viennese brand of anti-Semitism composed of commercial envy and traditional religious prejudice.

The fact remains that, at that period, the number of outstanding exponents of the creative arts who were of Jewish origin was out of all proportion to the population as a whole. In 1938, therefore, it was very difficult for the rulers of the Third Reich to persuade people that a large proportion of the writers and poets who, up till a few weeks before, had been regarded as the crème de la crème, had now, because Jewish, become bad, incompetent and repulsive, if indeed they had not always been so – Arthur Schnitzler, Hugo von Hofmannsthal, Franz Werfel, Stefan Zweig, Karl Kraus, Raoul Auernheimer, to name only a few.

In Vienna, a city in which music and literature had always played such a pre-eminent role, it was embarrassing suddenly to have to discard as the inferior products of a third-rate culture a large proportion of the works hitherto performed in the theatres, the Opera and the concert halls. A particularly amusing case was that of Johann Strauss, in whose veins there had been a drop or two of Jewish blood. Dr Goebbels and the Viennese cultural panjandrums succeeded in hushing up this defect since it was unthinkable ever to put the dear Führer in the position of learning that the King of the Waltz he so greatly revered had belonged to a group which, according to *Mein Kampf*, was incapable of true artistic achievement.

The sudden disappearance of large numbers of culturally creative people necessarily left gaps which could be filled only with the utmost difficulty, if at all, by recruiting artists able to produce a certificate of Aryanism. No one, for that matter, had a very clear idea of what Aryanism was. Aryan supermen, or so the doctrines of Alfred Rosenberg and other exponents of racism had it, were tall, fair-haired, blue-eyed and in all respects the successors of the Teutonic race of gods. But as everyone knows, neither Germans nor Austrians are in the main tall, blue-eyed, broad-shouldered, swift as a greyhound or hard as Krupps' steel, nor were these external manifestations of Aryanism discernible even in a minority of those at the top of the tree in the Greater German Reich. Neither Hitler nor Göring, neither Goebbels nor Alfred Rosenberg, and least of all Streicher, the infamous Gauleiter of Nuremberg and editor of the leading anti-Semitic organ *Der Stürmer*, bore the remotest resemblance to those Teutonic giants in whose likeness the German people was expected to evolve.

However, if these Nordic prodigies did not exist in the flesh, some attempt might at least be made to nordicize one's children by giving them Teutonic names. All of a sudden the sons of National Socialists were no longer called Karl, Leopold, Ludwig, Franz or Fritz; instead, abecedarians embarking as good little Germans on their school careers tended to have names like Hagen, Siegfried, or Rüdiger tacked on to surnames of unmistakably Czech, Hungarian or Polish origin. Nor was there any lack of similarly Teutonic names for girls, Gudrun and Siegelinde being particular favourites with which petty officials of the Nazi Party were wont to launch their daughters into life. The business also had its drawbacks, for later on, when the fortunes of war had turned, Teutonic names were something people would have gladly discarded. However, this was more easily said than done so that, several decades later, it is possible to tell from a person's Christian name whether or not his or her parents were supporters of the Third Reich.

The more foreign-sounding the surname of a Gauleiter or other leading party functionary – for instance, Globocnik or Zalesak – the greater the lengths to which he would go to prove himself a loyal German. Or, if at all possible, he would do even better and actually change his name. And, indeed, in the hope of obtaining advancement in the SA or SS, if not the upper reaches of politics, many a man who had embarked on his career in the thirties with an honest-to-goodness Czech, Hungarian or Slovene name, would suddenly turn up with a Teutonic version of it.

It was a time when political jokes proliferated as never before, something that is bound to happen under a dictatorship, where there is no other outlet for the expression of criticism or dissident opinion. Here, by way of an example, is a story about the controversy between the Catholic church and the Third Reich. Relations between the Vatican and the Reich government were going from bad to worse. Finally Hitler sent for Göring, ordered him to proceed immediately to Rome and settle matters with the Pope, cost what it might. Having taken note of the order, Göring set off. Two days later Hitler got a priority telegram from Rome which read: 'Reichsgau Vatican annexed. College of Cardinals converted. Pope shot while trying to escape. Tiara perfect fit. Heil Hitler. Hermann I, Pontifex Maximus.'

In March 1939 Otto moved off with his unit to the Znaim district of southern Moravia, then already part of Niederdonau, as the Nazis had renamed Lower Austria. He took part in the occupation of what remained of Czechoslovakia, finally ending up in Mährisch-Weisskirchen. Czecholsovakia became the Reich Protectorate of Bohemia and Moravia in which a Czech puppet goverment, led by Hacha, was set up to carry out the orders of a German Reich Protector, the first being the former German Foreign Minister, Freiherr von Neurath, later succeeded by ss-Obergruppenführer Heydrich. The latter was assassinated by Czech patriots flown in from England and dropped by parachute in the neighbourhood of Prague.

As a result of this assassination the Czech village of Lidice was razed to the ground and its inhabitants murdered. In the course of the war Czechoslovakia was to experience many other, if less publicized, atrocities of a similar kind, and there can be no doubt that the Czechs, who had always resisted annexation by the Third Reich, suffered intolerably under Hitler. On the other hand, it should be pointed out, though not at all in a spirit of denigration, that the Czechs were better off than the other subject peoples of the Third Reich. For instance, after their incorporation into the Greater German Reich, the Austrians and, of course, the Sudeten-Germans were subject to compulsory military service, as were the German-speaking inhabitants of the 'Protectorate', whereas right up to the end of the war the Czechs were never compelled to join the forces. Thus they were spared the terrible sacrifice in terms of human life inevitably undergone by the warring countries. No did they ever really have to face the possibility of air-raids on their cities, whereas the Allied bombers meted out much the same treatment to Austria as, for instance, to so many German towns. It was part of the bitter price the Austrians had to pay for the 're-incorporation' into the Reich of 'their beloved Führer's homeland'.

The countries that were occupied by German troops in the course of the war, such as Poland, Norway, the Low Countries, France, Yugoslavia, Greece and Russia, suffered terribly, if only as a result of the fighting. One only has to think of the bombing of Warsaw, Rotterdam and Belgrade, of the battle of

Lenigrad or of the way in which the Polish and Russian populations were maltreated, to realize that German rule in Czechosolvakia up to the time of Lidice was relatively mild. Before the assassination of Heydrich, Czechoslovakia was well treated by the Germans, who wished it to be a peaceful spot; and even after Heydrich's assassination, they were still at pains to spare Bohemia and Moravia as an integral part of the Reich and one obviously not earmarked by the Allies as a target for their bombers.

The Czechs have never been open to the reproach of failing to combat annexation, a reproach constantly and not altogether unjustifiably levelled against the Austrians by every Allied radio station in the years between 1938 and 1945. As early as July 1940 the Czechs formed a government in exile which Beneš, the former President of the Republic, was to lead with great skill throughout the war. The fact that, after the war, Beneš was unable to put up any adequate resistance to the Russians and that, in the end, Czechoslovakia had perforce to go the way of the other communist-occupied countries in eastern Europe, is neither here nor there.

Whatever the case, in the years after 1939 the average inhabitant of the Greater German Reich regarded the Bohemian and Moravian territories as an almost unattainable paradise. We knew that there was enough to eat there, we knew that there was no compulsory military service and we all lived in the hope of obtaining, on some pretext or other, a special dispensation that would enable us to enter the Reich Protectorate. I myself succeeded in doing so on two occasions, first in 1942 and again in 1944. When I was on my way back from Russia in 1942 my troop train stopped at Prague and a kindly military police sergeant at the station put a stamp on my movement order entitling me to break my journey for seventy-two hours. This I did with the utmost pleasure and, for the first time, was able to take a look at the most beautiful city in Central Europe. I still remember wandering about the streets of the Little Quarter and the Old City and realizing, as never before, how very much Prague was, in effect, a German city – though not in the sense supposed by the National Socialist rulers – or, to put it another way, how greatly the Bohemian-Czechoslovakian area had influenced the history of German-speaking Central Europe. And, thirdly and lastly, the extent to which the symbiosis of Slavs and

Germans in Prague, despite all antagonisms and difficulties, had put its stamp on the city, thus creating over the centuries an atmosphere such as would be unimaginable anywhere else.

The second time I stopped in Prague was in 1944. I was travelling with forged papers as Sergeant Steinhauser from Vienna to Berlin and had been held up in Prague by an air raid warning. On this occasion, I was again able to get a decent meal and a good glass of Pilsner at a public house.

The mood in German-occupied Prague was, however, utterly different from what I had been led to expect by *The Good Soldier Schweik* which, though banned, was still in our library in Vienna. It was a sombre mood, with no trace of that sardonic nimble-mindedness with which the Czechs had once tackled imperial rule in Bohemia, no trace of the skill with which, by this little trick or that, they had succeeded in ridiculing its pomposities. It was an uncanny silence, a defensiveness which, even in the absence of all outward manifestation, could hardly have made itself more plainly felt. I recollect two little stories of that time which reflect very clearly what the situation was like in the Prague of those days.

The scene of the first is the Wenceslas Bridge in the heart of the city. A man leans too far over and falls into the water. Despairingly he shouts in German: 'Help! Save me, I'm drowning!' Another man watches amiably from the bridge. Also in German, but with a broad Bohemian accent, he replies: 'Your German's not much use now. You ought've learnt to swim.'

The other story also takes place in Prague during the Second World War, aboard a tram that is about to stop outside the museum. Now, under the German occupation all names of streets etc had to be in two languages – Czech and German. As the tram stops, the conductor sings out: 'Museum, *Museum*. That was German, that was.'

It was gallows' humour and acerbic into the bargain. Nostalgically, people harked back to the days of the Dual Monarchy. I noticed the same thing at Brno, where I once spent the day. Conversation between Czechs was almost invariably punctuated by lamentations over the abolition of the monarchy in 1918 and their own foolishness in having allowed petty issues such as language differences to blind them to the real advantages they had enjoyed. 'We called it the "four nations' prison",' they would say. 'But now, under the Third Reich, we've come to know what a prison really is.'

Neither the Balkans nor the Danubian region has ever experienced so protracted a period of peace as under Austrian rule. Even if this was sometimes marred by inefficiency and the all-too-reactionary and conservative views of those in power, or jeopardized by quarrels between the various national groups, the balance was invariably restored. It was a time of cultural, economic and even political ferment. In 1914 Austria possessed a working democracy – a democracy, that was, at any rate, infinitely more representative and efficient than any to be found today in the east European countries, the so-called successor states of the old Austro-Hungarian Empire.

In the spring of 1939 there occurred in the Osterleitengasse an event of some importance to Fepolinski and Waschlapski, namely the arrival of Neda Rukavina, our cousin from Croatia, who had been invited by my mother to stay with us for a few months in order to improve her German or, in other words, to have a good time in Vienna. Nedica was a great success with the family as my parents, and my mother in particular, had always wanted a daughter but had so far had to make do with a brace of sons. Being two years older than I, Nedica was almost grown-up, and I thought her entrancing – the first time, in fact, that I had ever found a woman entrancing.

Otto was stationed at Mährisch-Weisskirchen with the 2nd Panzer Division and only came home for an occasional weekend. Father was working in the Jasomirgottstrasse where a weekly, the *Südost-Echo*, was issued by the German Economics Ministry in the hope of drumming up enthusiasm for the German economy in the countries of the Danubian area and the Balkans. After the destruction of the *Presse*, father's job as a librarian was a *pis-aller* which, while it had many drawbacks, possessed one inestimable advantage in the person of Elli Heringer, who had gone with him to his new office. Aided and abetted by her, he was able to face the many hazards of the Third Reich with comparative equanimity.

At all events father did at least have a temporary post which enabled him to work, earn money and keep his family. My mother, for her part, was very elated, for the autumn of 1939 at last saw the publication of her first big novel, *Pave und Pero*, which marked her breakthrough into the field of prose. The book got rapturous reviews and was sold out within a few weeks. A second edition was likewise quickly sold out, as was a third, and only then was the publisher, Otto Müller of Salzburg, refused further supplies of paper, first because my mother, being a markedly Catholic writer, was not considered acceptable by the Third Reich and, second, because the whole outlook of the publishing house of Otto Müller was antipathetic to the regime. For the time being then, the atmosphere at home was still perfectly cheerful; it seemed as though it might yet be possible to arrange our lives under the Third Reich so that we could withdraw into our own shell and not allow the outside world to impinge too much.

The dream was short-lived and did not even outlast the summer, for, by the end of August 1939, it was plain that war would break out; thus there could no longer be any question of withdrawing into our own shell.

Mother came back from Croatia, where she had been staying with her brother Peter. Harald Innerhofer and I had been to Germany, where we had hitch-hiked through the Ruhr Basin to Berlin and thence back to Austria. Otto was no longer getting leave. Yet still the German people persisted in the belief that Hitler would again succeed in bluffing the Allies. It was assumed that there would be another Munich conference, and there seemed small likelihood that the French and British, who had already allowed Hitler to engulf Austria, Czechoslovakia, the Sudetenland and the Memel territory, would choose to lay down their lives for Danzig. When, during the last week of August, the radio and press carried news of the Russo-German pact signed in Moscow by Ribbentrop, people in Germany either felt deeply depressed or tremendously elated, according to their point of view. In our case and that of our friends, depression prevailed, as might have been expected, although tempered a little by the relief of knowing there was not going to be a war, that Otto would not have to go to the front and that the danger was over, at least for the time being.

Then, as a complete surprise, came the German attack on Poland and the Anglo-French ultimatum. For a number of days there had been no news from Otto; we were not supposed to know where he was, though it was clear that his division was on its way to the Polish frontier. On the third or fourth day of the Polish campaign, the Wehrmacht communiqué reported that the 2nd Panzer Division had distinguished itself in the capture of the Jablunka Pass, through which it had thrust its way into Poland.

Not having had any direct news from Otto, mother sat pining at home but at last, after a week, a field postcard arrived; he had evidently got through unscathed and gave an account of his adventures – an armoured battle with a Polish cavalry regiment during which mounted Polish cadets had, with signal courage, but quite pointlessly, charged the German tanks, only to pay for it with their lives a few minutes later. He also described the capture of Cracow, in which his unit had taken part. And soon, barely three weeks after the campaign had begun, it was all over.

In November Otto was back, having been given Christmas leave in Vienna, after which he and his division were sent to the West. During the winter he was stationed in Darmstadt, where he went for long walks with his friend Robbi Baier, in the course of which they hatched a scheme for setting up after the war a kind of European forum or, as he put it, 'a college'. It was to be somewhere in Austria, in the mountains, and was to consist of students and professors from all over Europe, its object being to promote European unity. When he told me about it at the time the whole thing seemed to me somewhat fantastical, but in later years I have learned to take Otto's fantasies rather more seriously than I sometimes used to do at their first appearance for eventually, six years later, that college really did materialize and today it has been in existence for a good thirty years.

At school we had difficulty in keeping pace with the German victories. The appearance of the big map on the classroom wall, upon which German conquests were recorded with pins and little flags, was continually changing. In March 1940 it was the turn of Denmark and Norway. Father had assured us that the British Navy would undoubtedly succeed in defending Norway. Unfortunately his prognostications, like those of so many others during these years, were usually wrong. Within a few weeks the Germans had occupied the whole of Denmark and Norway and were holding Narvik. Before we had time to recover from our surprise and dismay, Otto announced that he was being moved from Darmstadt to an area which he was not allowed to name but which, through a certain understanding

we had come to about place names, we were able to identify
as the Eifel Mountains.

A few weeks later Otto was in France, his motor-cycle battalion being the first unit to reach the English Channel at Abbé-
ville. France capitulated and the greater part of it was occupied
by the Germans. At the beginning of July, however, Otto and
his division made a triumphal entry into Vienna from the
direction of St Pölten. I still remember how mother and I stood
at the Hietzing crossroads near what is now Kennedy Bridge
and waved to Otto as he roared past on his bike, wearing the
Iron Cross and smiling gaily.

On our way home that day mother and I did not exchange a
single word. Only when we had got out of the tram and were
walking from the Gatterburggasse down the Döblinger Haupt-
strasse to the Osterleitengasse did we both remark on the utter
grotesqueness of the situation. Her son – my own brother – had
returned victorious to Vienna, she and I had smiled and waved
as he went past, and yet the victory had filled us with despair.
The situation was even more grotesque for Otto and his like,
those thousands of soldiers in the German Wehrmacht who
fought gallantly, but nevertheless recoiled from every victory
won by the army.

In France, as before in Poland, Otto had done his duty as a
matter of course. He had done what every young man in a
similar situation must needs do – advanced with his comrades
and gone into action. Naturally he had done his best to ensure
that, in his own particular sphere, things turned out well and not
badly. There was, after all, no other alternative if he was not
to go out of his mind. That he was nevertheless unhappy about
the victory and did not derive as much satisfaction from his
Iron Cross as he might have done at some other time from some
other war medal, goes without saying. And this was a tragedy,
not only for him, but for many of his generation who shared
the same fate and underwent the same sufferings.

The summer of 1940 marked the climax of Germany's victorious advance and, indeed, at this time almost everyone in
Germany and Austria, no matter what his affiliations, assumed
that the Germans would win the war. We believed that Britain
would be forced to conclude a negotiated peace after being
brought to her knees by the German bombing. We noted the
powerful alliance between Germany and Russia, a state of

affairs which we hardly supposed Hitler would do anything to alter; nor was there any sign of an enemy who might still be capable of subduing Germany. Only a year later, all this had changed, for many who had set out as conquerors had lost their lives in the vast expanses of Russia.

But in the summer of 1940 it seemed, even to those in the Greater German Reich who were very far from hoping for victory, that everything had gone according to plan and that they would more or less have to reconcile themselves to the fact that the Third Reich would endure, if not for another thousand years, then at least for several generations. For a boy like me, just turned sixteen, the prospect of spending a lifetime under a regime which rejected him and which he rejected was not exactly rosy, knowing as he did he would have no real opportunity of doing the things he wanted to do. Well, I have never been given to introspection or to outbreaks of despair, and even at that time, after initial feelings of depression, I soon recovered my good spirits.

The war did not affect our lives very much. True, Otto's friends had now all been called up, but practically no one had been killed. None of our closer acquaintances had fallen victim to the war. Indeed, the German armed forces had suffered relatively few losses in the course of their first successful offensives and victorious campaigns of aggression. Life still went on as usual and there was plenty of food; in fact, so liberally was it doled out that, though rationing had been imposed, we scarcely noticed it. People could go about as they pleased within the Greater German Reich; theatres were open; new films were constantly coming out, each more lavishly produced than the last. By the same token, Dr Goebbels was determined, war or no war, to keep the German people and its armed forces supplied with luxury articles. There was still much to be had including, all at once, the spoils from the various occupied territories – French champagne, for instance, which was on sale in every little German shop. It began to look as though the Germans might now take over the legacy of the British and, for a generation or two, enjoy the fruits of other people's toil.

In the autumn of 1940, Otto was temporarily released from the forces in order to spend a couple of terms at Vienna University. We were all happy to have him at home again and it almost seemed as though the year 1940 might also see the end of hostilities. Italy's entry into the war was regarded as a joke – rather than a cause for additional concern; it was as though, with the armistice just round the corner, the great Duce was bent on securing Nice with, perhaps, some small part of Greece thrown in.

Vienna, having long since ceased to be a capital city, most unexpectedly experienced a sudden revival of diplomatic activity. The Belvedere Palace was the scene of meetings between the prime ministers and heads of State of the Danubian countries – Roumania, Bulgaria, Hungary and Yugoslavia. Sundry pacts were concluded. Italy's Foreign Minister, Ciano, repeatedly visited Vienna, where he stayed at the Hotel Cobenzl. In short, a curious period of intensive negotiations – diplomatic, political and economic – had now set in, a period during which Germany successfully liquidated what had once been the Little Entente. One could hardly go out in Vienna without seeing a procession of Horchs and Mercedes speeding along with, fore and aft, an escort of German military police on motorcycles. Inside the cars one might catch sight of Horthy, Ciano, Antonescu or, perhaps, the Yugoslav prime minister Cvetković who, at this time, was constantly seeking to strengthen his ties with Germany.

Only one thing had seriously deteriorated and that was the supply of news. Until the outbreak of war a few foreign papers had still been available, though not the *Zürcher Zeitung*, which was banned. We had, however, been able to get the *Pester Lloyd*, the largest German language daily in Budapest, and the *Agramer Morgenblatt*, and also Italian newspapers, whose reporting was then still relatively outspoken; in addition to these, French-language papers from Switzerland were also freely available. But in the early part of 1940 all this changed abruptly.

The only journal still to be had, aside from the conformist papers from the German Reich, was *Der Grenzbote*, the daily paper of the German minority in Slovakia. While this newspaper religiously conformed to the National Socialist line, it also continued until well into 1942 to publish the news it received from the United Press – a fact which must have been overlooked by some censor or other. For the paper subscribed to the UP news service and it was not until war had been declared between Slovakia and America at the end of 1942, that this last source of relatively objective news from the world at large completely dried up.

By that time, however, people had long since accustomed themselves to listening to 'enemy' broadcasts. It was a pretty risky business because punishable with imprisonment or hard labour, while to pass on news so heard was a capital offence. Nevertheless, there was hardly anyone who did not listen to some foreign radio station. The most popular was the BBC with its Austrian programme. Later, too, there was the 'Voice of America' and, of course – because relatively close and easy to obtain – Beromünster, the Swiss national broadcasting station. These services all had hundreds of thousands of grateful listeners in the German-occupied zones and in Austria, many of whom might not have survived the war without this source of news. For some would have fallen prey to hopeless despair, while on many crucial occasions others would not have been able to adapt themselves quickly enough to the contingencies of war.

5

The Liesl

In the presbytery in the Canisiusgasse a group of us sat boasting about the adventures we had during the summer holidays. It was mid-September 1940. We were about ten boys, most of them friends I had made in the short time I had been at Schotten Grammar School. The presbytery was housed in a hideous building dating back to 1900 or thereabouts; it adjoined the big Canisius church and was a quiet spot, not as yet under observation or visited by the Gestapo. We felt free and safe there.

Someone suddenly exclaimed: 'By the way, did you know the Don Cossacks are coming to Vienna next week?' 'You mean the *Kuban* Cossacks,' said another boy. There ensued a brief argument after which it was enthusiastically agreed that we should go in a party to hear the Russian folk songs.

For the benefit of those unacquainted with the youth movement, I should say that its members had a passion for folk songs and soldiers' songs including, of course, those of the Cossacks, which they would sing for hours on end round their camp fires and while on the march. Among our favourites were the Russian songs 'We sing of Platov the hero' or 'Beyond the Kuban, beyond the river, a Cossack rides', to mention only two. So it was understandable that we should be determined at all costs to visit the concert hall and listen to the Kuban Cossacks.

Eight or nine days later we met at a little café on the Graben and set off together for the concert hall, which we aimed to reach on the stroke of seven, when the doors of the pit opened. On entering, we found to our absolute amazement that there were at least four hundred other lads there, dressed exactly like ourselves, in shorts and stockings. And like us they wore, tucked into one garter, a short aluminium tube known as a DT or drinking tube, but which served many other purposes besides that of imbibing water. It was the hallmark of the youth movement and formed an integral part of what we called our 'gear'. After 1938 non-Nazi uniforms had, of course, been banned, and so had badges. But we still retained our grey shorts and grey, pull-on, buttonless blouses – the outfit which, though devoid of badges, distinguished us unmistakably from the Hitler Youth.

So there we were, all together again – several hundred members of the various illegal Viennese youth movements. Many we knew from former excursions, if not pitched battles, others we knew by name, while some were complete strangers. But we all came from the same stable and everyone greeted each other.

The concert began and we thought it terrific. Even during the interval we had begun, quite spontaneously and of our own accord, to chant in unison the names of the songs we loved – 'Kolchak' and 'Platov', whose opening words are 'Slavin Platov hagiroia'. And after the interval the Cossacks, carried away by our ovations, began to sing what we had asked for. Our enthusiasm knew no bounds; we joined in all the songs and our rapturous applause elicited six encores. The conductor was partly turned towards us so that he could at one and the same time conduct his choir and the enthusiastic audience. The concert hall re-echoed to the rafters and, as for us, we were happier than we had been for many a long day.

When, in a state of elation, we finally left the hall to go home, we found the Gestapo – easily recognizable by their leather coats and jack-boots – lying in wait outside the exits. In the street some fifteen or twenty 'Green Henrys', as prison vans are called in Vienna, were standing in readiness, and in these the whole lot of us were conveyed to Gestapo headquarters in what, up till 1938, had been a quiet hotel in the Morzinplatz.

Though the prospect of being taken to Gestapo headquarters was not particularly pleasant, we were still young and inexperienced and the whole thing seemed to us a tremendous lark. On this occasion we only stayed at the Morzinplatz long enough for our particulars to be taken, after which we were bundled back in the 'Green Henrys' where, to the intense surprise of the uniformed police, we proudly and defiantly resumed our singing. Later I was told by one of the policemen that they hadn't witnessed anything like it for years or, more precisely,

snce the winter of 1937–8. Then it had been members of the
Hitler Youth or other young Nazis who, when they were being
taken away, would sometimes sing in the prison vans.

We sang until we reached the 'Liesl'. This last was, as it still
is, the remand centre in the Rossauer Lände beside the Danube
Canal, a street which, up till 1918, had been called the Elisabeth-
Promenade. The remand centre therefore owes its charming
name to the beautiful Empress Lisi.

For me, as no doubt for most of the other rapturous concert-
goers inside the Green Henrys, this was my first taste of prison,
and I looked forward with considerable curiosity to what lay
ahead. Having been made to form up in long rows, we were
again asked for our names and particulars and then 'frisked'.
The policemen on duty were all members of the Vienna force
and had nothing to do with the Gestapo. All objects that might
be used for suicide, such as knives and shoe-laces, or for trans-
mitting information, such as pens and pencils, had to be handed
over. Nine or ten of us were assigned to cells which were
normally meant for four, though admittedly neither at Gestapo
headquarters nor at the Elisabeth-Promenade had they anticipated a fresh intake of several hundred persons that night.

I was later to discover that a former adherent of one of the
non-Nazi youth groups, now a Hitler Youth leader, had also
gone to hear the Cossacks. During the interval he had informed
the secret police that an organized band of some four or five
hundred young anti-Nazis had forgathered in the concert hall to
stage a political demonstration. On arriving outside the hall the
Gestapo officials did indeed hear youth movement songs that
had been banned in the Reich being sung at the tops of their
voices by the rash but enthusiastic boys within. This seemed
to confirm what they had been told about an anti-Nazi demonstration.

The 'Liesl', a massive edifice, was built around the turn of
the century. Its hub was – and presumably still is – what is
known as the 'Run'. The Run is an outsize, many-storied stair-
well with metal staircases and landings; there the life of the
prisoners is enacted. On the ground floor were the rooms in
which the prisoners had to give up their civilian clothing and
where personal inventories were made. If one was assigned to a
cell in the Run, one was more involved in the comings and goings of that drab, circumscribed world than if one was housed

in a side wing. News would reach one sooner and there was, moreover, a persistent rumour that inmates of the Run were at an advantage where food was concerned. For its distribution began in the Run, and the greater the distance from the centre, the smaller the portions were apt to be.

The food, contained in large tubs, was carried on little trollies and was ladled out into the prisoners' mess-tins. Usually it was a kind of watery stew, on some Sundays there might even be meat, and in the evenings we got bread with sausage or cheese and sometimes noodles. And every morning they poured us out some sort of liquid of which it was hard to say whether it was substitute coffee or substitute tea. With it went a piece of bread.

There was an exceedingly efficient system for the transmission of information between individual cells by tapping on the walls. Experienced old prisoners had acquired great ingenuity in establishing communications, not only between cell and cell, but from one floor to the next. We spent hours and hours passing on information to a cell that might be no more than a hundred yards away. And it invariably reached its destination, though the reply, having perhaps to travel up or down several floors, might not arrive till half a day later.

The daily routine was unfailingly monotonous. At six am we got up and washed; the plank beds were folded back against the wall; then we sat around on benches. Sometimes there might be newspapers – only Nazi ones, needless to say – sometimes not. Long-term prisoners were allowed to borrow reading matter from the prison library, but it was a complicated process. To combat boredom we played chess and fashioned small figures out of breadcrumbs, an occupation confined to the early part of the war, for bread became too valuable later on. The day ended at 8 pm. Lights were dimmed and prisoners had to lie down on their plank beds.

The prison cells were relatively large and had windows of which the lower half was of frosted glass. The upper half, of clear glass, was sometimes opened. Then, through the bars, one could see the wall of a house, a roof or a piece of sky. The sky, whether grey or blue, always looked beautiful and aroused feelings of nostalgia.

At the Liesl, by contrast with the Grey House, the enormous convict prison about which more anon, there was singing and laughter, a habit, however, that was not proof against a more protracted spell of imprisonment. On one's arrival, one learnt the 'Song of the Green Van':

> One harmless word, one little song
> And the green van'll come along,
> It'll take you away, you don't have to pay
> First stop Rossauer Lände.
> They swipe your matches, fags and pen,
> And take away your clothes, and then
> It's into the cell you go.

In October 1940 we only stayed a couple of weeks in the Elisabeth-Promenade, some of us less, some more. My cell-mates were Fritz Hansen-Löve, his brother Oge, Harald Innerhofer and my classmate, Harald Frederiksen, the latter having come to his imprisonment like a lamb to the slaughter, for on the eve of the Cossack concert he had heard me talking about it at school and asked whether he might go too, though he had never belonged to the youth movement. In this way we all made our first acquaintance with the Gestapo and their prisons. Later, as a leader and one of the most gallant members of our resistance group, he was to spend many months locked up in the Liesl.

My second stay there early the following year was no longer surrounded by an aura of adventure. Nor was the fact of missing school adequate recompense for a Gestapo interrogation. I was taken with a few other young people by Green Henry to the Morzinplatz. For psychological reasons most such interrogations took place at night. The authorities had been keeping an eye on those they regarded as the hard core of the concert hall contingent, and whom they suspected of being involved in the activities of some anti-National Socialist group.

That hard core consisted of the people who had been at Parthenen in the summer of 1938 and, indeed, Otto had been arrested at the time and charged with conspiracy. The Gestapo had succeeded in getting hold of a list of the participants and I was suspected of being a kind of contact man between the Parthenen group and the concert hall demonstrators. The Gestapo tried to prove that I had been in touch with Clemens von Klemperer, now in America, whom they believed to be operating on behalf of an active political underground group as its backer and overseas wirepuller. In this respect I was fortunately able to answer them perfectly truthfully and frankly. I could not then have been in touch with Klemperer, for war had long since broken out and correspondence with America was a virtual impossibility.

The conditions under which interrogations were conducted were still tolerable. True, we were left standing in the corridor half the night, but we were not beaten up. They shouted and threatened us but we were, after all, very young; it was a year of victory for the Third Reich and the Gestapo had absolutely no cause to feel jumpy and unsure of themselves. During subsequent periods of detention I was subjected to repeated interrogations at the Morzinplatz, each one harsher than the last. It was then that I became acquainted with the 'kindly' treatment specially reserved for political prisoners.

I had the doubtful pleasure of finding myself face to face with the then chief of the Gestapo in Vienna, Parteigenosse X. (Not that the name eludes me. But unlike the Gestapo, I am no advocate of the system of extending liability to kith and kin, and gladly refrain from mentioning his name, which has since been Teutonized.) Today I still have four small scars caused by cigarettes being slowly ground out on the back of my hand, a method particularly favoured by the Viennese secret police and one which also appeared to afford great pleasure to the aforementioned X. On two occasions he sat on the edge of his desk and watched attentively while the Gestapo interrogator gloatingly busied himself with his cigarette on the back of my hand. It hurt a good deal but I did not feel faint, as I did on one or two other occasions, when they made me stand to attention throughout an all-night interrogation and would not let me go to the lavatory. That was real agony. When they hit us, the spots they preferred were the backs of the knees, and the cheeks, nose or throat.

While such methods of treatment did not kill, they induced a sense of unutterable degradation. On the other hand, they helped one to become inured, and to endure worse things with greater resilience. My parents were interrogated far more rigorously than I, my mother in particular being subjected to outright torture of an exceptionally vile kind such as can only be applied to women. And when my father was released from prison and we were reunited again months after the war had ended, he showed me the great, unhealed welts that had resulted from his being flogged with a rawhide whip.

When we were released on this first occasion, the headmaster of our school sent for us and catechized each of us in turn, telling us that another arrest would undoubtedly bring down upon us the so-called 'Reich ban', in other words we should be excluded from every school in the German Reich. Not a very pleasant prospect since we should not, in that case, be able to matriculate.

Life returned to normal. But much had changed. Thanks to the secret police, dozens of young people had become acquainted who were unanimous in their rejection of National Socialism. From being lone wolves, these youthful critics of the regime became a confederacy. Gradually we began to create an underground network of active cells and organized resistance. Initially this consisted of co-operation between individual parish youth groups like those of the Canisiusgasse, the Schottenstift and the parish of St Paul in Döbling. Through our concert hall group we had come into contact with former members of other youth organisations opposed to National Socialism, in particular a circle of *Wandervogel* origin. And we eventually succeeded in getting into touch for the first time with the remnants of active resistance groups that had been completely disrupted in 1939 and 1940 and whose leaders, Alexander Auer, Rudi Strasser and Viktor Reimann, had been sentenced to long terms of imprisonment. Other contacts were the three Austrian Freedom Movements which had been disbanded in the summer of 1940 after being denounced by the actor, Otto Hartmann. As a result, two hundred and forty people had been imprisoned, and nine executed, including their leaders, Roman Scholz, Hans-Georg Heintschel-Heinegg, Gerhard Fischer-Ledenice, Dr Jakob Kastelic and Dr Karl Lederer. After the collapse of the Freedom Movement, a number of Catholic priests reacted quite admirably and, had it not been for them, we might well have been unable to do any serious underground work at all.

On returning home after my release I found my mother alone and in a state of utter despair. Father had been placed under the Ostmark ban, which meant that he was not allowed to reside in Austria. As I mentioned earlier, in the circumstances he could consider himself fortunate that Seyss-Inquart and some of his Dutch friends were able to help him obtain the post of librarian to a German-language weekly appearing in Holland. There was hardly any news of Otto except that he was somewhere in Poland with his unit, awaiting orders to move. My mother's unhappiness was compounded by the news that her beloved brother Ivo, a captain in the Yugoslav Navy, had been taken prisoner during the fighting that followed the German and Italian attack on Yugoslavia in the spring of 1941, and taken to a prisoner-of-war camp near Turin. Knowing Ivo's love of liberty, my mother was convinced that he would soon make a bid for freedom and thus, or so she feared, put his life in jeopardy.

She had also had bad news of Peter, her younger brother, a perceptive poet, playwright and journalist to whom she was deeply attached. He had fallen seriously ill and had gone to a sanatorium high up in the Sljeme Mountains not far from Zagreb where, a few months later, he died.

By now Hitler had discarded his non-aggression pact with the Soviet Union and June saw the beginning of the Russian campaign. In the drive towards Smolensk, Otto's armoured division got as far as Tula, a town some 150 kilometres south-east of Moscow, where it was brought to a halt by an unseasonable fall of snow. Otto himself, suffering from severe frostbite and a strained heart muscle, was sent in the late winter of 1942 to a field hospital in West Russia, and thence to the Pfalzburg Hospital in Alsace for convalescence, after which, to mother's intense relief, he was to be employed solely on duties behind the front lines. Indeed, the following winter he was given leave to study in Vienna and was then posted to a POW camp near Rathenow.

Early in 1941 I had decided that I would take the first opportunity that offered to make my way to the Allies. Not only was I fed up, but I loathed prisons and deprivation of liberty. I had no desire to go on living in the German Reich, where we were entirely surrounded by enemies, while hopes of liberation seemed increasingly remote. Unless I went abroad, I felt, there would be no prospect of doing anything worthwhile for Austria. I therefore decided to try and get out and join the Austrian Legion which, according to a BBC broadcast, had been brought into being by the Allies.

In the summer of 1941 there seemed to be a real chance of my being able to do so. I managed to obtain a travel permit without much difficulty, and went to visit father in Holland. I arrived in Amsterdam at the beginning of August, was met at the station by my father, and spent a few days with him in the city. He was living at the Amstel Hotel and had arranged for me to stay at a tiny pension in Zandvoort, a small sea-side resort. My father had friends in Holland, where he had lived at the end of the First World War when in the Austrian diplomatic service. In this way I got to know a few young people, who told me there might be an opportunity of getting to England by fishing vessel, several of these having already succeeded in making the crossing.

Fired with enthusiasm, I asked whether I might go too. When my Dutch friends contacted the men who arranged such trips, they found that I was at first regarded with some suspicion. For though Austrian, I was, of course, a German citzen, nor was it exactly a recommendation that Seyss-Inquart, who had befriended my father, was the German Reich Commissar in the Netherlands, and both an Austrian and a Nazi. Finally, however, they promised that they would take me over to England as soon as possible.

I missed the first boat, which in any case, as I later heard, was spotted by a German aircraft when half way across and set on fire. Another vessel was due to leave a few days later, not this time from anywhere near Zandvoort but from the north of Holland. I lived in hope, waiting to be told when the boat was due to sail. We should, it seemed, have to wait for favourable weather and a time when the moon was neither full nor new. As the days went by I grew anxious and eventually began to despair, for the permit authorizing me to stay in Holland was running out, and for me to have remained there illegally would have seriously compromised my father.

At last came the news that we should be leaving next day. In accordance with my instructions, I travelled to Groningen in the company of a Dutch friend. We spent two hours waiting in the station restaurant. When the intermediary, with whom my friend was acquainted, eventually turned up, he told us that the trip had been postponed. In despair, I took the train back to Amsterdam, waited another day and then returned to Groningen. The intermediary arrived and we took a bus to a small village some six kilometres away where we were to wait until dark.

At about six o'clock another Dutchman whom I did not know came to tell us that the trip was off. While on her way to our rendezvous, the ship and her crew had been intercepted by a German speedboat. A number of weapons and concealed fuel tanks had come to light, from which the Germans had rightly concluded that she was not going fishing but was en route to England. The crew had been arrested.

Feeling miserable and very downcast, I returned to Amsterdam and thence without delay to Vienna. A day or two later the Gestapo appeared in the Osterleitengasse, where Aunt Gabriele, being the only member of the family then in Vienna, was holding the fort. When the Gestapo asked for me, she could only tell them that I wasn't in. That evening, two minutes after I had come home, the Gestapo reappeared and took me away. They had posted men in the garden to await my return. Somebody who knew my name had been arrested in Holland, from which the Gestapo had concluded that I had been trying to find a fishing vessel to take me to England. The easy-going days were over; interrogations had grown more rigorous and the charges more compromising. I was transferred to the Grey House where, to soften me up, they put me in one of the so-called 'death cells'.

The 'Grey House', the Regional Criminal Court of Vienna, is an extensive complex containing not only a prison but also a place of execution; before 1938 this was in what was known as 'gallows yard' and, after the *Anschluss*, in a ground floor room where a guillotine had been installed. The 'death cells' in which condemned men awaited their execution – or, in rare cases, their pardon – were situated on the ground floor round what had formerly been gallows yard.

The Gestapo's psychological expertise was considerable, for the resistance of a seventeen-year-old could hardly be expected to withstand the tremendous mental stress to which he was exposed in a condemned cell. In my case, thanks to internal and external circumstances, they eventually failed in their design. But never in all my life shall I forget those ten days.

There were four people with me in the cell, including a peasant from the Burgenland, condemned to death for hiding a British pilot who had been shot down. He had certainly never dreamed that he was risking a death sentence when he gave the Englishman shelter. He was just a kindly chap who hid the stranger in his barn, gave him half a ham and told him what direction to take for Hungary. After only a few miles, the escaped pilot was captured and the peasant who had sheltered him tracked down. The British officer had long since gone to a prisoner of war camp, whereas his host from the Burgenland was having to pay with his life for the help he had given him.

My second cell-mate was a Catholic army chaplain from Poland who had sheltered Polish POWs in Vienna and had thus, it seemed, become involved with a resistance group. He had been caught and condemned to death.

The third inmate was a harmless thief. True, he had had the misfortune to be caught at night while attempting to steal forces' mail from a post office van in one of Vienna's stations. The theft of army postal packages under cover of darkness was a 'blackout offence' and, as such, punishable by death. The young man, who was, perhaps, twenty-three years old, had not understood the implications either of his offence or of the verdict. During the short time I remained in the cell he was the only one to be fetched away for execution. After receiving extreme unction from a priest, he was led away completely dazed.

My early release was due to the vigorous action of our old family lawyer, Dr Josef Ezdorf, who had been called in by my despairing mother. After considerable effort he succeeded in getting my case out of the hands of the Gestapo and arranging for the whole business to be dealt with, not by the People's Court, but by the Juvenile Court, under whose jurisdiction I properly belonged as I was not yet eighteen. Thanks to the backing of well-intentioned magistrates, I was eventually charged with menacing behaviour and illegal leisure activities. Somewhere along the line the charges of conspiracy and treason preferred by the Gestapo and accepted by the Public Prosecutor – charges which might have earned me the death penalty – had disappeared from the file.

Nevertheless, I was faced with a sentence of eight years' imprisonment, such being the period stipulated by the Public Prosecutor. Dr Ezdorf was anxious to postpone the main proceedings for as long as possible. For at this time, in the late winter of 1942, it was known that Hitler was about to issue an order whereby all prisoners under eighteen and serving a sentence of less than four years were to be given an opportunity of volunteering for the Wehrmacht and rehabilitating themselves at the front. The reason for the order was all too apparent, namely the appalling losses in the east wrought by the winter of 1941–42. In the race for Moscow and Leningrad whole German armies had been engulfed in the snow and ice of the Russian winter. The Führer needed soldiers and where he got them from was, by now, a matter of comparative indifference to him.

So I was not shut up for very long. After sentence had been passed, I was transferred from the relatively humane detention centre for juveniles to the Liesing convict prison. There I appealed for the remission of the remainder of my sentence and, at the same time, volunteered for service at the front.

The horror I felt at any deprivation of freedom undoubtedly became even more intense as a result of an experience at Liesing. I had been caught helping to smuggle a message out of prison, for which I was given forty-eight hours on bread and water in an unlit cell. I was taken to that cell at ten o'clock in the morning. It was down in the cellars of the prison. As I was pushed in, and for the brief moment during which the door remained open, I was able to take stock of my surroundings – a low, windowless place, furnished with a wooden stool, a plank bed, a minute table and, in one corner, a pail that did duty for a lavatory. The warder, having dumped down a can of water, told me he would bring me some bread during the afternoon. Then the door slammed to, the bolt was shot and I was left sitting in complete darkness. I stood up and, in an attempt to find my bearings, stumbled and knocked over the water jug, spilling all its contents. This did not matter at first as I was not particularly thirsty. While still in the old cell I had been told that I should try and count for an hour, think for an hour and then spend another hour counting. After about twenty minutes I lost the rhythm and couldn't tell how long I had been counting, so I gave it up. That afternoon the warder who should have brought me bread failed to appear, nor did he come during the evening. It was midnight before he turned up. I asked him why he hadn't come in the afternoon.

'Silly bugger,' he said. 'It *is* afternoon, just turned four.' I had been in the darkened cell for only six hours but had imagined that at least fourteen had gone by. According to my estimate it was midnight. The warder gave me a piece of bread and, being a nice chap, also refilled the water-jug. The following morning I knew that it was not the warder who had forgotten to come but that it was I who had again grossly overestimated the passage of time. He appeared at six o'clock, opened up the cell and left the door ajar for a couple of minutes while he stood in the doorway. It was extraordinarily decent of him, for it gave me a chance of reminding myself what light looked like. I knew of other prisoners who did not see any light for the whole forty-eight hours because the warder would only open the door a crack and turn off the light in the corridor so that nothing at all was visible. This made the forty-eight hours seem like five or six days. But my confinement in the dark was as nothing compared to that of a comrade in the Grey House who had once spent forty days under such conditions. He thought he'd been there a year.

From Liesing I was transferred to Kaisersteinbruch concentration camp, only to be released a few weeks later. My appeal had succeeded and I was instructed to report to the Wehrmacht depot in Vienna. There I was examined by a doctor, passed as fit but in need of sick-leave, and sent home. A further examination, carried out after pressure from three medical friends of the family, showed that I was suffering from the after-effects of the diptheria I had contracted in gaol, and I was given a three months' extension of sick-leave. After a spell in hospital I returned home and was able to spend the rest of my leave recuperating from my time in camp and prison.

Even then, in the first glorious weeks of my regained freedom, I began to suspect that the experiences I had accumulated in prison would prove more of a help than a hindrance in days to come. I had become familiar, at least in broad outline, with the methods used by a dictatorship to induce political conformity, and I had seen what effect a concentration camp can have on its inmates. True, Kaisersteinbruch also comprised a camp for young offenders and its methods were consequently a good deal less harsh than those of, say, Mauthausen, Ebensee or Flossenbürg, but many who mounted the steps leading up to it were destined never to come down them again.

The time I spent in the condemned cell turned me once and for all into an opponent of capital punishment. I readily concede, of course, that my inability to take a wholly objective view of the problems surrounding the death penalty is due in part to the nodding acquaintance I was to have with it later on. But it was the total lack of any just relationship between cause and effect, the utter failure to take account of the individual case, the stroke of the pen whereby my cell-mates, the humble Burgenland peasant and Strizzi, the light-fingered Viennese thief, were sent to the guillotine, which inevitably turned me into an advocate of everyone's right to live, no matter what the circumstances.

After my experiences in sundry Viennese gaols, the word freedom has acquired a new significance. Only someone who has been a prisoner can properly appreciate certain pleasures of everyday life: what it means to be able to decide for oneself whether to get up in the morning or whether to lie in for a little while; whether to have tea or coffee for breakfast; whether to read the paper or listen to the radio. Only someone who has spent some time locked up in a cell can know the joy of simply being able to open a door and go out.

I should not be doing justice to the truth if I were to pretend that my time in prison did not have its humorous side. This last I owe almost exclusively to my friends in the criminal fraternity. From them I gained for the first time a thorough knowledge of the Viennese dialect and also a broader insight into the city's underworld.

I shall never forget Leo – it would be indiscreet to reveal his real name – who, while we were in prison together, used to pour out his woes to me. He had, he said, formerly had a marvellous barrister who had repeatedly extricated him from the toils of justice, but who had been forced as a Jew to leave Austria at the end of 1939. Now Leo had been fobbed off with a defence counsel who might just as well have been a public prosecutor. Instead of help, all he got was homilies about how a good citizen ought to behave in the Greater German Reich. Poor Leo was completely at sea, for the whirlwind of the Third Reich had wrought havoc with the hallowed traditions of the underworld he knew – you were condemned to death and had your head chopped off for theft; your defence counsel behaved like a prosecutor; things that had always been taboo even to the small-time crook were now openly perpetrated by the new rulers. In short, without a proper lawyer Leo felt utterly bereft and asked me to help him.

After my release, therefore, I sought out the various people whose addresses Leo had given me. All, without exception, were members of Vienna's underworld who, Leo hoped, would help him find another defence counsel. And, in fact, I was 'given the straight tip' and told where to find a suitable man. On arriving at my destination, I was scarcely able to believe my eyes. In the grand office I had tracked down in the Inner City I found a dignified gentleman whom I should have taken at the very least for the legal adviser to Vienna's Jockey Club if not to the Order of Sacred Heart; in fact, he was the Viennese underworld's number one barrister. Thanks to his circumspection, it was soon my friend Leo's turn to be released. After the war I chanced to run into him. He had become a key figure in the city's black market in the Resselpark, where he had turned over many millions of dollars. Whenever I needed anything, he willingly helped me and always dealt with me fairly, supplying my needs at preferential rates. And every now and then he would turn up bearing a gift – coffee or cigarettes: ' 'Cos we can't leave an old chum out in the cold.'

After I had more or less recovered from my spell in prison, I enjoyed the last carefree holidays I was to have. I went to stay with a friend, on the Wolfgangsee – parties as in peacetime, flirtations and admiring glances from girls when they heard I had been in prison. A few marvellous days spent in the Ramsau Mountains near Schladming, with Monika and Justine who were running their parents' farm like proper peasant-women. And, finally, back to Vienna. My call-up papers read: 'Report 2 July 1942 to 1 Coy, 482 Infantry Depot Battalion in Mistelbach on the Zaya.'

As I boarded the Mistelbach train in Vienna's Nordbahnhof, I caught sight of the tram-stop where I had sat waiting after my discharge from Liesing, with the prison still visible in the background and, on my knees, my bits and pieces wrapped in newspaper. I was happy because I was free. Along came the tram; the conductor asked: 'Just out of Liesing?' 'Yes.' 'Then there's nothing to pay,' he said.

6

Punishment Battalion

After training in the Steinhammer exercise area in Upper Silesia the whole battalion, numbering some six hundred men, had been brought by rail to Kiev and set down in a temporary marshalling yard outside the town. We had now been there for three days and were awaiting forward transport. The air was thick with rumours, though the pundits in the orderly room, who prided themselves on their omniscience, told us we should be moving further east to the Rostov area.

This was early in September 1942; the German offensives aimed at the Caucasus and Stalingrad were in full swing and everything seemed to be going very well. It was expected that the late autumn would see the fall of Stalingrad and the collapse of the Russian front in the south. Here at our station near Kiev there was much activity. Day after day entire divisions rolled in from the Reich, changed trains, and continued on their way. From the east came the hospital trains; serious cases were taken to local field hospitals, while those fit to travel proceeded on-wards, either to the *Generalgouvernement*, in other words Poland, or to destinations in the Reich.

The consensus in the battalion was that we should do better if we were to move up closer to the front. In northern Russia there was said to be another probationary battalion – the polite name for a punishment battalion such as ours – whose members had serverd a three months' probationary term at the front and then been posted to normal units. We therefore hoped that, after a successful spell in the line before Stalingrad, say, or in the Caucasus, we would similarly be excused a further period of probation by the army commander concerned and sent to normal units in the field. Needless to say, everyone dreamed of this possibility, which, however, soon proved to be an illusion. There was every incentive to get out of a punishment battallion as quickly as one could, for experts had calculated that its members had a ten per cent chance of survival and an expectation of life of no more than six months.

But in other respects, too, service in a punishment battalion was one of the most unpleasant ways of spending the war in uniform. In Kiev things were not too bad, but at Steinhammer we had been driven mercilessly for up to fifteen hours a day. And since the corporals, and also some of the officers, had been transferred to the battalion on disciplinary grounds, morale as a whole was understandably low. The corporals were at pains to make soldiers of their charges as quickly as they could, for the harder they drove them, the more likely they were to rehabilitate themselves as NCOs and, perhaps, regain their former rank. Most of our corporals had previously been sergeants or even second-lieutenants and naturally wished to be so again.

About a third of the men had been transferred on disciplinary grounds, having been found guilty of some particularly grave misdemeanour, another third because they had repeatedly contracted venereal disease, in other words had ignored the 'Prophylactic Regulations', a form of 'refusal to obey an order', while the remainder consisted of so-called PUs, of whom I was one. Anyone marked PU in his service dossier was held to be 'politically unreliable'. Most of them had entered the Wehrmacht direct from concentration camp or prison. Our numbers had risen considerably in recent months, following the Führer's directive of early 1942 ordering the release of a great many young men from various German prisons and concentration camps. The best soldiers were those who owed their presence in the battallion to their frequent bouts of venereal disease. All had been completely cured and were perfectly normal people. Those transferred from other units on disciplinary grounds because of grave misconduct were usually alcoholics, or youths on the fringes of crime; many were potential thugs – knifers and the like.

The politically unreliable were also quite unreliable as soldiers. As people they were, it is true, very sympathetic types, but they had had less training than the rest. Months or years of confinement in prison also meant that they were physically unequal to the exertions demanded of them and hence they were

a burden on all the others. The platoon and section commanders did their best to take as few PUs as possible, but this
worked greatly to our disadvantage, since all the really disagreeable jobs and details came our way. So far I had scraped
along tolerably well. An NCO in the company office had, for
some reason, taken a liking to me and found employment for
me during our move and then in Kiev. My task was to prepare
strength and equipment returns, count stores and so forth.

The nights were our only real consolation, for the weather
was consistently fine. We lay in the open on large bales of
straw near the railway coaches, while overhead the indescrib-
ably clear sky grew slowly darker. For the first time in my life
I applied myself to a close study of the stars. Unfortunately I
had no book to help me identfy them but, by drawing on my
knowledge of certain of the constellations, I devised a chart and
proceeded to give imaginary names to the stars I did not know.
Later on I derived great kudos from this, for I was instantly
able to explain and give names to the more beautiful constellations for the benefit of those who, like me, knew next to nothing about astronomy. Everything was perfectly correct except
that the names, being the fruit of my imagination, were always
wrong.

We never visited Kiev itself, for the battalion was refused
passes as a matter of principle and our only chance of getting
there was in the course of some duty or other. I did once set out
in a truck that was to collect potatoes from an army ration
depot, but unforunately it broke down about half a kilometre
from our camp and we had to walk back. A week went by and
we were still outside Kiev in our vast marshalling yard when
suddenly – in the Wehrmacht it was always a case of several
weeks' waiting followed by a tremendous rush – the battalion
was ordered to be ready to move.

This time we travelled by truck, heading north-west up one of
those Russian highways that might better have been described
as dirt roads. They were at least thirty to forty metres wide, and
on them one would often see, side by side with the heavy transport of the Wehrmacht, small local carts drawn by three horses,
a pair, or even one. In the Wehrmacht one was seldom told
one's destination. The fear of spies was too great; the enemy
might be listening. In the case of a probationary battalion the

rule was, of course, even more strictly observed, since its members might themselves belong to the enemy.

So we continued our journey throughout the day, before halting that evening near a small ruined town where we bivouacked. Sentries were posted, indeed they were doubled. Hitherto they had always faced inwards to ensure that none of us made off. Now they also had to be on the alert for an attack from without. Next day we pressed on and, at about midday, reached a big village, also largely in ruins, which was occupied by an ss unit. This, we discovered, was to be our headquarters for some time to come.

The battalion split up into its six companies, after which we marched to a nearby hamlet which was used as a base for operations against the partisans. The hamlet lay on the edge of a large marshy area and had been totally abandoned by its inhabitants. Most of the houses had been burnt down, but there were still a few barns and stables that could at a pinch be put in order again. This was our first job. At roll call the next morning our company commander, a lieutenant, briefed us on our allotted task. No. 3 Company was to act as pathfinders to an ss brigade which was hunting the partisans. The latter had withdrawn to islands in the marshes, in other words to patches of firm ground within this large swampy region. Partisans, it was impressed on us, were Jews, Poles, gypsies, riff-raff, and must be tracked down and destroyed. That would be attended to by the ss brigade; our job was simply to reconnoitre and mark the tracks through the swamp, therby enabling their lordships, the ss, to clear the area and make it secure without running the risk of drowning.

At first we didn't quite grasp what it was we had to do. But by the next day we were in no doubt that an intriguing task lay ahead. Together with my section I was allotted to an ss-Oberscharführer, the equivalent of a sergeant. Two trucks carried us along a kind of sunken track which suddenly debouched into flat country before it entered the marsh.

Evidently the extent of the marsh varied according to the season or the amount of rainfall; there was no doubt that vehicles had previously driven further along this track, since we could see tyre marks running straight ahead into the marsh. For a distance of ten metres from a quite easily identifiable point the depth of the swamp was about twenty to thirty centimetres, after which it increased considerably. That was where we started to work. We had brought marker-poles equipped with small flags and our task was to discover whether the ss, and especially their vehicles, could use the track. Three men carried the heavy marker-poles, while two or three of us went ahead armed with sticks. Behind us came our corporal and the ss-Oberscharführer. No weapons were trained on us, for our chances of escape were non-existent. We would have been swallowed up in the swamp immediately.

All went fairly well for the first five hundred metres, though we had to take care when feeling our way ahead along the narrow strip of firm ground. The route was partially identifiable, for the flowers in the marsh differed from those on the strip and, provided one was careful not to stray, little could go wrong. About twenty minutes later, however, one of the men ventured rather too far ahead.

We heard a sudden shout and ran towards him. By then he was already up to his knees in mire and trying desperately to extricate himself. There were two of us and we managed to drag him out. He owed his rescue to the fact that we were able to pull him out of his 'ammos' or marching-boots, which disappeared without trace into the marsh and were never seen again. We noticed that the marsh kept 'working', that is to say it was in some kind of motion, possibly akin to the tides at sea. Now we knew we had to take care. By the evening we had marked out about three kilometres of track. On our return we were ordered to mount guard at the edge of the marsh, in case anyone should remove the markers during the night.

It was the first cloudy night since I had been in the Ukraine and, at about two in the morning, it began to rain. We had neither greatcoats nor tents and were soon soaked through. Early next day the ss-Oberscharführer reappered, whereupon our truck left for the village to collect our kit and whatever was needed to set up a temporary camp. The task of marking proceeded as usual and the morning passed without incident until just before twelve, when we were about to break off for half an hour to eat our midday meal of bread and tinned sausage. Suddenly we heard shouts up ahead. I was one of the party bringing up the markers. We hurried forward, but by the time we arrived Hugo Brettwich had gone. Hugo came from

Berlin and had been one of my fellow PUs. He had only managed to call out twice. During the final ten seconds he had
evidently been too frightened to shout any more.

When we had finished our midday meal by the side of the
track, we were ordered by the corporal to plant a cross close
to where Brettwich had been sucked under. We fetched his helmet, which he, like the rest of us, had left behind, for we found
them tiresome to wear all the time and in any case there was
no enemy around to shoot at us. It was a strange sensation to be
present at what was for me the first death of the war, a death,
moreover, that had come about in the way it had. I had been
able to visualize people struck down by bullets or hit by bombs,
but the possibility that death might mean simply sinking into
a swamp had never occurred to me. At midday, after another
man had been lost in similar circumstance, the corporal marched
us back and took the truck to the company command-post which
was about four kilometres away. Evidently he discussed the
matter with the lieutenant commanding our company, for early
the next day a second party was sent out to join us.

We now fashioned crude implements intended to help us
determine the location of the negotiable track. We also built
platforms which we pushed ahead of us, since it was clear that
a better distribution of weight would lessen the danger of our
sinking in. After that our losses diminished, though hardly a day
went by without our leaving at least one man behind in the
marsh. However this did not apply solely to us, for the company had four such parties in operation, only one of which was
better off than ourselves, thanks to the easier going they had
encountered. It was to cost them dear, as they were the first to
reach an island, where they came under machine-gun fire. There
was, of course, no cover on the marsh with the result that three
or four men were killed instantly. Life in that spot was hardly
a bed of roses, nor were we exactly enamoured of our SS-Oberscharführer.

On the fifteenth day of our stint on the marsh, the island we
were aiming for came into sight. In view of the experience of
the other party, it was decided to call a halt before attempting
an approach by night. Our corporal reported back to the company and returned with the news that the attack was to be
carried out by SS troops. It was evidently feared that we might
desert, in itself a grotesque idea, since to desert would mean

sinking into the swamp, if nothing worse. So we returned to spend the night in our camp on the edge of the marsh.

The ss detachment, numbering some fifteen men, drove in two Kübelwagens (the military version of the Volkswagen) for about five kilometres up the track we had made across the marsh to the point where it became too narrow for vehicles. From there onwards they continued on foot. About an hour later we heard firing and could see tracer, muzzle-flashes, and then the glow cast by flamethrowers. Our corporal informed the company and the company informed the ss. Later that night two more companies of ss arrived, evidently to support the party up ahead in the marsh. But by now a mist had come down and they were unable to proceed.

Early next morning, several of the ss men who had set out for the island the night before were found to be still alive; the detachment had been badly knocked about and approximately one third was missing, presumably swallowed up in the marsh.

To complete the track we had begun was thus something of a problem. Accordingly a kind of protective parapet was erected, though not without difficulty, since in places the path was only half a metre wide. But the partisans had apparently lost the inclination to fight at this spot. Two days later we reached the shore of the island and our work came to an end. We were at once sent back, for, as I have already said, it was feared that we might desert.

We reported to the company and, on the following day, were assigned to other sections, since there had been very heavy casualties. Eighteen days before, when the company had arrived at the edge of the marsh, we had numbered some 110 men; now there were probably no more than sixty-five of us. I was extremely lucky, for next day, while patrolling the edge of the marsh, I was grazed on the leg by a bullet and taken to hospital. On this particular occasion I was only detained for two days, after which I was returned to the company for further duty. My first stop, however, was battalion headquarters, where I was ordered to unload an ammunition truck. In doing so I strained a heart muscle and collapsed.

It was probably a consequence of the diphtheria which I had managed to survive while in prison, but had never thrown off properly after my release. Once again I was promptly removed to hospital, first to one in the neighbourhood of Kiev and then, a day or two later, to a base hospital near Lvov. This was a large, well-equipped establishment that had been requisitioned from the Poles by the Wehrmacht for the treatment of chronic and serious cases. I was placed in the ward for internal diseases.

There the doctor, a young captain from Hamburg, took me in hand. He was an extraordinarily nice man and he used to give me long accounts of the old Hansa town and the voyages his father – presumably a ship's master or something of the sort – had made all over the world. He also enjoyed conversing with me about other matters and was interested to hear what I thought about the war, though naturally we did not go into detail. One evening he told me he had been in Lvov during the afternoon and had bought some books at the German field bookshop. He wondered whether I might like to have a look at some of them. The books he removed from his large Wehrmacht-issue briefcase were the clearest possible political confession of faith. They included Ernst Jünger, Rainer Maria Rilke, *The Wedding in Magdeburg* by Gertrud von Le Fort and a book of German poetry. I told him my mother was a writer and he knew her name at once. Indeed, he had read a number of her poems, though not as yet her latest novel. After he had left me that evening I lay awake for a long time. The conversation with the captain had suddenly removed an obstruction from my mind and I began to look back over the previous eight weeks.

First there was the long haul to Kiev, our stay there and then our struggle with the swamp somewhere on the edge of the Pripet Marshes, my first experience of war at close quarters, our first dead. Then there was the Waffen-SS (the fighting arm) – supermen as they were forever reminding us, while we were regarded as the dregs of humanity, only a little better than the partisans, the Russians, Ukrainians and Jews, whom they made clear by words and gestures they considered totally sub-human. Then I thought of the forlorn band of PUS, my comrades in the company and the platoon, none of whom had yet come to terms with life in the Wehrmacht, to which they had been sent virtually as auxiliaries, or 'Auxies', as the Wehrmacht's Slav or other supernumeraries were usually termed. In this world a man had barely time to find his feet before he was dead, either killed by partisans or drowned in the marshes.

All this passed through my mind that night, and for the first time I made some attempt to sort out and digest the many impressions of my spell in Russia. Of one thing I was certain and that was the importance of the will to survive. The PUS in my company and in the battalion as a whole were undoubtedly all more or less hostile to the regime. Nevertheless, during our operations in the marsh each of us had done his duty as a matter of course, just as all the others had, whether or not they were Nazis. For along with the will to survive was the axiom that the closed community, the forlorn band, call it what you will, to which you belonged, took precedence over everything else. To survive you had to stick together. At home in our own country, we had not been so aware of this, for back there we were at odds with each other; back there my friends and I had been anti-Nazi and in consequence had been locked up by those bastards the Nazis, who, in their turn, regarded us as bastards. Now, here in Russia, although the Nazis remained our enemies, although they had pushed us into a punishment battalion and had treated us badly and inhumanly, somewhat different standards prevailed. When we were out on an operation, we stuck together and supported each other. And even though we may not have been exactly broken-hearted when the ss suffered casualties during an engagement, we would never have dreamed of doing anything that made their task more difficult. A community thrown back on its own resources can only exist if it sticks together. The moment it ceases to do so, it goes to pieces. That was one lesson to be learned from those two months of war in the East.

Another was that the methods of warfare were altogether different from what we had imagined. My brother Otto had told us a lot about the war and the campaigns in Poland, France and Russia. But that was a front-line war, a war in which the crack panzer divisions of the Wehrmacht formed the spearhead of the victorious armies. It was war fairly fought and, if prisoners were taken, they were decently treated. Then, when victory had been won, as in Poland or France, the troops returned home, having handed over control to the despised 'golden pheasants' or party bigwigs, to the police and the ss.

The war I had got into was quite a different war. It was a war between supermen and sub-humans, where no quarter was given on either side. And quite by chance, without my having had any say in the matter, I had landed on the side of the supermen.

That the supermen in turn looked on us as almost sub-human lent added piquancy to the situation.

During the few weeks in which we had the ss as our neighbours we naturally conversed on occasion with these young men, who carried out guard duties just as we did and accompanied us on operations. They were volunteers, idealists beyond doubt, but also beyond doubt members of a killer squad, for the task of this unit was to exterminate partisans and other 'riffraff'. From what we saw and heard, the operation they had carried out with us had been something of an exception. For the fact that the partisans had returned their fire and on some days had suffered fewer casualties than the ss, was regarded by the latter as an amazing and 'shocking' sign of the times. Up till then they had been 'mopping up', as they themselves put it, in the rear areas. No one had opened fire on them and their losses had been virtually nil. However it was quite clear that the men of this brigade had not volunteered for their task out of cowardice. On the contrary they had, they told us, previously been engaged on what were certainly more dangerous operations in the Balkans and elsewhere. Political fanaticism had drawn them into the ss and they were convinced that it was of crucial importance to the German people, the honour of the Waffen-ss and the achievement of their aims, that the East should be made subject to the German master race. The fact that countless human lives would be lost in the process was neither here nor there.

Final victory and the purification of the German race were the overriding aims to which all else had to be subordinated. As one of the young lads from the ss unit put it: 'Like the Catholic Church, we believe that the end justifies the means.' Here then was the second lesson to be learned from those weeks in Russia, or rather the Ukraine.

This insight into the attitude of the National Socialist rulers and their elite units came as a revelation; it shocked me profoundly and forced me to revise my ideas. In the long run it would not be enough to join in Cossack choruses, or even, perhaps, to be thrown into gaol, or to try and extricate myself from my predicament by leaving through the back door – in my case from Holland by boat to England. If these people were to win the war and impose their ideology there would, presumably, no longer be any point in existing in this world. That was the most important conclusion I had managed to reach during my nights in hospital at Lvov. I realized that if I wanted to survive I would have to do something more positive.

Next day the captain reappeared and examined me. My bed was in a large ward which I shared with ten other soldiers. He said he would have me fetched for a full ECG (electro-cardiograph) check-up. Next morning, after my removal from the ward, he examined me from top to toe; the ECG was done and I was subjected to every imaginable check. When it was over he wheeled my bed into a small room and began to talk at length about the state of my health. I should, he said, make a complete recovery, but he would have to put me down for at least six months LD followed by two years GDH: LD meant light duties, in other words employment in the rear areas as a clerk, for example. GDH meant garrison duties at home, that is to say you were sent to the Reich. This was splendid news, for in no circumstances would I have to return to the Eastern Front.

He then went on to say that he had sent for my personal papers and had happened to notice that certain records were, unfortunately, missing from my service dossier. Now, it should be understood that the service dossier contained all essential material in the way of documents and records in respect of each member of the Wehrmacht. One copy accompanied the soldier from unit to unit, while the original remained with the appropriate military district. My dossier contained particulars of my arrests and the reasons for them and it also included the inauspicious entry: PU.

But the captain had given me to understand, as it were casually, that my dossier had arrived incomplete. This surprised me, for it had been handed to me in a sealed envelope on my removal to Lvov from the field hospital in Kiev and I had actually had it on my bed. Then I caught on. He had evidently gone carefully through the dossier and realized what my fate would be if he was to return me to the punishment battalion via my depot battalion. In one 'probationary unit' there had been a hundred per cent turnover in the company strengths within the space of a year at most, in other words the number serving in it twelve months before corresponded to the number since killed. The doctor, who was clearly well-disposed towards me, also knew that he would not be able to send me to a different depot battalion unless he abstracted certain parts of my service dossier.

This was precisely what he had done; and he had also told me
as much in a roundabout way, so that I should be able to conduct myself accordingly.

I had already gained sufficient experience of the Third Reich
to know that I must, of course, give no immediate sign of having understood. It was an unwritten law that even people with
similar views never spoke absolutely frankly to one another, for
they could never tell whether they might not be overheard, or
whether one or the other might not be tortured until he finally
came out with things he had had absolutely no intention of
saying. So I simply thanked the doctor politely and added: 'I
quite understand what you have told me about my health, sir,
and about the deficiencies in my service dossier.' 'That's settled
then,' was all he said. 'We shall be seeing each other again.'

Back in my ward and, during the days that followed, on a
splendid veranda bathed in autumn sunshine, I had ample time
to think about the doctor. In all likelihood he had saved my
life.

There was no chance of my repaying him adequately, but I
felt impelled to let him know somehow or other that I realized
what he had done for me and was grateful. I had with me a
copy of *Praise God in the Mountains*, my mother's latest volume
of poetry, which had come out before the *Anschluss*. She had
written an inscription for me on the flyleaf. I took the book
and copied out for him five lines from a new poem my mother
had written during the previous winter, so that he would realize
what I knew and what I thought of him. The verse runs:

> We're frightened. All the demons are out,
> And under the door trickles blood.
> With shriek and with shout and in furious rout
> Past the house goes the devil's brood.
> We're frightened. No one is good.

On the day before I was discharged as cured, I presented
the doctor with *Praise God in the Mountains* containing the
earlier inscription by my mother and my new inscription to
him. He looked at me kindly, read the inscription, held out his
hand and said: 'I don't imagine we shall see one another again
and I also think it would be best for us to forget the conversa-

tions we have had. Thank you for the beautiful book.' In deference to his wishes I have deliberately forgotten his name.

As the doctor had predicted, I was sent to a pool for men
discharged from hospital who no longer belonged to a specific
depot unit. This was a depot in Liegnitz in Silesia. There I
again had time to draw up a sort of balance-sheet of everything
Fepolinski and Waschlapski had seen and experienced during
their service in the East. Eight weeks on active service, the contest with the swamp, the contest with the partisans, a super-
ficial wound in the leg, a serious cardiac disorder, forty-five of
my own company lost in the marsh, some twenty-five of the
attendant Waffen-ss killed, an untold number of partisans dead.
All things considered I had come off lightly, especially when
one remembers how events were shaping at Stalingrad and in the
Caucasus during those months, or what had happened prior to
this in the northern and central sectors of the Russian front.

By comparison with those countless dead, that ocean of
suffering, what was a mere operation against the partisans, a
few men lost in the marsh? But for me it was enough and to
spare.

In the two and a half years that followed, that is up till the
end of the war in May 1945, the experiences I was to accumulate
were for the most part far more significant than those I had
been through in the Pripet Marshes. Nevertheless, it was this
first experience of the war in the East that made a deeper impression upon me than any other. Here I had learned what was
meant by the words: 'The sharks of the deep have awakened.'
Here I had seen the sharks for the first time, and here I had
come to know what fear was.

Here, too, I had discovered the meaning of comradeship in
its purest and most immediate form: how someone handed
you a mess tin of soup; how they supported you in that moment
of helplessness when, for the first time, you stood before a
soldier's grave; how they placed the dead man's helmet on the
wooden cross and how one of them, embarrassed, began to
stammer out the first words of the Lord's Prayer before the
others haltingly joined in, relieved that they were still permitted to pray.

In the final analysis, then, after the first months of the pitiless
reality of war, after the first shock and the first awakening, there
was nevertheless a ray of hope, and with it the touch of human

warmth that an eighteen-year-old must have if he is to survive: the doctor in the hospital who helped without being asked or bidden, who came and started to talk about Rilke, thus restoring the sense of security I had not known once since leaving home, and who, in his matter of fact way, as though everything had been settled beforehand, contrived by tampering a little with my records to set my life on a new course and, in so doing, probably saved it. This doctor was a symbol of the humanity and helpfulness I was never again to lose sight of throughout the war. To Fepolinski in that autumn of 1942 he came as a great and joyous revelation.

Nowhere was one completely alone; it was not just the shelter of the parental home or of old friends or of one's family in which mutual aid was taken for granted. The same thing held good of the outside world, whether Russia, France, Germany, Poland or Italy. There would always be somebody who suffered and thought as you did, somebody to whom you could turn. The brutality and mercilessness of Hitler's world had found its opposite pole in the helpfulness, kindness and sincerity of those who stuck together to defy and resist the powers of evil, the sharks of the underworld. In the coming years, the black horde of haters and destroyers that had overrun the Continent was to encounter ever greater opposition from a brotherhood of the humane, helpful and kind until war, misery and murder finally came to an end.

More than thirty years later I read *The Gulag Archipelago* and learned of Solzhenitzyn's experiences in the Siberian camps. Much of it seemed closely akin to what had gone on in the Third Reich though a good deal was unfamiliar to me, since the two were, after all, poles apart. But one thing stands out, and that is that where there is evil there is also good. Where there are people who disrupt, destroy and torture there are also, beyond all doubt, others who help, heal and support.

7

Living Like a Lord

In defiance of Notre Dame, in defiance of the Champs Elysées
and in defiance of the other splendid buildings, bridges and
squares by which Paris is graced, that hideous steel giant, the
Eiffel Tower, has, of all things, become the symbol of France
and her capital. But however that may be, the builder of the
monster, M Eiffel, besides putting up the tower and doubtless
thanks to the fame this had brought him, also built a small,
elegant mansion in the best part of Paris, in the Rue Matignon
just behind the Rond Point in the Champs Elysées.

When I entered the Palais d'Eiffel for the first time in
November 1942, I was received by a bored Wehrmacht lance-
corporal, a sort of cross between a French concierge and a
German orderly. He looked at my movement order and
motioned me towards one of the velvet-covered Empire arm-
chairs that stood around the hall. For a private soldier newly
arrived from a punishment battalion in Russia it was an unusual way to wait.

There was more or less constant coming and going in the
hall which led out on to the courtyard, this in turn being
separated from the street by a wall with two large arched gate-
ways. Like hundreds of others the place had been built in the
style customarily adopted in the latter half of the last century
for a grand town house. But I did not discover this till later.
Civilians, men as well as women, kept arriving and departing,
the latter dressed in what I took to be fashionable clothes,
though I was, of course, no judge of fashion. Then, too, there
were German officers in uniforms that had obviously been
made to measure. Everyone greeted each other with such
languid grace that it was almost like watching a film. Parcels

were delivered, bunches of flowers were borne by orderlies to the upper floors.

I sat there open mouthed, feeling that, provided they did not immediately chuck me out, I had unquestionably made a big step forward by comparison with the preceding months. About ten minutes later an elegant young man came down the stairs. He wore riding boots, black breeches and a uniform tunic undone at the neck. The narrowness of his shoulder-cords proclaimed him to be what was known in Wehrmacht jargon as a 'narrow-gauge officer', or Commissioned Specialist. He wore a moustache and had an amiable and very Austrian air. There was a hint of arrogance about the mouth, perhaps, but the eyes had a smile in them. As he walked towards me, I rose, clicked my heel and saluted.

'Hello, hello my dear fellow,' he said. 'Do come upstairs and make yourself at home.' I thought my eyes and ears were deceiving me. That was how the actors in the Josefstadt* used to greet one another on stage when representing the gentry of pre-1914 Austria in plays by Schnitzler or Hoffmannsthal. He gave me a friendly handshake, put an arm round my shoulders and steered me upstairs to his office. This was a small room on the second floor overlooking the gardens of the Champs Elysées and containing an elegant desk with small, slender legs. I was directed to a sofa while he sat down at his desk on a no less elegant chair.

'We make ourselves pretty comfortable here, you know,' he said. 'Would you care for a cup of coffee, or something a bit stronger, perhaps?' I was still speechless, but almost at once found myself back in the world I knew so well in Vienna. It was as though it was not in fact Riki Freiherr von Posch-Pastor who was sitting there, but rather my cousin Niki Preradović, or Poldo Parneck, or any one of a host of other friends, school-fellows and companions of my youth in Austria, the inhabitants of the familiar world of the old order with which I had lost touch during the past year, first in prison, then at the training camp with the punishment battalion and, finally, at the front. Now there they all were again, as though nothing had happened.

*The Theater in der Josefstadt was a famous Viennese theatre, known for its *fin-de-siècle* performances.

So Riki ordered coffee and I made myself 'at home'. He asked me whether I had had a good trip and what things were like in the Reich. I was giving him my impressions of Germany and Russia when he interrupted me. 'They haven't a chance,' he said. 'Just you wait and see. In two months' time Hitler will come a cropper, they will never capture Stalingrad, and they won't be able to hold the Caucasus and then it will be backwards all the way. Put her into reverse, that will be the order. Ah well, we'll have to hang on here as best we can; it would be too idiotic to be pushed off to Russia at the very last moment.' I agreed wholeheartedly and he assured me that I should find life quite tolerable. He had apparently seen my name on a transfer list and at once put a tick against it, thereby ensuring that I was not, as originally intended, sent on to a branch in Normandy, but kept in Paris as an interpreter on the German Procurement Staff in France. I then told Riki, as he had asked me to call him – the familiar *du* or thou was taken for granted – that my knowledge of French corresponded at best to that of a child in the bottom form of a primary school.

This did not worry him in the slightest and he merely remarked: 'But surely you know English, say, or Italian?' When I admitted to a knowledge of both, he answered: 'That's perfectly sufficient. We have to do business in English and Italian as well. An interpreter you are and shall remain, and you'll be attached to me. So that's settled. Now, where would you like to be put up?'

Once again I was struck dumb.

'I don't quite understand what you mean.'

'Where would you like to stay?'

The question, addressed as it was to a private soldier who only recently had had the choice between a hospital, a bed of straw in Russia and a hero's grave, could not but arouse astonishment. Finally I found myself billeted in the Wagram, a small hotel on the Avenue de Wagram about three minutes' walk from the Etoile. It was a charming little place which had previously been an establishment, though of a superior kind, where rooms were let by the hour. Now it was inhabited by half a dozen German officers, NCOs and men employed on the large staffs that had proliferated round the Etoile.

Riki lived in grander style, partly in the Hotel Claridge on the Champs Elysées and partly in a small apartment he had commandeered for himself. He had been in Paris for some time, knew France, spoke perfect French and was thoroughly conversant with the world of pre-war Europe about which I knew next to nothing, apart from what I had learnt from books. His grandfather had been Austrian Ambassador to the Holy See and had written quite a well-known history of the papacy. The family was of Tyrolese origin and Riki was a 'Lord and Yeoman of the Tyrol'. Sometimes, when he felt mischievous, he would place round his neck the green ribbon with its gorgeous Tyrolese eagle, which the lords and yeomen of the Tyrol were wont to wear on ceremonial occasions. He was a first-rate, extraordinarily helpful companion, cheerful, high-spirited and constantly on the look-out for an opportunity to put down the great German Wehrmacht. He could hardly have been better suited to the staff on which he was employed.

The German Procurement Staff in France was under the direction of a general and its task was to buy essential articles and goods on the black market in both occupied and unoccupied France. 'Essential articles and goods' comprised pretty well everything from ball-bearings to naval guns, or champagne and caviar to British aircraft. The most bizarre transaction during my time concerned two or three Spitfires which had been placed at the disposal of the Portuguese Air Force by the British, and were now to be dismantled and transported by a devious route via Spain and unoccupied France to a workshop south of Paris, in exchange for spare parts for passenger aircraft of German provenance, namely the Ju 52, plus a substantial sum in convertible currencies, in this case pounds and Swiss francs. The pounds and Swiss francs that exchanged hands in the course of transactions like these were, moreover, still genuine. It was not until 1944 that the Germans flooded the market with hundreds of millions of counterfeit British pounds and American dollars. Payment in pound and dollar notes could still be accepted without misgivings.

The officers on the German Procurement Staff consisted of some twenty-five or thirty administrative advisers and commissioned specialists, most of them former directors of large banks and industrial concerns. Like all the others who worked in the Palais d'Eiffel – clerks, orderlies and a dozen for the most part exceptionally pretty German and French secretaries – they might have been living on another planet. Everyone was

polite to one another and military protocol was dropped as
soon as one stepped inside the door, if not sooner. General
Thönisen invariably addressed those he was talking to as
'Gentlemen', irrespective of whether they were colonels, senior
economic advisers or humble privates. In short it was a different world with a different tone, and it was exceedingly agreeable.

We worked from 8.0 am to 12 midday and from 3.0 to 7.0
pm, such hours being not unusual in banking and industry.
On Saturdays everyone knocked off at midday, an unheard of
state of affairs in a military establishment, but then again it
was perfectly normal for the heads of a business to knock
off on a Saturday. On Sundays we would go out to the race-
courses, or perhaps take a stroll in the large park. Virtually
everyone had a car, even me, Riki having supplied me with
a minute Simca which he had got hold of somewhere. Unfortunately it was of little use at first as I could not drive and I
therefore took lessons from the general's driver. On Sundays
we would go out to the Bois, where I learnt the basic principles.
This was not particularly dangerous either to others or to
myself as there was relatively little traffic in France, even in
Paris, at that time. Admittedly I could use the car only on
Saturdays and Sundays, for on weekends it was inadvisable
for a member of the Procurement Staff to go joy-riding in a
private car with French number-plates.

Riki Posch-Pastor thought it intolerable that we should have
to go about in uniform all the time and accordingly obtained
permission for us to wear civilian clothes. In this way we
travelled the country concluding various deals, the intricacies
of which were somewhat above my head, since I had virtually
no knowledge either of business or of barter, let alone of buying and selling. Not that it mattered, since he had brought me
along partly for company.

One day I telephoned the German Embassy and asked to
speak to a young woman by the name of Ulli Rüdt von Kollen-
berg. Ulli, who had heard from her aunt, Jannerl Gatterburg-
Stockhausen, that I was in France, at once arranged to meet
me at the Hotel Claridge. In the vestibule I was greeted by a
graceful, fair-haired, exceptionally pretty young woman and
there, in the heart of wartime Paris, the opportunity arose for
my first serious flirtation with the most charming member of

the Baden aristocracy I have ever met. Moreover Ulli was subsequently to play a central role in our underground activities. After her transfer from the German Embassy in Paris to the Archives Commission of the Foreign Affairs Ministry in Berlin she rendered incalculable service to our cause. But for her, Otto would in all likelihood no longer be alive today.

Every so often we would wander through the French capital enjoying life. The war was very remote. Paris was an extraordinarily peaceful place and to me it seemed that the French were neither interested in the conflict nor hostile to the Germans. Naturally they could not suspect that I was an Austrian and an opponent of Hitler. I was, of course, usually in uniform, but even so I never heard a single unfriendly word; invariably the French were pleasant and obliging. On my departure from Paris I thought how utterly unnecessary this war between French and Germans had been. Such expressions of criticism and disapproval as were to be heard in Paris in 1942 were levelled at the British who, after the Allied invasion of North Africa, were then in process of occupying Madagascar. Naturally enough this infuriated the French and there were big protest demonstrations. Admittedly it was quite obvious that German propaganda and the efforts of Laval's government were largely responsible for this attitude, but it was also quite obvious that at this stage the forces hostile to the Germans could not yet venture to come out into the open.

As to the hatred which was so much in evidence after the war and which had allegedly been a dominant feature of the French scene even in the early years of the occupation, I for one could see absolutely no sign of it. On the contrary, I had the utmost difficulty in tracking down active members of the resistance in Paris. This again was not surprising, since my French was atrocious and in any case my contacts were too few, at least during the early months. I used to meet friends of friends who would then open up new possibilities, but it was not until February 1943, unfortunately just when I was about to be posted away, that I finally made contact with the resistance through the person of Jean Menier, a charming and in other respects thoroughly unwarlike chocolate manufacturer.

In the meantime, however, I was more preoccupied with the pleasures of life. We went to the theatre, Ulli helped me to understand French plays, we ate out together and rode in the bicycle rickshaws that thronged the streets of Paris, small, elegant contraptions very similar to the rickshaws of the East. Traction was provided by a normal bicycle or tandem, while at the back was a small aluminum cart with room for one or two people. It was a somewhat slow, extremely comfortable form of progress and undoubtedly a complete anachronism by modern social standards. But at the time everyone thought it most agreeable.

We went for walks by the Seine and browsed through the bookstalls, which were still where they always had been. Here one might light upon titles that would have met with considerable disapproval from the representatives of the Third Reich. Many of the émigrés of the years between 1933 and 1939 had obviously arrived in Paris with countless books and had subsequently disposed of them piecemeal. Over the months I discovered at least forty or fifty volumes that were on the blackest of the Third Reich's black lists and these helped me substantially to improve my still very scanty knowledge of the non-Nazi and anti-Nazi literature of the preceding twenty or thirty years. It was there that I was able to get hold of my first copies of Thomas Mann, Franz Werfel and Stefan Zweig and gain access to a body of literature hitherto unfamiliar to me. For at home, when I had taken up reading in 1938, everything of that description had been hidden away, while the officially approved fare we were dished up with was insipid and, on the whole, thoroughly boring.

In France I lived like a lord. There was no doubt that we were dancing on the edge of a volcano, nor was there any doubt that it could only last for another month or two, but we did not worry. Riki Posch-Pastor, Ulli, a few other friends and I wandered about Paris, just as any young people would if given the chance of exploring the city. We talked of books and art, went to plays, visited museums and art galleries and sat for hours in the cafés of the Champs Elysées, clinging with both hands to those starlit hours, that fleeting moment when, or so it seemed to us, the exploding star had, all of a sudden, ceased to explode.

I doubt if I ever enjoyed anything so much in my youth as those three or four months in Paris. This may seem incomprehensible to many people today, but that period was a dream, the dream of a world as it may have been in the past and might – though not for decades – become again, a world in which the young could be young, lighthearted and free, a world in which they could become absorbed in things that had nothing to do with war, bloodshed and suffering. To enjoy this dream world we obviously had to keep the curtains closely drawn so as to prevent the raw air of the outside world, the reality of war, from intruding. Though we did not manage to do so for very long, the brief respite we had been granted was the more wonderful for that.

In the early part of 1943 I was given ten days' leave and went home to Vienna. Otto was also there; he had finally recovered and had been granted student's leave. On my returning to Paris I was greeted by a somewhat agitated and jumpy Riki Posch-Pastor. The 'Hero's Friend', he announced, was about to descend on us. The Hero's Friend was a general, answering to the apt name of Unruh (trouble, commotion), who had been entrusted by the Führer with the task of seeking out superfluous 'base wallahs' in the rear areas, especially in France, and packing them off to the front. Horrifying rumours and stories preceded his arrival. In Belgium, so we learnt, it had taken him only a fortnight to produce three divisions exclusively from the base staffs and much the same thing had happened in Holland. He had promised Hitler that in France he would raise two army corps. To me it seemed perfectly possible to round up sufficient men for two army corps from among the idle soldiery employed on administrative and other agreeable duties in occupied France, especially as there was then no apparent need for any serious military activity in the zone.

So General Unruh arrived in Paris, set up his HQ in the Hotel Majestic and, within a few weeks, the German Procurement Staff in France had been disbanded. A heavy blow to us all, as also no doubt to General Thönisen, our chief. Riki contrived to stay in Paris for the time being, but I was posted to Berlin with the prospect of being sent on further east. Great lamentations on all sides, a round of farewells, final evenings in the Bois, final visits to the cafés, then the Gare du Nord.

I stood at the window of the German leave-train that was to take me to Berlin via Aachen, Cologne and the Ruhr. Below, on the platform, stood Ulli, small, endearing, somewhat

tearful. She did not know how long she would be staying in
Paris, nor I where fate would lead me. My movement order
read: 'To Depot Battalion Spandau for reassignment to combat duties Eastern Front.' We gazed into each other's eyes,
then up to the murky roof of the Gare du Nord, exchanging
no more than an inconsequential word or two, for our flirtation and the mutual love that had us firmly in its grip had
also brought the discovery that we saw eye to eye over things
that were then of paramount importance, namely rejection
of dictatorship, rejection of the Third Reich and the certainty
that something must be done to combat them.

Fair-haired little Ulli was more positive and more uncom-
promising than I. I had the advantage of her only in the sense
that I already had some experience of prison and the Gestapo.
She, however, was endowed with the certainty of those who
know precisely what is good and what is necessary. Never for
an instant did she hesitate to become involved in matters that
might at any moment have cost her her life. From the start
she was never in any doubt that such and such a course was
right and therefore must be followed. For me Ulli became a
symbol of those 'other Germans' of whom my knowledge and
personal experience had hitherto been limited by the fact of my
being an Austrian and hence, perhaps, a bit of an outsider.
Later on I was to meet many other people of this kind, but
virtually none possessing greater integrity or single-minded-
ness.

As the train at last moved out after half an hour's delay,
for which we both were deeply grateful, I watched Ulli gradually disappear from view on the platform. She gave me another wave with one of her beautiful Parisian scarves, while I
leaned so far out of the window that I was nearly struck by a
gantry as the train went speeding by.

I was hauled back by a sergeant.

'What the hell you up to, boy?' he enquired. 'Want to be
court-martialled for self-inflicted injury?'

Once more I was caught up in the reality of the German
Wehrmacht. Through the winter's night the leave-train steamed
towards Berlin.

8

Corporal Sedler

In the early days of 1943 Berlin still had almost a peacetime air. The bombing raids were only just beginning and the fronts appeared to have been stabilized again after the heavy defeat at Stalingrad and the loss of Libya. In Tunisia the Afrika Korps had moved into strong positions, while in Russia a new line had been established on the Don. Speaking at the Sports Palace in Berlin on 18 February, Goebbels had proclaimed 'total war'. When I arrived in Berlin in March to await my posting from the Spandau depot, the advertising pillars were all plastered with gigantic posters bearing the slogan: 'We want total war.' But the impression made by Berlin itself was that of a cosmopolitan city. Admittedly there were many uniforms to be seen, but the civilians still dressed well, while the bustle in the Kurfürstendamm or near Potsdam station was reminiscent of peacetime. And one could, at a price, eat tolerably well in a restaurant.

As a soldier you were treated kindly and life in Berlin was by no means unbearable. Especially for me, as I had various friends and relations in the capital. An uncle, Karl Straubinger, lived in Berlin and worked at the Ministry of Food, while my godfather Professor Heinrich Mitteis and his wife Lidi used to come to Berlin to see me. Mitteis, an Austrian by birth, had been professor of the history of law at Heidelberg and Munich. As an opponent of the Nazis, however, he had lost his post and moved to Vienna in 1935 to teach, at which time he also assumed the onerous duty of being my godfather. When Hitler annexed Austria in 1938, he had to leave Vienna and was transferred to Greifswald.

The chief subject of any conversation was, of course,

whether Hitler might still win the war. By early 1943 most of his opponents were already of the opinion that he had lost it. The only question now was how much longer hostilities would last, and whether one ought not to do everything possible to bring the horrors of war to an early end.

It was at the home of Hilda Krummbach, a friend of my mother's, in the Berlin suburb of Zehlendorf-West, that I had my first meeting with members of the German resistance. While I had been on leave in Vienna the previous Christmas, Major Alfons Freiherr von Stillfried' had confided to me that he and several friends of his from the former Austrian officer corps were about to set up an active military resistance group in Austria. Though he had not, of course, mentioned any names, he had nevertheless give me an address in Berlin which proved to be that of one of Colonel Erwin von Lahousen's liaison centres. Until 1938 Lahousen had worked in the Austrian intelligence department responsible for counter-espionage. He was then sent for by Admiral Canaris, head of the Abwehr, and installed in his headquarters in Berlin. Both men obviously saw eye to eye, not only as intelligence experts, but also in political matters.

Some ten days after I had delivered Stillfried's letter of introduction at Lahousen's office, I received a message to the effect that the colonel – he later rose to general – could not see me just then as he was not in Berlin. I was therefore all the more astonished when, two days later, on being taken out to supper at a restaurant near the Adlon Hotel by my Uncle Karl. I was introduced to Lahousen, who was already sitting at our table.

Even in German uniform Lahousen still looked the typical Austrian officer and very much a man of the world. He obviously wanted to know more about me and asked numerous questions. When my uncle brought the conversation round to my stay in France, Lahousen inquired about the morale of both the Germans and the French in Paris and about other related matters. Finally he asked me about my experiences with the Gestapo in Vienna, though it seemed to me that there was little I could tell him that he didn't already know.

As we were saying goodbye, Lahousen turned to me. 'I shall drop you at Spandau,' he said. On the way to the car he suddenly paused, took out his notebook and asked: 'What unit do you belong to?' Having jotted this down, along with the name of my commanding officer, he continued: 'It would be as well for you to go to Italy. No. 2 Economic Administration Centre is forming a new unit and you ought to be one of the party. I shall see if I can make the necessary arrangements. You will be hearing from me again.' It was plain that he had had absolutely no intention of giving me a lift back to barracks, but had simply wanted to talk to me alone. So I took my leave and walked away.

I did not see Lahousen again. Not long afterwards, however, I was posted to a new unit, then still in process of formation, which was about to move to the Chiemsee in Upper Bavaria and whose ultimate destination was Italy. So far as I was concerned, the Chiemsee and even Italy presented a prospect that was, to say the least, better than a return to Russia. A few weeks elapsed before the unit, which had been raised in the utmost secrecy, was transported together with its vehicles by special train to Prien on the Chiemsee. There it set about organizing itself for the task that lay ahead.

In the early summer the Chiemsee was an exceptionally pleasant place to be stationed at, an added advantage being that I had the opportunity of visiting my parents, who were spending their holidays with our relatives, the Straubingers, in Gastein. My mother was intensely depressed and was writing long, despairing elegies. Whenever she felt that things were becoming too much to bear, she would seek refuge in her writing. My father, calmer and more optimistic, thought the war could not last more than a year at the outside. Various straws in the wind had led him to believe that, after their victory, the Allies would restore Austria's independence.

Without mentioning any names, I told my parents that I had made contact with a resistance group in the Wehrmacht and that my transfer to Italy had some connection with this. Both of them approved, but they naturally told me to take as much care as possible; they also offered their help should need arise. From then on everything was easier for me. I had greatly feared that my parents would disapprove of my decision to join the resistance. But during the course of a conversation on an evening walk to the Grüner Baum, an inn in a valley that branches off the Gasteinertal, I found I was wrong.

We spoke at length about the problem of the oath of allegiance, though for me, at any rate, the subject was merely of theoretical significance, since a kind dispensation of fate had absolved me from having to swear allegiance to Hitler. For I enlisted in the summer of 1942, my first posting had been to the infantry depot battlion at Mistelbach for training and, of course, for attestation. But because of an unexpected and extremely quick transfer to the punishment battalion at Steinhammer in Upper Silesia, I left Mistelbach two days before the ceremony. In Steinhammer, also, everyone had already taken the oath, with the result that I slipped through without being attested. Hence, having never taken the oath, I could not possibly break it.

But the theoretical question still remained, of course, and for many soldiers it also proved a serious problem in practice. Father himself was of the opinion – and here he had the support of my mother, officer's daughter though she was – that not too much should be made of the matter. Austria, he argued, had been forcibly occupied by the German Reich; none of us had wanted the *Anschluss* and we had all done everything possible to prevent it. An oath sworn under compulsion could not entail any obligation to keep faith with the leader of a foreign country. Besides, a pledge could be binding only vis-à-vis a moral authority. Since Hitler's accession to power, however, National Socialist Germany had committed countless acts that were absolutely contrary to all moral principles, both human and divine. Even had we not been Austrians but Germans, the Hitlerian form of oath would, he maintained, have ceased by now to have any validity for us. By and large I had always thought as much, but I was very glad to hear that such a stickler as my father was of the same opinion.

We were due to leave for Rome in July. Our unit had received orders to move into billets in a village near Frascati and an advance party had already left. Suddenly all plans were changed. Mussolini had fallen from power on 25 July and was under arrest, and a complete readjustment of Italo-German relations seemed likely. Throughout August we received a constant stream of orders, each one countermanding the last. Finally, at the end of August, we set off via the Brenner for South Tyrol and from there proceeded to Rovereto.

On arrival we were assigned the task of disarming the

Italian troops in the Rovereto area, Badoglio's government having concluded an armistice with the Allies on 8 September. Our personnel consisted largely of administrative experts, interpreters and the like, in other words of people with little inclination for feats of heroism. Hence, operations such as these developed exclusively upon the relatively few younger members of the unit.

In due course six of us sallied forth to disarm the Italians in Rovereto barracks, which contained elements of an Alpini division. To our amazement they surrendered without making the slightest attempt at resistance, after which the entire barracks were 'held' by six humble members of the Wehrmacht until the German military police finally arrived to organize the removal of the Italians to POW camps. To me the whole business was an utter mystery. Had the Italian armed forces resisted for no more than five minutes, the German seizure of power, not only in Rovereto, but in Milan and elsewhere, would have proved completely impossible. The Italians had obviously been abandoned by their superiors. None of them knew what they were supposed to do and in any case they were all fed up and simply wanted to go home. It was a mood reflected in the song sung by Italian soldiers everywhere:

> We're sick to death of this bleeding war,
> So back to our homes we'll go once more.
> Down with Adolf, down with Benito,
> Down with England, basta, finito.
> All we want is dolce far niente
> With a trim little piece who's sweet and twenty.

After a few more days in Rovereto we drove along Lake Garda, first to Garda and then to Salò. Here we again halted for a time. On the third day an enormous party of German and Italian generals suddenly made their appearance, followed by Benito Mussolini himself. The Duce certainly bore little resemblance to the image I had of him from the newsreels and illustrated papers. Here was a weary, rather stout old man who walked as though weighed down by a heavy burden. No trace remained of the glamour with which he had been invested as a dictator and tribune of the people. He was visibly distrait, if not bored, as he inspected a company of Black-shirts, after which he quickly disappeared through the door-way of a villa. A short while before he had been a prisoner of the Royal government on the Gran Sasso and had been rescued on the orders of his friend Hitler by a swashbuckling ss officer named Otto Skorzeny in the course of a daring action. After his visit to Hitler at Führer Headquarters, the Duce had formed a Fascist government in the part of Italy still under German occupation. In this rump state he abolished the monarchy and proclaimed the Republica Sociale Italiana, with himself as head of both state and government. His en-tourage consisited of a few Fascist leaders and generals who had remained faithful to the party. Saló was the seat of govern-ment. Initially Mussolini kept to his castle, the Rocca della Caminata, and paid only brief visits to Lake Garda. It was on one of these trips that we saw him.

We now moved on to Milan, where we installed ourselves in the Albergo Gran Turismo. Before long we began to meet severe competition, since No. 2 Economic Administration Centre (Upper Italy), to which we belonged, was at daggers drawn with the so-called Stab Ruk, the Armaments and War Production Staff, which was based partly in Milan and partly in Como. The task of both organizations was to boost the con-tribution of Italian industry and commerce to the war effort or, in plainer terms, to harness Italian factories to the require-ments of the Wehrmacht and, where expedient, dismantle their machinery and send it to the Reich. In addition, raw materials of all descriptions were, of course, commandeered in central and northern Italy by the so-called Economic Administration Centres and despatched to the same destination. We always furnished the most detailed figures relating to their value, but I cannot say whether the Italians ever really set eyes on their money.

Between 1943 and 1945 that part of Italy not as yet occupied by the Allies was a most curious form of state. In fact it was not a state at all but rather a conglomerate of more or less organized administrative systems which existed side by side and in some cases overlapped. There was the Italian civil service, which had been taken over from the monarchy along with the provincial officials, who continued to function much as they had done prior to July 1943. Besides these there were German

military and, especially near the German border, civil adminis-
trative agencies, all of which, whether under the auspices of
Wehrmacht, ss, Party or Reich, competed with one another.
Finally there were all manner of local Fascist potentates who
ruled under the aegis of the Germans. And, from September
1943, there was the government of the Republica Sociale
Italiana, which actually had an army at its disposal, for several
Italian divisions consisiting of ex-POWs had been raised in
Germany and northern Italy. Besides these, however, were the
Fascist private armies, the most famous being the Decima
Mas.

The Decima Mas had originated in a naval special service
unit which had been equipped with one-man torpedoes to
operate against the British fleet in the harbours of Gibraltar,
Alexandria and Malta. In the autumn of 1943 its commander,
Prince Junio Valerio Borghese, had placed his services and
those of his thirteen hundred men at the disposal of the Germans and, later, of Mussolini, because, as he put it, his code
of honour bound him to the alliance and forbade him to go
over to the other side. Even though Prince Borghese stressed
that he was in fact no Fascist, the Decima Mas was soon to be
hardly less feared than the ss.

The great majority of Italians were neither Fascist nor anti-
Fascist. All they looked for was peace and quiet. Just as they
had not been exactly over-enthusiastic about the Duce before
the war, so now they were neither pro-Ally nor pro-German;
at bottom they wanted to be allowed to go about their own
business or *fare affari*. At the same time their political standpoint was proclaimed everywhere on the walls by the slogan:
Abbasso tutto, or down with everyone.

Possibly this reflected more faithfully than anything else the
political despair prevailing in Italy in the years 1943 and 1944.
The people were assuredly not pro-partisan, since the partisans
might kill you and would certainly take away what little food
and money you had. And they were undoubtedly not pro-
German, for it was the Germans who carried you off to the
Reich as a 'foreign worker'. Neither did they favour Mussolini,
who, after all, had already lost his empire and was on the point
of disappearing from the scene. But nor had they had any love
for the Allies, who not only dropped bombs on their country,
but regarded it as a third-rate power.

Indeed they were anti-everyone; anti-Graziani, the Italian general on Hitler's side who had been appointed Commander-in-Chief of the Italian troops in the German occupied zone, anti-Badoglio, the Italian general who had concluded the armistice with the Allies and was now continuing the war on the latter's side. Everything was at sixes and sevens, yet life went on. Indeed, you could get hold of anything you wanted on the black, the grey or the off-white market; everything had its price and was dealt in accordingly.

The air raids were not so much unpleasant as downright disagreeable, but they were confined to a few of the larger cities such as Rome, Milan, Bologna and, curiously enough, Treviso, which was particularly badly hit. By and large, however, the Allies went for military targets, though that was small consolation to the railwaymen, say, or truck drivers whose occupation required their constant presence within the target area.

The situation in Italy differed fundamentally from that in Germany. First of all, the German secret police never really succeeded in penetrating the Italian community. Their numbers were too few and the war was already much too far advanced. The Italians had to see to their own internal security themselves and the Fascist police were relatively innocuous. It was a different matter where anti-partisan operations were concerned; here there was much bloodshed.

Mussolini had also launched a retributive campaign against those who had brought about his downfall in the summer of 1943, that is upon nineteen out of the twenty-nine members of the Grand Fascist Council, including his son-in-law, Count Galeazzo Ciano, who had been his Foreign Minister until February 1943. Ciano was tried in Verona in January 1944 and, like Marshal de Bono and many other erstwhile Fascist leaders, sentenced to death by firing squad.

There were, of course, several partisan organizations: the Communists with their Red Brigades, the left-wing, but not exclusively Communist, Matteotti Brigades, the Garibaldi Brigades, the Liberal Fiamme Verdi, as well as the groups of Christian Democratic persuasion. Within the movement as a whole it was the Communists and Socialists who were most important. The partisans were in some cases subordinate to their local chiefs, in others to the party central committees which by now were functioning legally in the South. Finally, they were influenced to a very large extent by the Americans and British, from whom they received arms, ammunition and other supplies. During the last months of the war there was also a Comitato di Liberazione Nationale Alta Italia (CLNAI), the high command of the Italian resistance movement, which was headed by General Raffaele Cadorna, a son of the Italian Commander-in-Chief in the First World War.

For the most part the Italian population was very friendly towards the Germans, though obviously there were exceptions especially in places where, for example, hostages had been shot. The Germans also behaved very well towards the Italians, SS permitting. Quite often, comparatively close and cordial relationships sprang up, certainly more cordial than, say, in France.

In the winter of 1943–44 the partisans controlled various isolated mountain districts, mainly in the central Apennines and the Piedmontese Alps. Subsequently they extended their control to the highlands round Sondrio and, later still, to the Udine region. They did not infiltrate the towns except in the form of underground cells, which had certainly been operating since 1943 in, amongst other cities, Turin, Bologna and, from my own observation, Milan. During 1944 and the early part of 1945 they proliferated still further until, in the end, only the main trunk roads and the large cities remained under the control of the Germans and their Fascist allies. Elsewhere, provided no German division was quartered in the region, there was little sign of German or Fascist domination during the last three or four months of the Second World War.

The autumn of 1943 which I spent in Milan was a most interesting and pleasant time. In the first place I had never before had an opportunity of living in an Italian city and, secondly, I was soon able to build up a circle of friends to whom I was later to owe my survival. Within a few weeks I had got to know the Faccincani della Torre family through their children Gianfranco and Renata. Gianfranco was a student and a fervent patriot who was to die fighting in the Piedmontese mountains in the winter of 1944. In fact, it was he and his sister Renata who helped me appreciate not only the youth of Italy at that time, but the mentality of Italians generally, their thoughts and emotions. The Italy I came to know then was quite different from what it was after the war. These young people were great idealists with a capacity for enthusiasm that can hardly be imagined today. There was something fascinating about the pair of them. It is commonly said that Italians are small and dark-haired, but the Faccincanis were quite the opposite, tall, slim, with fair hair and broad features. Both were exceptionally handsome, indeed Renata was a real beauty, and both took a tremendous interest in the world about them. They spoke German, French and English almost as well as Italian.

While it was Gianfranco and Renata Faccincani and then their charming mother who first made me welcome in their house in the Via Goldoni which was later to play such an important role in my life, others were not slow to follow suit. My cousin Lori Possanner brought back happy memories of past summer holidays in Prein. She had lived for some years in Milan, where she owned a firm, if firm it could be called, that did a great deal of business with all and sundry, and entertained lavishly in her home. Then there were two other friends of mine in the city: the first, Kurt Baumgartner, at that time a senior administrative adviser to the military and a man with whom I had much in common, especially a love of the mountains; the second, Lieutenant Franz Schromm, a Viennese journalist in civil life. Finally, and most important of all, my friend and comrade Corporal Count Franz Otting, a sensitive, lovable man of almost boyish appearance and a devotee of the arts and literature. He was a Bavarian with a very pronounced Austrian streak and, like most of those I have just mentioned, he was to play an extremely active part in the resistance later on.

Thanks to my knowledge of Italian I got on very well in Milan. Not only was I indispensable to the Economic Administration Centre, but for several weeks was actually engaged on duties that contributed in no small measure to my sexual education, namely as interpreter to the German brothel patrol, or 'crumpet picket'. This was a most interesting and memorable job, our orders being to keep a daily check on the Milan brothels that were out of bounds to German troops.

There were only three 'legal' brothels, or Forces' Social Establishments as they were termed, one for officers and two for NCOs and men; all were under regular medical supervision.

Members of the Wehrmacht were strictly forbidden to patronize any brothels other than these, and it was our job to ensure that this regulation was observed. The work was far from disagreeable, since the madames of the various establishments overwhelmed us with hospitality, serving up champagne and excellent food in order to concentrate our attention on culinary matters and prevent us from keeping a careful check on the visitors to the establishment. We felt it our duty, in the interests of good order and military discipline, to take vigorous action only in the case of ss officers; our comrades were usually allowed to carry on.

Each brothel was equipped with an intriguing device in the form of small peep-holes through which the ladies could be observed at work in their rooms. Hence the assignment was not uninstructive, but unfortunately it lasted no more than three weeks. The man I had been standing in for returned from leave, thereby putting an end to my tours of the brothels dressed in uniform and wearing the well-known 'dog-label' or metal gorget-plate of the military police round my neck.

Just as I was really beginning to enjoy myself in Milan, a man appeared who identified himself with the code-word of our friend Stillfried. He said I must arrange to be transferred to a certain division in the line and there report to a Lieutenant Steffke of the division staff. This was not a particularly simple task. However I knew some of the people at Wehrmacht headquarters in Milan and therefore went and told them I wanted to be sent into the line, by then a somewhat unusual request. At first they were utterly taken aback and thought I had gone mad, but finally they resigned themselves, as much as to say, 'Oh well, if he absolutely insists. . .'

First I had to report to Economic Administration HQ in Treviso, where I spent about a fortnight, after which I was posted south. At Orvieto, my first stop, I acted as interpreter to the town major on an inspection of the wine cellars and was able to sample the best of the local vintages. From there I proceeded to the front, first near Monte Cassino, then in the coastal plain near Anzio and Nettuno where the Americans had landed in January 1944, initially without much success, for the Germans, by restricting the extent of the beach-head, had been able to contain the assault for four or five months.

My army career was taking the usual course. While serving

in Italy I was promoted to lance-corporal and gradually began
to feel like an old hand. This struck me particularly whenever
I shared a trench with raw recruits who had been newly thrown
into the line. One then realized what it meant to have had
two years' service in the army and several months in action.
Every month of front-line experience helped one to survive.

My unit, which had suffered fairly severe casualties in the
fighting south of Rome, was finally pulled out and moved to
central Italy, or rather the Arno valley in the heart of Tuscany,
to rest and to assist in the creation of new infantry battalions.
To this end a kind of training establishment was set up in
Pescia and Borgo di Buggiano. It had a headquarters which
operated in harness with divisional headquarters and comprised several training cadres, a considerable number of long-
serving senior and junior NCOs and, finally, a small squad of
interpreters, of which I was one.

We knew that we should be staying there for several months
and everyone was greatly cheered by the prospect of spending
the spring in the Arno valley. The only annoyance we had to
contend with at the beginning was the daily attentions of the
Allied fighter-bombers. Of these I have a lasting memento,
for in March 1944 I was wounded by shell splinters when a
large Wehrmacht truck immediately next to me was shot up
by a fighter-bomber. The splinters struck my face and a number of small steel fragments lodged in my upper jaw. As a
result, I lost most of my upper teeth along with their roots
and thus presented a far from pleasing appearance. In the
months ahead this was to prove a great disadvantage in other
respects also, since it was a simple matter for the military
police to append the words 'gap in upper front teeth' to my
name on the wanted list.

One day a corporal by the name of Günther Jäger turned
up at our headquarters. I soon became friends with him, as
also with several other comrades of his, and presently discovered that these were the people whom Stillfried had said
I should find in the 356th Infantry Division. Lieutenant Steffke
had long since told them of my existence and through some
channel, the exact nature of which I myself never discovered
but which certainly passed through Lahousen, they had been
warned of my arrival.

One evening I was invited to take a glass of wine with them.

I soon gathered what was afoot, for they informed me that they belonged to a resistance group, the ramifications of which were of course kept secret from me. In fact there were, in this and neighbouring divisions, a number of officers who later participated in the events of 20 July 1944. However they did not confide in me to that extent, nor was there the slightest call for them to do so. All I learned was that, for the time being, I would be employed on perfectly normal duties concerned with the procurement of goods and foodstuffs for the division from the Italian supply depots in Florence. During these visits, however, I was to make contact at a particular café with an Italian by the name of Franco Baldi.

It was most exciting to be given a special pass for Florence. Never having been in the capital of Tuscany before, I took in the sights before starting my long negotiations at the Italian supply depot. Finally I made my way to the small café near the cathedral where, according to instructions, I asked for Franco Baldi. Half an hour later my man arrived. The main result of our conversation was to convince Franco Baldi of my good faith and vice-versa. I gathered that he didn't yet really know what he was supposed to discuss with me, while on my part I was completely unaware of the purpose of our meeting.

The conversation was therefore restricted to generalities about the weather and the vileness of the coffee; we agreed, however, to meet again. The next time I was rather less naive and asked Corporal Jäger to enlighten me. He finally told me that my trips to Florence were connected with an attempt to make contact with Italian partisan units in the area of the central Apennines. I was to find out whether these people might be prepared to hold a discussion in the near future with a man who would, of course, have more authority than myself. I put this cautiously to Franco Baldi, who said he would first have to discuss the matter with other friends of his, since he himself was not sufficiently in the know. Finally, at a third meeting, it was agreed that two people, both of them unknown to me, should forgather early in May 1944 in a trattoria in Pistoia. All I knew, or had any cause to know, was that the German representative was a senior officer in our division. The Italian, as I discovered much later, was a liaison officer, employed by the British air-landing units in Bari, who had been trained by the British and had then parachuted into the central Apennines. He was to come down from the mountains for the meeting with our man.

In the meantime, I had also been in more frequent contact with my friends in the Vienna underground and, towards the end of April, I received an urgent request via the military postal service to come to Vienna as quickly as possible. Thanks to the good relations I now enjoyed with our headquarters, I was at once granted short leave 'on compassionate grounds' and accordingly set off for Vienna. Otto was also there, as was Cousin Nedica, who had left Croatia and had now made Vienna her home. I also saw Ulli, who was visiting the city for a few days and staying with my mother. This, the last leave we were all to have together, was a great joy to my mother, since both her sons were present as were her 'adopted daughters', Neda and Ulli. I spent only five or six days in Vienna, for the journey from central Italy had already become a wearing and lengthy business. The line was under constant bombardment and one often had to spend two or three days in the train.

In Vienna I had a discussion with Stillfried and two other representives of the military resistance group, one of whom was Captain Biedermann, who was to be hanged by the Nazis in Floridsdorf for his activities prior to the liberation of Vienna. My instructions were to try and get posted back to the Milan area as soon as circumstances permitted, since it was hoped to recruit an Austrian partisan group from the German HQS and other formations in Lombardy. My task was to place this unit on a proper organizational footing with the help of the Italian partisan leaders. On top of that I had to decide where it should operate from, a provisional choice being the Campo dei Fiori near Varese, which was a place already known to me. At the same time I had to maintain communications with the Italians. From the Campo dei Fiori I was expected to try and make my way into nearby Switzerland and get in touch with the British Consul in Lugano, where a representative of the British secret service had been nominated to act as our spokesman and intermediary. This was quite enough to be going on with. However the chief difficulty, as I saw it, was to get a posting to Milan from a division shortly to be ordered back into the line.

So I returned to Borgo di Buggiano, where everything

seemed to be going very smoothly. Evidently the preliminary talks with the partisans had now taken place, since I learnt that my meetings with Baldi were no longer necessary. However I was to visit Florence in a week's time to meet another Italian. I was also assured that my posting back to Milan would go through and, as a first step, was ordered to report to the MO, who expressed the opinion that my heart trouble had been aggravated by the severe infection of the jaw resulting from my wound. Thanks to this 'unfavourable' diagnosis, I was once again put down for LD, or light duties, and thus could no longer remain in a fighting unit. The next step would be a posting back to my former unit, in other words to Milan. So far everything was going swimmingly.

On the day before my visit to Florence, I joined Lieutenant Steffke and Corporal Jäger in a small trattoria in order to be briefed about the trip. In the midst of our discussion both of them suddenly got up and beckoned me to follow. We made for the door of the café, which faced our HQ offices in Borgo di Bugganio, and, as soon as we were outside, Steffke turned to Jäger with the words: 'Sedler is spying on us.' Sedler was a lance-corporal in the office of the Senior Staff Officer (Operations) and had been wounded at Monte Cassino. After some further discussion about the dubiousness of Sedler's character and his propensity for poking his nose into other people's affairs, Steffke urged us to be very wary of him. I myself hardly knew the man, having merely passed the time of day with him now and again, but in the very near future I was to have cause to remember this conversation.

Next day, having concluded my official duties, I again made my way to the little café near the cathedral, where I met a friend of Franco Baldi's by the name of Giuseppe Trentini. By the afternoon I had completed all my business and set off home. Just before the point where one turns off the Lucca road for Borgo di Buggiano, I was hailed by a German soldier. As I stopped the car, I saw to my dismay that it was Lance-Corporal Sedler. What on earth did he want? Surely he wasn't waiting for me of all people to take him the two kilometres to Borgo. Not wishing to behave oddly, I had no alternative but to offer him a lift. 'Get in,' I said, opening the door.

'On the contrary,' he replied, 'it's you who had better get out.' I was utterly mystified. 'Exactly what do you mean?' I asked him. In considerable agitation he quickly told me his story. At midday the secret police had suddenly appeared and arrested, among others, Steffke, Jäger and, apparently, Sedler's own chief. Sedler had been on orderly duty at the time and had learned all this at divisional headquarters. Having seen me in company with Steffke and Jäger, he had assumed that I must be among the suspects. And the police had, in fact, inquired about me as well. Accordingly, as soon as his duties were over, he had set out to warn me.

I still couldn't quite take it all in. Here, facing me, was this scruffy, somewhat lop-sided and really rather unprepossessing lance-corporal with whom I had hitherto exchanged barely twenty words and who was now trying to save my life. And in so doing he was, of course, also risking his own. All I could do was thank him. But he went on to give me some further advice. 'You'd do best to try the Abetone,' he said. 'There's a road block up there, as you know, but if you can get past it you'll find it all the easier to disappear. Anyway, push off as fast you can.'

I clasped his hand and suddenly noticed the immense kindliness of his deep-set grey eyes. I thanked him once again, reversed the Topolino and drove back towards Florence. At Montecatini I turned left and, keeping to side roads, headed for the mountains and the Abetone pass. Fortunately I knew the district well, having visited it often when buying black-market supplies from the peasants.

I drove for some fifteen kilometres northwards of a line Buggiano-Pescia, taking care never to lose sight of the Strada Nazionale dell'Abetone e del Brennero. The Passo dell'Abetone, 1350 metres, to which it led, is the least used of the central Apennine crossings and connects the Arno valley with the Modena region. For months the partisan groups, who had established themselves in the wild country of the Central Apennines, had regularly made it a target for their sabotage operations in an effort to disrupt German traffic.

That was why, early in 1944, the Commander-in-Chief of Army Group South-West had placed restrictions on the use of the pass. Thereafter only two convoys a week were permitted in either direction, their control and protection being the responsibility of the ss or military police. I was familiar with these convoys, since on one occasion I myself had been engaged with my unit in escorting one of them. A few days before my present trip, however, the partisans had spotted and attacked a small convoy. The ensuing gun battle had ended with the hurried departure of the Germans for Modena, from where they had set out. Since then the Abetone had been closed to all traffic and instead the Germans had been using the, in any case shorter, better surfaced and more readily controllable routes via the Futa and the Porretta.

I was in no doubt that they would reopen the pass in a matter of days, since it had hitherto received virtually no attention from ground-attack aircraft and thus had been the first choice for slow, heavy loads. However, I hoped to get across before the army began sweeping the area for partisans.

Some twenty-five kilometres south of the top of the pass the Germans had set up a road block, which I circumvented by using secondary roads. On passing quite close to the spot in the early dusk I could see that it was guarded by a couple of tanks. Twenty minutes later and about three kilometres north of the obstruction I rejoined the main road and continued on for a little way, needless to say without lights. However I now became afraid of falling foul of either an SS patrol or a group of partisans. Since neither of these eventualities was particularly appealing to a man in my situation, I took the first opportunity that offered and sought concealment in a dilapidated road-mender's hut that stood behind an embarkment.

Time passed relatively quickly, for I had to consider what to do next. I resolved to get to the top of the pass next day, as usual making use of such side-roads as might be available. From there I would strike out for Sant' Andrea Pelago, a small village close to the pass where the bush telegraph had reported the presence of partisan units in the nearby mountains. These I proposed to join. At some point I must have fallen asleep, for I was woken by the sound of a man's voice. Beside the Topolino stood a shepherd with his flock; he was addressing his dog. I got up and greeted him. He was perfectly amicable, evidently thought there was nothing unusual about our encounter, and continued on his way with his charges. The time must now have been about 5.30 am and, as it was already light, I decided to take advantage of the early hour and push on. The chances of running into a patrol at that time in the morning were very remote.

I could no longer use the side roads since the going had become too precipitous. However I encountered nothing but a few horse- or ox-drawn carts and another shepherd or two and by about 8.30 am, had reached the top of the pass. There I noted several bullet-scarred buildings and beside them a group of wrecked Italian tanks and German trucks. There was also – much to my relief – a number of corpses on the roadside beside a barn. This was obviously where the convoy had been attacked, after which the Germans had hastily retreated northwards. The partisans must have withdrawn somewhat later, taking their dead and wounded, while the German dead had been left lying where they had fallen.

I climbed to the highest point of the pass and looked round. Not a soul in sight. I selected a corpse with bullet wounds in the chest and neck, dragged it over to the Topolino, put it aboard and continued on northwards. After a couple of hundred metres or so I drew up at a suitable spot by a breast-wall where, with considerable difficulty, I manoeuvred my passenger into the driver's seat. Next, I dressed him in my uniform tunic and hung my identity disc round his neck, after which I placed in the breast pocket sundry documents bearing my name – ration cards from Florence, a divisional pass and similar items – though not my paybook since that seemed too risky. I then shot out the windscreen with my machine pistol, sprinkled the contents of the spare can over the Topolino and set it alight.

As soon as the car was well ablaze, I gave it a final burst with the machine pistol before taking my departure. I had reached the group of houses on the pass and was about to climb towards a line of trees, when suddenly I heard the sound of engines in the distance. Some fifteen minutes later a convoy hove into view, led by an ss armoured car. Next came about six armoured troop carriers and perhaps five or six heavy German trucks which had been fitted with additional armour. More troop carriers and armoured cars brought up the rear. In all the convoy must have comprised about twenty-five vehicles and two hundred and fifty men.

As they breasted the pass they opened fire on the village before proceeding to the spot where the Topolino was still smouldering. From my place of concealment at the edge of the pinewood above the village I could just make out a group of SS officers standing round the smoking wreck. Then came the sound of whistles and the convoy moved off. Possibly they suspected that the car was a trap and, because of their relatively small numbers, decided to drive on. Their destination must have been Modena, for they had come up from the south.

I spent the morning in my hiding-place, observing the country round me. I had ample time for reflection, since there was no movement within my range of vision other than in the village of Abetone, where people would occasionally emerge from their houses, look round, and disappear again.

Sitting behind my screen of young pines, I cast my eyes over the splendid mountain scenery. Higher up, in the direction of Monte Cimone, which rises to over 2,000 metres, the view was reminiscent of the Alps. Lower down, towards Modena, the large pine and fir woods were a particularly striking sight in so southerly a region; at intervals deep gorges descended into the valley. Here, at 1,350 metres, I was surrounded by a dream landscape not unlike parts of the Salzkammergut, though I was, alas, in no case to enjoy it properly.

Indeed my situation was a wretched one. I had a machine pistol and an automatic, it is true, but virtually no ammunition. A mere thirty rounds or so remained for the machine pistol, thanks to my excessive expenditure of ammunition on the burning car, and three magazines, say eighteen rounds, for the automatic. Otherwise I had nothing, neither rations nor equipment, for the trip to Florence had been only for the day. Luckily I had bought some chocolate there and this was all the real nourishment I now possessed. I had enough money – a count revealed about 3,000 lire and 120 marks, not that this would take me very far, but it was ample for the moment. The map I had brought with me covered the whole of northern Italy, but in the area of the Abetone pass it showed only the main road; not one of the villages was marked.

As my knowledge of the district extended only as far as the top of the pass, I was uncertain how to proceed or, for that matter, how to get through to the partisans in the mountains. All I knew was that they were occupying the district round Monte Albano beyond a village by the name of Sant' Andrea Pelago, which could be reached via Fiumalba, further down the road to Modena. In or near Sant' Andrea Pelago there was said to be a parish church and my intention was to seek out the priest. For the rest, there was absolutely no doubt in my mind that my name would by now be on the wanted list and that the army, ss and police would be searching high and low for Lance-Corporal Molden, F. What ought I to do? I decided to wait until the afternoon to see whether anything happened on the road, and then set out under cover of dusk for Fiumalba and Sant' Andrea Pelago. I had no idea of the distance, since neither of these places was shown on my map.

I had landed myself in a pretty pickle; ten days ago I had been on leave in the Osterleitengasse with my parents; two days ago I had still been leading a peaceful existence with my comrades in Borgo di Buggiano; yesterday I had been in Florence, unsuspectingly buying chocolate instead of more important provisions before driving back along the Arno, oblivious of everything. Now, here I was in a plantation of young pines on the Abetone, distinctly at a loss and, for the first time, dependent wholly on my own resources. Hitherto I had always been one of a unit, of a group, whether of prisoners, fellow soldiers or friends. Now there was nobody within miles to whom I could turn for advice. It was up to me to decide what to do next.

I had never been much of a hero and in action, first in the Pripet Marshes and, later on, in the line, I had often been extremely frightened, though probably never so much so as during my time in prison. Now I was faced with an entirely different situation. That morning I realized that fear would get me nowhere; rather it would weaken my resolve. So I made up my mind to cease thinking about the negative aspects and instead concentrate on the positive. I would surely succeed in sticking it out. The war could not last much longer. By the look of things, the Allies would soon break through to Rome. Moreover the nearest prepared position the Germans now possessed was the Gothic Line beyond the Apennines.

A withdrawal was inevitable and, provided I managed to remain in concealment for the next few weeks, I should automatically be left behind as the Germans retreated. Until then it was essential to go to ground either in the mountains or in some village before joining up with the Allies. In three or four weeks' time, certainly not more, everything would be all right. There was obviously the possibility of my being caught before that, but I should manage somehow. After all, I spoke Italian and the Italians were not the sort of people to give one away. I could only be thankful that, in this respect, they were far superior to the Austrians, for in Austria one was constantly on tenterhooks; even one's relatives often held different political opinions and, if Nazis, were honour bound to denounce a kinsman or schoolfellow. From that point of view, therefore, I was better off where I was.

By midday it had become fairly hot so I lay down on the grass behind a clump of bushes to get some sleep. An hour later, I was awakened by the roar of engines. Below me six or seven German tanks were entering the village. They had obviously come from the northern end of the pass, since their guns were pointing south. After an hour of inactivity they proceeded to shoot the place up. Whether this was to bolster their courage or to flush out partisan stragglers, I couldn't tell. Shortly afterwards one of the tanks detached itself from the rest and drove up to my Topolino. Ten minutes went by, then fifteen. Finally it turned round and re-entered the village. Half an hour later the whole lot of them faced about and departed in the direction from which they had come. On the assumption that that would be the last performance of the day, I waited for half an hour, then made my way downhill, using the bushes as cover, until I reached a large meadow. This I crossed at the double, every so often flinging myself to the ground, and at last gained the road. Not a soul was in sight.

I walked up to my once proud Topolino, a sorry spectacle now, blackened by fire and riddled with bullets. The doors were open and the corpse had gone. Obviously they had taken it with them. But had they, I wondered, assumed it to be Lance-Corporal Molden, F.? This was a question of the utmost importance so far as I was concerned. Months later I discovered that the deception had indeed been successful, since my name had been removed from the wanted list at the beginning of June. Not until very much later did I learn that I had nevertheless been sentenced in absentia by No. 1012 Military Court in Bologna, along with those who had been arrested in Buggiano and Pescia on that fateful day. Subsequently I used to say jokingly that, if I ran away at the time, it was because I hated executions and was opposed to capital punishment. In fact I ran away because I was afraid. But is the distinction really so great? On that afternoon on the Abetone, however, all I knew was that my doppelgänger had gone. I only hoped they would give him a decent burial. In any case, I decided that it was time to be off.

I set out along a path leading down to Fiumalba and beyond. For the first part of the way it ran alongside the main road, before bearing westwards through mountain forests. Sooner or later I was almost bound to arrive at Sant' Andrea Pelago and there, perhaps, meet people who could direct me. As I walked I tried to conjure up Sedler's face in my mind's eye. Without him I should assuredly be sitting in some cellar at the mercy of the secret police, perhaps already beaten to pulp. I was no longer able to visualize his features and kept mixing them up with those of the dead ss man who now bore the name of Lance-Corporal Molden, F. Lost in though, I made my way through the twilit woods below the Passo dell'Abetone.

9

Rendezvous Goldoni

Luigi Brentini, student, of 11 Via Roma, Pisa, son of Pietro Brentini and Erna Innerhofer, born 9 May 1921 in Bressanone, formerly Brixen, sat in the waiting-room of Francesco Demeti, a Milan dentist, suffering from severe toothache. He went there every day at an unusual hour, namely 9.30 pm. For Demeti, being a very busy man, always had other patients to attend to in the afternoons, whereas Luigi Brentini had plenty of time on his hands. He did not even pursue his studies but lazed around and was readily available even at night. Thus, evening after evening he would sit in Demeti's surgery and, what is more, sit there in the dark. Evidently the dentist was a parsimonious man.

From the darkened room Brentini would look down into a street that was no less dark, for this was in the spring of 1944 and there was an air-raid warning almost every night. However, Milan had not as yet been seriously knocked about.

Brentini needed a fair amount of dental treatment. Some wartime accident had badly damaged his front upper teeth, most of which could, indeed, be described as non-existent. Demeti was engaged in the task of providing Brentini with false teeth, but first he had to extract what was left of the nerves and roots. In fact the task was rather beyond his competence, for Demeti was not a dental surgeon but merely a jobbing dentist from southern Italy, driven north by the war. He had not even got a licence and worked, as it were, privately; nor had he any business to provide a new set of teeth, a job which was in fact the responsibility of the hospital. But Demeti could not send anyone to hospital, nor could Brentini possibly present himself there for fear of causing raised eyebrows by his inability to produce either a plausible explanation for his accident, a letter of admission or, indeed, any document except a *carta d'identità* issued on 5 April 1943 in Pisa.

For Brentini's name was not Brentini at all; rather, it was Lance-Corporal Molden, F., formerly known as Fepolinski and Waschlapski, who had disappeared from Borgo di Buggiano at the beginning of May 1944 and been found dead high up on the Abetone Pass. Brentini was very glad to have discovered Demeti. From the moment a fortnight earlier, when he had rung the bell late one evening in the Via Goldoni, unkempt, famished and almost completely exhausted, his Milanese friends had helped him in every sense of the word. He had been sheltered by Renata and her mother, who had procured papers for him – those, in fact, of Luigi Brentini – and had assisted him in every possible way. He was sorely in need of help for, in the course of his arduous journey from the Central Apennines to Milan, Luigi Brentini, now reborn in Sant' Andrea Pelago, had been through a great deal.

After his adventures on the Abetone Pass he had taken refuge with a Catholic priest while attempting to contact the partisans. When some of these eventually turned up, they took him for a spy and proposed to shoot him out of hand. With considerable difficulty he succeeded in persuading them that he really was on the run from the Germans and they agreed to take him with them into the hills of the Monte Cimone region. There he remained for several weeks until, after a partisan raid on a German convoy, a big mopping-up operation led to a general clearance of the district. Most of his comrades of Brigata Matteotti No. 3 were either killed or taken prisoner. The rest escaped into the remoter parts of the Apennines.

Luigi Brentini then made his way to Bologna. He had a friend there, an inn-keeper called Camillo Dall'Ollio, who owned the trattoria of that name that lay in a little arcade at the edge of the old city, below the Porta Saragossa. Camillo Dall'Ollio was a genial, portly man whose house had been much frequented by Luigi Brentini on those occasions when, as Lance-Corporal Molden, he had been stationed at Bologna. The old Bolognese inn-keeper and the young Austrian soldier had made friends. They conversed happily together about this and that and soon realized that they had much the same political views. Camillo was married to a charming signora, a real lady, not herself a true Bolognese but a native of a small town, almost a village, just outside Bologna and called, I think, Casalecchio di Reno. After an air raid we would often go and sit there of an evening, or might even spend the whole day in the little place if raids were frequent.

For Bologna lay exactly beneath the path taken by the Allied bombers from their bases in Bari to the Brenner and Germany, and there were numerous anti-aircraft batteries in the area. When these proved unduly troublesome, the bombers would simply drop their loads on to the town so that their approach was a signal for a general sauve-qui-peut, either into the hills above Bologna or into the vast plain to the east of it. Looking down from the hills and seeing the town in flames at one's feet, one felt it must have been like this when the devil tempted Jesus, so beautiful and yet so ghastly a spectacle was it.

Camillo also had a pretty daughter and a mass of regular customers, all of them simple, decent Italians, typical sons of Bologna, with whom, during long nights spent at the inn, Lance-Corporal Molden had struck up many a friendship. This time, again at night, he had returned in rags; true, he still boasted a pair of shoes but only one sock, while his pockets were empty apart from forty lire and a pistol without ammunition. Signor Dall'Ollio took him in, addressed him thenceforward as *caro* Luigi, and found hiding-places for him. One night it was a barrel where Brentini all but succumbed to the fumes of alcohol, another time it was under a cask. He had to remain in hiding because, a fortnight earlier, the German military police had been to the inn and inquired after Lance-Corporal Molden, F., who was known to have been a frequent customer there. He was wanted for a court martial, they said. Camillo professed an ignorance that was perfectly genuine at the time; later he was sufficiently well-informed to keep Brentini safely tucked away. It was plain that he could not remain in Bologna. But how to get him out? The town was most carefully cordoned off with a view to stemming the tide of refugees and picking up deserters, partisans and other 'riff-raff'.

At last an opportunity presented itself. Dall'Ollio had to go out to one of the villages to replenish his supplies of wine. To this end he obtained a *permesso* and likewise a lorry propelled by wood-gas onto which he loaded his empty barrels, one of them again providing a hiding-place for Brentini. Then they set off, old Camillo and a friend as driver. At the barrier they showed their *permesso*. Everything was in order. Twenty minutes later they stopped outside a small farmhouse, Camillo opened the barrel and said, '*Luigi, tutto va bene.*' But Luigi, again rendered unconscious by the fumes, did not reply. He was, however, quickly brought round with a bucket or two of water.

Once again all had gone well. He said goodbye and, having been given two salami sausages and a loaf of bread, set off on foot. He always moved at night and spent the day sleeping in maize fields, where the crop was already well-advanced and provided a perfect hiding-place. One night when he had nothing left to eat – this was somewhere near Reggio Emilia – he knocked at a peasant's door. The latter asked few questions, gave him food and shelter and, what is more, presented him with a pair of civilian trousers and a jacket. Brentini had discovered that no Italian would ever betray him. So every night, no matter where he was, he would knock at someone's door, and in every case he would be given shelter, a bed, food and sometimes even money.

Finally he reached the Po. The bridges were heavily guarded and he had no Camillo Dall'Ollio to arrange a jaunt in a barrel. There was only one thing to be done – find a place where there were plenty of sandbanks and swim across. It was about the end of June and very hot. Brentini decided to wait until darkness fell. Then he took off his clothes, tied them into a bundle and, holding them above his head, crossed the Po. It all went without a hitch, except that he trod on a bee on one of the sandbanks and was therefore unable to put on his shoe the next day. But that wasn't the worst. Far more disagreeable was the persistent pain from his broken teeth and festering gums. Nevertheless, he kept going until he got to Pavia, where he boarded a tram and travelled to Milan without a ticket.

Late one evening – in Normandy the Allies' battle to break out of the beachhead was then at its height – Luigi Brentini rang the bell at 19 Via Goldoni; the door was opened by Renata Faccincani, who flung her arms round his neck. They, too, had been asked whether they had by any chance seen Lance-Corporal Molden, F. They admitted to having known him when he had been stationed in Milan, adding, however, that that had been a long time ago and they had never set eyes on him since.

Thenceforward not only Luigi Brentini, but also Pietro de Lago, Hans Steindler, Ernst Steinhauser, Peter Stummer and Jerry Wieser, to mention only a few, were to turn up regularly at the Via Goldoni and find a welcome there. A whole procession of chaps with brown hair whose shade varied according to the time when, and the expertise with which, the dye had been applied. Chaps with false teeth and, in due course, respectable moustaches. Just now, it happened to be Luigi Brentini, whom the dentist had at last succeeded in fitting out with a temporary set of false teeth. He felt a new man.

Meanwhile he had also found somewhere to live. Thanks to the Faccincanis and their friends, he had got to know old Colonel Spignese d'Elena, a respectable regular army officer now retired, and a sincere opponent of the Fascist regime. Spignese had numerous friends, both in the underground and amongst the partisans, and promised to put Brentini in touch with the right people. So it was that, a few days later, he was able to go out to Varese and meet his partisan contacts. Together they went to take a look at the Campo dei Fiori, a mountainous and still peaceful district which the partisans had not as yet seriously considered taking over. German troops were stationed in Varese itself, and also at frontier points on Lakes Maggiore and Lugano. But up in the Campo dei Fiori, which could be reached by an old-fashioned funicular, the peace was only disturbed by an occasional weekend hunter.

Brentini returned to Milan, where he had arranged to meet Franz Otting, Franz Schromm and one of two other friends he had made during his previous stay there. It was decided to form a band consisting of Austrian deserters and civilian resistance men which would be located in the mountains round about Varese.

In high spirits he made his way home along the Galleria to his temporary lodgings and was surprised to find Colonel Spignese waiting for him in the street. The colonel came to meet him and, drawing him into a doorway, advised him to move off without delay, for two of the contacts with whom he had spent the previous day had been arrested that morning by the Fascist militia. It must be presumed that all clues would be followed up and that one of them would undoubtedly lead to Spignese d'Elena who, a week before, had sent a note to one of the detained men recommending Luigi Brentini of 11, Via Roma, Pisa, as one who could be relied on as a friend. Spignese said that he, too, intended to leave Milan and retire to a country estate near Bergamo owned by a distant cousin of his. Having politely thanked the colonel, Brentini once again found himself at a loss what to do next. It was high time, at any rate, to ensure that Luigi Brentini of 11 Via Roma, Pisa, disappeared from the scene.

I spent that evening at Lori Possanner's. My cousin Lori, who had shared our holidays at Prein and been teased by Otto and Niki because she was so fat, had meanwhile grown up and turned into a slender and lovely young woman. She kept open house in Milan and, when I had been previously stationed there, had welcomed me most kindly. It is greatly to her credit that she was prepared to help me despite all her fears. Obviously I should have to drop my nom-de-guerre of Brentini and temporarily relinquish the contracts I had so carefully built up with the Milanese partisans. Nor, for the time being, would it be possible for me to get into touch with Renata direct.

I therefore remained in hiding at Lori's for several days, and this in a room immediately adjoining the big drawing-room where she used to hold court every evening and receive her many friends, including German officers of all ranks. Lori dealt extensively with the Germans, amongst whom she had numerous acquaintances, which meant that she could pull a great many strings. First of all, she succeeded in finding out almost at once that, while I was still on the wanted list, the actual search had been called off. After a couple of days Lori also discovered that the hunt was on for Brentini, Luigi, of 11, Via Roma, Pisa, suspected of pro-partisan activities. At vast expense she then procured for me a new identity card in the high-sounding name of Carlo Fontana. It was a fine name but an indifferent card. For it was perfectly clear that the particulars it contained did not tally with the photograph. But at least it was my photograph. So although able to venture out into the street again, I felt far from happy about it. In the meantime a message from Alfons Stillfried had arrived at the Via Goldoni which eventually reached me at Lori's. From it I learnt that a courier would contact me within a day or two in Milan, but via the address in the Via Goldoni. I conveyed the news to Renata by a roundabout route and she arranged things with the courier. It was thus that I met him at a small café not far from Lori's house.

The courier, a German officer of Austrian origin, neither introduced himself nor asked for my particulars. We had established our identities by exchanging code words. He gave me my instructions, which were that, as already arranged in April in Vienna, I was to go to Switzerland, ring up the British Consulate in Lugano and ask for a Mr de Coundes, identifying myself by means of three code words. As soon as this had been done my task would be to establish more concrete relations between the Austrian resistance movement and the Allies, for whom de Coundes was acting in Lugano. I was then to return to Milan and, despite what had happened, make a further attempt to organize the partisan groups in the Campo dei Fiori. Finally, I was to communicate with Vienna again as soon as possible. The courier went on to say that he would return to Milan in ten days' time, when he would again contact me via the Goldoni station. I was a trifle confused by the many new tasks I had been set. Our leave-taking was brief. Evidently he assumed I should have no difficulty in getting into Switzerland with the help of the Italian partisans.

Thus my time in Milan was drawing to a close. Much had happened there. From being a soldier in the German army. I had transformed myself once and for all into a dark-haired Italian, had revived old friendships and made new ones, and begun to find my way about in a new world which, though largely built on sand, was nevertheless reasonably secure. I was constantly having to change my identity and name, always having to invent new parents and a new childhood, but this was soon to become second nature to me. The Via Goldoni with the Faccincanis and their friends, Lori Possanner and her little world, Franzl Otting and many others in Milan – these were to provide the firm stanchion for the nerve-racking wire I had to walk between the Allied and the German camps, between Switzerland and Vienna, on my many journeys between the two worlds.

The Via Goldoni spelt home, security, warmth and affection. Helpfulness and friendliness were the very raison d'être of those who lived there. For me they were typical of the Italian people whom I had come to know and love, a people who always inquire, first after your human needs, and only then after your politics. With the inhabitants of the Via Goldoni and their friends, with the peasants in the Emilia, with the young partisans of the Brigata Matteotti No. 3, with Camillo Dall'Ollio and his regulars, to mention only a few, I had established bonds of sympathy and esteem which nothing could now sever. The Goldoni station had about it a permanence that would outlast war, Fascism and partisans. And, quite apart from anything else, Fepolinski had fallen in love again, this time with a beautiful, fair-haired Milanese girl, Renata of the self-same Via Goldoni.

With her help it took me two days, if that, to make the necessary contacts with a group of partisans operating on the borders of Switzerland, helpful souls who might more unkindly be described as smugglers. In return for adequate remuneration they undertook to get me across the frontier near Mendrisio.

In those days cash was a major problem. Though I had arrived at the Faccincanis with no more than five lire in my pocket, they not only gave me a heart-warming welcome but actually lent me money, indeed quite a lot of money, first for a new set of teeth, then for forged papers and, finally, since I had to live, for my subsistence. Help was also forthcoming from Lori Possanner and a couple of other friends who were still in the Wehrmacht. I knew that plenty of money was available in Vienna but there was no way of getting at it. Eventually, by fair means or foul – probably the latter – a friend of mine on the Armaments and War Production staff was able, within a few days, to rustle up the sum of fifty thousand marks, which he handed over to me for use in future operations. Later on, too, he was to be of great assistance to me and this I was able to repay in some measure when, in April 1945, he was about to be strung up out of hand by partisans, drunk with victory and intent on revenge. I arrived at his lodgings only just in time. Already securely bound, he was about to be taken by jeep to the same square in which, much to the glee of the assembled populace, Mussolini's corpse and that of his mistress, Clara Petacci, had been strung up by the heels a few days before.

Thanks to this man, then, I had fifty thousand marks at my disposal, which was a very large sum indeed in those days. I was able to pay my debts and the balance was placed to my credit by Lori so that my account now contained at any rate half the amount I required. Renata and I went to Varese, and from there we proceeded by a minute branch line towards Porto Ceresio on Lake Lugano. We got out two stations before Porto Ceresio, went to a little inn, and there sat waiting in a shady garden. After an hour we were joined by two friendly individuals of somewhat bucolic appearance – the partisans who were to get me across the frontier. Renata then boarded the train for the return journey and, as we said goodbye, we both assumed that we should be seeing each other again a couple of days later in Milan.

The two men and I made for the frontier, through a wood, across several meadows, now crouching, now running. Twice we had to go out of our way to avoid Italian police patrols whom we had sighted in the distance, but otherwise nothing untoward happened. Finally, after running through a plantation of young tree, we came to a barbed-wire fence over which we climbed. Another stretch of forest and we were in Switzerland. My two companions, who had already had their fee, took friendly leave of me. We agreed to meet next day at 4 pm on the road leading out of Menrisio. They had told me exactly what route to follow and all went smoothly. Once a Swiss vehicle came into view on the little country road. Not wanting to draw attention to myself I dived into the bushes and let it go past. Then I proceeded on my way.

10

A Sane World with Rösti and Coffee

I walked as in a dream, a dream in which huge, full-fat Emmental cheeses went rolling down carefully swept roads. It was along those roads that my path to Mendrisio lay. The few houses I had passed had been neat and trim, and all of them, perhaps because of their proximity to the frontier, had big flags adorned with the Swiss cross hanging out of their attic windows. At last I came to the little town which lies about half way between Chiasso and Lugano, in the southernmost extremity of the Swiss canton of Ticino.

To me, it was like a revelation. The gates of a paradise flowing over with chocolates, cigarettes and the *Neue Zürcher Zeitung* had opened up before me. Here was a sane world in which even Fepolinski and Waschlapski might feed on sausages, rösti* and coffee. I was twenty years old, had experienced five years of war, six years of Nazi rule and eleven years of dictatorship, and had now, for the first time since reaching the age of discretion, set foot in a free country.

I had had no idea what a country was like where there wasn't a war on, a town in which you could go into a shop and buy anything you wanted. For years I had dreamed of being able to buy uncensored papers with news of what was actually happening. I had also dreamed of being able to buy chocolate and cigarettes as a matter of course. In my pocket I had sixty Swiss francs procured for me in Milan by Lori Possanner's banker friends – a lot of money. So I sauntered through Mendrisio, bought myself some chocolate, sauntered on, bought cigarettes and eventually came to the station. Mendrisio is on

*A Swiss national dish resembling potato pancakes.

the St Gotthard line and I had to take a train to Lugano and there contact my intermediary at the British Consulate.

I entered the station building, bought a ticket 'Lugano e ritorno', and waited for the next train. In Italian Switzerland the railways then still bore the delightfully old-fashioned name of 'Strade Ferrate Federali'. In Italy, where people were more up-to-date, they already spoke of the 'ferrovia', but in the Ticino, now as before, it was still the Strade Ferrate Federali. As a railway enthusiast, I found this quite enchanting, being also much taken by the cleanliness of the station. Then, on one of the platforms, I caught sight of a small kiosk. On approaching it I espied the *Neue Zürcher Zeitung*, for a journalist's son a dream come true. I bought it, also the *Baseler Nationalzeitung*, the *Baseler Nachrichten*, the *Berner Bund* – all the newspapers they had, in fact, not forgetting the *Weltwoche* and the *Nebelspalter*. Then I made my way back to my fine seat on the beautiful, clean, unbombed platform of the Strade Ferrate Federale Svizzere in Mendrisio, in the beautiful canton of Ticino, placed the newspapers beside me in a great pile, and deemed myself a millionaire. Next, I opened a packet of Player's Navy Cut, which was also to be had in Switzerland, took out a cigarette, lit it and felt utterly content. Replacing cigarettes and matches in my pocket I picked up the *Zürcher Zeitung* and began to read.

'Mi scusi, Signore,' said a friendly voice, 'lei ha un fiammifero?' Do you happen to have a match?

'Naturalmente, Signore, per favore,' I replied, glad to be able to help a Swiss. I got out my matches and gave the man a light.

'Grazie, grazie mille volte,' Very many thanks, he said, adding politely: 'Prego, ma li lasci vedere i fiammiferi?' I was a bit taken aback; why should he want to look at my matches? Then I realized that this time all was not well. For the matches were of Italian make.

And here the cunning Brentini, Fontana, Molden, F., Fepolinski and Waschlapski, had reckoned without his Swiss host. No one had yet succeeded in catching him, neither the Gestapo, nor the Italians, nor the Wehrmacht patrols, and now he had gone and got himself caught by, of all people, the Swiss. With a smile, the man identified himself, Aliens Department of Cantonal Police, and asked to see my permit. Unfortunately I had none to show. He invited me to accompany him, took me to Mendrisio police station, asked me to take a seat and to lay my possessions on the table. I was allowed to retain cigarettes, matches and newspapers but not my penknife. After a short telephone conversation the policeman said he would have to take me to Bellinzona, the capital of the canton, where my case would be attended to.

We therefore left by the train for which I had been waiting. I was somewhat but not greatly depressed for, after all, nothing very dire could happen to me in Switzerland. True, I would be unable to meet my Englishman, which was galling, but I comforted myself with the thought that 'tomorrow is another day'. It was a lovely, clean train – the policeman had booked us second class so my own third class ticket remained unused in my pocket – in which we travelled through the summer landscape of the Ticino, past Lugano, to Bellinzona. There my new friend took me to the cantonal gaol.

I was put into a magnificent cell with a view of the mountains. A few minutes later a pleasant, elderly woman appeared, introduced herself as the new wife of the chief warder and gave me my supper – coffee and rösti and, on top of that, because of my starved appearance and because this was the Ticino, a dish of spaghetti. It all seemed wonderful to me; here I was with the newspapers I had bought, able to read them and turn the light out whenever I liked. For the first time in years I went to sleep without fear of arrest by the Gestapo, safe and content in this lovely Swiss prison.

Early the next day another affable gentleman arrived and began to interrogate me. I, no less affable, said I was sorry, but I could not tell him anything and asked him to set me free.

'Very well,' he said, 'where do you wish to go?'

'I'd like to go back to Italy.'

'Very well, that's easily done. This afternoon we shall hand you over to the Italian authorities in Chiasso.'

Now that didn't suit my book at all, for it was perfectly clear what would happen next. The Italian authorities would lose no time in discovering that I wasn't an Italian and would promptly hand me over to the Gestapo, who also had an office in Chiasso. Sooner or later, the latter would inevitably find out from No. 1012 German Military Court, Bologna, or from

Gestapo headquarters in Vienna exactly who I was and how matters really stood with me. Since, as already indicated, executions have never been my cup of tea, I was extremely reluctant, in short, to adopt the course proposed by the affable gentleman. I told him as much, whereupon he said: 'Well, if that doesn't suit you, then it might be best if you were after all to tell me who you are and what you are really up to here.'

At this I told him that I was an Austrian patriot, that I had business in Switzerland, but that I could not inform him of the purpose of my journey, though I was prepared to discuss matters at a higher level.

'Very well. You will be hearing from me tomorrow,' he said and left, but not before placing on the table copies of *Sie und Er* and the *Schweizer Illustrierte*, kindly observing that it must be a long time since I had seen a picture paper. How right he was!

That evening the married couple in charge of the prison invited me to join them in a game of cards. I wasn't much of a partner since I didn't know how to play their Swiss game – *Watten*, or whatever its name was. They were delightful people – she was an Italian and he a native of the Canton of Uri – and both treated me kindly and sympathetically. I ought, they said, to spend some time with them so that they could fatten me up properly. But the pleasant interlude in Bellinzona was to come to an end the very next day. Another gentleman turned up, not quite so affable, perhaps, but nevertheless very correct, even if he did secure me to his person with handcuffs. We went to Bellinzona station and from there in a prison compartment – or rather, I was inside it, not he – by express train over to St Gotthard. It was the first time I had crossed the Alps in Switzerland and I thoroughly enjoyed the trip, although my view was somewhat restricted by the smallness of the window and the fact that it was barred.

We arrived at Lucerne in the afternoon and I was taken to the Hotel Schweizerhof, the headquarters of Swiss Military Intelligence, where I was received by several officers, some in civilian clothes, some in uniform. That evening I was questioned for about five hours, first by a single interrogator and then by two, the second being Major, later Colonel, Max Waibel, head of Military Intelligence and a member of the Swiss Army General Staff. Both of them were very polite and, to begin with, exceedingly reserved. I was given a room in the Schweizerhof and was kept under guard. But I was allowed out with my guards and even went to the cinema with them to see an amusing film called *The Ghost goes West* in the original English.

Three days later, when they had finished questioning me, I was told that I would be taken to the Dietschiberg, a mountain outside Lucerne frequented by excursionists and served by a small cable-car. There I would remain in a sort of temporary internment camp but would be fetched away again quite soon – as soon, that is, as my fate had been decided. I spent a week in this comparatively luxurious camp, where I worked in a large vegetable garden hoeing weeds, a skill I had not lost since my time in Liesing prison. There I had to hoe vast fields of turnips, here considerably smaller tomato and strawberry beds. It was an agreeable time, the food was good and plentiful and, while I waited, I could enjoy the view of Lake Lucerne and the mountains of the original Swiss cantons.

My fellow internees came from all over the world and were taciturn to a man. All were clearly people who had somehow found their way to Switzerland and were now intent on making some kind of contact with the Swiss secret service. No one talked much, no one introduced himself; conversation was restricted to politics and the war and everyone was at pains to talk in accents other than his own.

When I had been there six days, a tubby, genial man arrived on the scene, sent for me and introduced himself: 'I am Fritz Dickmann, of Basle.' That afternoon I became acquainted, in the person of Fritz Dickmann, with one of the finest, straightest and most likeable men I have ever met.

He was head of the Austrian section of the Swiss military secret service. Like almost all the Swiss, he was not a professional soldier, but a lawyer and notary who had joined up only for the duration and had been assigned to intelligence. The assignment could not have been bettered, for Fritz Dickmann, whose kind-heartedness was only equalled by his extreme intelligence, was as if cut out for the post and was, moreover, one of the most honourable men I have ever known. We got on splendidly from the first. He took me away with him there and then and this time not in handcuffs. We went down by the cable-car to the lake, where a small automobile awaited us. Dickmann drove me to the Schweizerhof and explained en route that all my statements had been checked and found correct. Waibel was therefore quite prepared to hold serious discussions with me about the possibility of collaborating with the Austrian resistance group I represented. There would, Dickmann said, undoubtedly be some hard bargaining, but I needn't worry for, having now found out who I was, his colleagues would trust me. In the Schweizerhof I was taken to a lounge where four or five men were sitting, amongst them Major Waibel.

There ensued long and detailed discussions. The gentlemen proved to be exceptionally well supplied with up-to-date information, not only as regards my own person but also as regards the position in Austria, Germany and northern Italy. They told me they were interested in maintaining contacts with Austrian underground groups. We should realize, however, that this in no way implied any recognition, whether official or otherwise, of our cause by the Swiss, or any degree of partiality towards it. Rather, the Swiss Army, no matter where its sympathies might lie – and where in fact they lay was obvious enough to me after what had happened during the past week – was interested in maintaining contacts with persons of whatever complexion who might help to preserve the neutrality and independence of Switzerland.

From these discussions it soon transpired that Switzerland had reason to fear an infringement of her territorial integrity, and hence of her neutrality, by the German armed forces. Allied air attacks on the Brenner, Reschen and Tarvis passes were making it increasingly difficult for the German Wehrmacht to supply their combat units in Italy or send goods from that country to Germany. The only Alpine passes that still remained intact were those inside Switzerland which, moreover, represented the shortest route between northern Italy and the south-east of France. True, the Germans were allowed to use the Swiss railways for the conveyance of goods but not for military purposes. For unlike, say Sweden, the Swiss had stood firm in the matter of their neutrality. There was an ever-growing danger, however, that Hitler would send his troops into Switzerland as being the 'shortest overland route'. But the underlying circumstances were changing, for the further the Allies advanced in Italy, the greater was the danger that the

German forces, and in particular the German South-West Army Group in Italy, would simply ignore Switzerland's neutrality and march across the country. The Swiss feared a similar breach of neutrality by the German army groups still in the South of France as soon as the Allies succeeded in cutting off the latter's communications with the main German forces in the central and northern parts of that country.

Again, the Swiss High Command believed that an American landing in the region of Genoa would disrupt communications between Italy and the south of France, whereupon the German forces there would be faced with the choice either of escaping into Switzerland or of capitulating. The second alternative seemed highly improbable at the time, in view of the consequences the commanders concerned would have had to suffer at Hitler's hands.

For all these reasons the Swiss military leaders were exceedingly interested in obtaining all available information about German troop movements in the south of France, northern Italy, Austria and southern Germany. Similarly, they wanted to know anything that might have any bearing on the so-called 'Alpine Redoubt'. For there was an increasingly persistent rumour that the Germans were planning an Alpine stronghold consisting of the Trento area (those parts of Italy north of Lake Garda), South Tyrol, North Tyrol, the Vorarlberg, southern Bavaria, and parts of Salzburg and Upper Carinthia. There they intended to make a last, desperate stand as the Allied armies advanced upon them from all directions. This much the Swiss knew and, true or not, it worried them. Hence their General Staff were naturally most anxious to obtain reliable and early information on the subject.

Such were the real reasons for the evident interest shown by Major Waibel, Dr Dickmann and their friends in establishing and developing contacts with the Austrian resistance movement and with myself as its, to them, first tangible representative. They in their turn were prepared to make important concessions, viz:

1   To place at the disposal of couriers and other authenticated members of the Austrian resistance movement who might enter or leave Switzerland, documents, papers, weapons and other equipment.

2   To permit representatives of the Austrian resistance
    movement, aided by the Swiss military authorities, to
    visit Swiss internment camps in search of persons of
    Austrian nationality (refugees or émigrés) prepared to
    work or fight with the resistance movement and go to
    Austria. Officially, of course, the Swiss military authori-
    ties had to take the view that all persons retrieved by us
    from such camps, either now or later, would be acting
    in the interests of the Swiss. But they certainly must have
    realized how difficult it would be to draw the line be-
    tween acting in the pursuit of common Swiss and Aus-
    trian goals and acting either solely on behalf of the
    resistance or solely on behalf of the Swiss. Whatever the
    case, the Swiss were to put a very liberal interpretation
    on these questions in the months that lay ahead.

3   To empower the Austrian resistance movement to estab-
    lish a communications centre in Switzerland. To this end
    I was given permission to contact Austrians domiciled
    in the country and to set up a small organization in
    Zurich.

4   To permit and assist our people to cross and re-cross the
    frontier, thus enabling us to introduce our men into Ger-
    man occupied territories from Switzerland and vice-
    versa.

5   To accord tacit consent to contacts between Austrian
    agencies and the representatives of Allied governments
    in Switzerland.

In return, our own duties were clearly formulated:

1   The representatives of the Austrian resistance movement
    would do their utmost promptly to place at the disposal
    of the Swiss authorities all available information, not
    only on German troop movements but also on all tactical,
    strategic, military or other developments in German-
    occupied Italy and Austria and within the German
    Reich.

2   The representatives of the Austrian resistance movement
    would do everything in their power to make instantly
    available to the Swiss authorities any information con-
    cerning possible plans on the part of German or other

agencies to infringe Swiss neutrality and, in so far as possible, obstruct such activities on the part of the said agencies.

3   The Austrian resistance movement and its representatives would in no circumstances so take advantage of the privileges accorded and the support given them by Swiss agencies as to infringe Swiss neutrality in any respect. In particular they would, while on Swiss territory, do nothing that was contrary to the law of the land.

Patently, it was the observance of the third clause that would present the greatest difficulty. But we always did our level best not to cause the Swiss any embarrassment, while they for their part similiarly did their best to turn a blind eye if, on occasion, we overstepped the mark in any way.

This agreement, which was set down in writing as a kind of aide-mémoire, marked a crucial turning point in the history of the Austrian resistance movement. For it provided us with our first opportunity of maintaining regular and reliable contacts with the free world. It also provided us with our first opportunity of organizing in Switzerland a communications centre for the active Austrian underground, an agency from which contacts could be established with the Allies and with those Austrians who were mustering in other parts of the world. Finally, and, perhaps, most important of all, it provided a unique chance of re-entering Austria from Switzerland and of supplying resistance groups in the field with weapons as well as the radio equipment and other means of communication required to set up an intelligence network.

The discussions went on for about three days, at the end of which we were all pretty well done-in, I more than anyone else for I was on my own, whereas there were five or six of them. But here I must admit that, unlike the others who were very busy men, I had nothing else to do. Eventually we reached agreement on all counts. Dr Fritz Dickmann was appointed our intermediary. Thanks to him and some of his colleagues, our close collaboration with the Swiss army proceeded without a hitch right up to the end of the war.

As from that day, the practical facilities I needed for my work in Switzerland were placed at my disposal, it being understood that, after about four weeks' stay there, I should return to northern Italy and from there to Austria. I went to Zurich and was issued with a refugee's permit, my choice of name on this being Gerhard Wieser. I was also allocated a room at the Evangelical Hostel in the Niederdorfstrasse, a very respectable, puritanical establisment where good lodgings with breakfast were to be had at very reasonable cost. All of a sudden I found myself established in Zurich, a free man – free to go sight-seeing, visit the cinema or eat out, which I did for preference at 'Die Hinteren Sterne'.

On the very first day of this existence I made an important contact. I was standing not far from the Bellevueplatz, on the bridge at the lower end of the Lake of Zurich where the River Linth has its source, and was looking around me full of delighted curiosity, when I saw a young man, with a pleasant, intelligent face, walking towards me. He might almost be an Austrian, I thought, if his appearance was anything to go by. And then, as he went past, I noticed that he was wearing a red, white and red badge. I decided to follow him. The young man entered a café, sat down and began to read a paper. I also went in, walked straight across to his table – which must have seemed odd, if only because nearly all the other tables were unoccupied – and in a strong Austrian accent said:

'Excuse me, is this seat taken?'

He looked up in some annoyance.

'But there's plenty of room elsewhere.'

'Yes. But Austrians are few and far between.'

He looked at me, smiled and got up.

'Well, and who are you?'

I introduced myself as Gerhard Wieser, adding that I was an Austrian refugee. With some hesitation the young man told me that his name was Hans Thalberg. Naturally enough, he was extremely reserved and it was plain that he didn't know what to make of me. Later, he was to tell me that he had at first taken me for a German agent.

It had, of course, also occurred to me that I might be falling into a German agent's trap, but so imperative was my need to contact other Austrians that the risk had to be taken. After we had both of us beaten about the bush for some time I eventually decided to try and draw him out. I therefore asked him if he happened to know a Herr Linder of Vorarlberg, some-time Social Democratic member of the Vienna parliament, whom I believed to be living in the Zurich district. I also asked him about Prince Schwarzenberg, a former Austrian diplomat, said by my father to be now in Geneva as Austrian delegate to the International Red Cross.

The effect was the reverse of what I had hoped. Thalberg grew even more reserved, evidently in the belief that my questions were designed to catch him out. We were getting no further and, since time was precious, I saw that I should have to cast caution to the winds. I told him a good deal though I naturally said nothing about my agreement with the Swiss, nor did I reveal my real name. After listening attentively, he said:

'I assume you're telling me the truth, but how can you prove it?'

Not knowing myself just how this could be done, I replied: 'Perhaps we could put our heads together and devise some way of proving it?'

He burst out laughing. 'Give me time to think it over, and we'll go into the matter,' he said. 'Where do you live?'

I gave him my address and he arranged to come and call for me that evening. As, later that day, I sat waiting in my little room in the Evangelical Hostel, I thought: 'Suppose the chap calls for me and takes me to some place where I'm drugged by the Gestapo and smuggled across the border?' I didn't even dare ring up Fritz Dickmann, who would undoubtedly have thought me a most terrible amateur and had me thrown out of the country. So there I sat and waited, reflecting that I was not really cut out for secret service work after all, and had behaved in a singularly unprofessional fashion.

Presently I left the hostel and went to the station, where I bought quantities of chocolate and, out of sheer desperation, ate the whole lot. On my return I posted myself in a doorway from which I could observe the entrance hall of the Evangelical Hostel. Hans Thalberg, I now saw, was already there with a female companion. So I plucked up courage and went into the little hall, hoping for the best. And the best happened. Thalberg greeted me and introduced me to Friedl, then a close friend and now his wife. She struck me as an unusually pleasant and trustworthy person.

Thalberg had been making inquiries and had found out as much as he was able. It seemed that some Swiss friends, while not divulging very much about me, had somehow convinced him that I was all right. He had also spoken to a Dr Kurt Grimm, who, in the months ahead, was to play a major role, not only in our activities, but in my life in particular.

First we all three went to a café and afterwards to a restaurant for a meal. I was reasonably forthcoming about the course of my life over the past few years, though I did not reveal my real name until some time later, when I was absolutely sure of them. In return Hans told me that, after 1938, he had come to Switzerland, where he had been able to continue his studies. For some time past, it seemed, his activities had been mainly devoted to charitable work and to an organization for Austrians domiciled in Switzerland.

All this was now to change dramatically. We talked until far into the night. The following day Hans Thalberg took me to see Kurt Grimm at the Hotel Bellerive au Lac on the shores of the beautiful Lake Zurich. After a short wait, we were taken up to the second floor and ushered into the sitting-room of a magnificent corner suite. Today I can still visualize that room and, standing in the middle of it, Kurt Grimm, obviously a very live wire indeed. It was not long before he and I were on good terms. Like Hans Thalberg, I immediately felt I could trust him, a sentiment that was, I am glad to say, reciprocated so that we were able to settle down to work together within a matter of hours.

When, on the evening of 20 July 1944, the Swiss radio broadcast the news of the attempt on Hitler's life, I was greatly cast down by the fact that it had failed. I had met several of the men whose names were to figure among the victims of the reprisals carried out by the Nazi leadership. When I was in Berlin in 1943 I had been taken to have coffee with Ulrich von Hassell, sometime ambassador to the Quirinal, by my Viennese defence counsel, Dr Josef Graf Ezdorf, who had many friends and relations in Berlin, amongst them a cousin in the Foreign Ministry. It was not until later, of course, that I learned that von Hassell was one of the central figures in the German resistance. Others present were Adam von Trott zu Solz also of the Foreign Ministry and, like von Hassell, executed after 20 July, and Bernd Gisevius, whom I was to meet again on a number of occasions in Switzerland.

Politics were barely mentioned during that meeting. With great affability von Hassell told me he had read my father's book on Metternich and, when I was on the point of leaving, asked me to come and see him again and tell him something about Austria. This I never managed to do, for I was posted away from Berlin a few days later. The next thing I heard about Ulrich von Hassell was that he had been arrested in connection with the attempt on Hitler's life. He was executed in September 1944. Also executed was a colonel in the Abwehr, Count Rudolf von Marogna-Redwitz, who had been closely associated with the 20 July rising in Vienna, and had worked hand in glove with General Erwin Lahousen. I had been acquainted with Marogna-Redwitz, having often met him on social and other occasions. He had been kept informed of our activities by Stillfried and, without his intervention, my movements in Italy, made on the former's instructions, would not have been possible.

Had the coup succeeded, the question of Austria's independence would have immediately become a crucial one. So far as our Austrian circle in Switzerland was concerned, there had never been any pan-German problem, either before or after the tragedy of 20 July. We were all agreed that Austria must rise again, and that a democratic government should be formed and free elections held at the earliest opportunity; in other words we wished to see the creation of a parliamentary democracy such as had existed before 1933. No one envisaged a return to the Dollfuss-Schuschnigg system, although our circle included men of the right as well as of the left. To us of the younger generation, who had not belonged to any party, things seemed far simpler and less problematical. The same could also be said of Kurt Grimm, however, who continually stressed the fact that his concern was with Austria rather than this or that political faction. At the time it did not take us very long to reach an agreement on basic principles which would be acceptable to all who worked with us in Switzerland, with the exception of the Communists.

The small group of Communist émigrés in that country was led by a Herr Kohn and a Frau Ilse Benedikt, daughter of Dr Ernst Benedikt, for many years editor of the *Neue Freie Presse* and my father's sometime employer. Frau Benedikt was sincerely anxious to take part in the struggle for liberation and would undoubtedly have co-operated with our group. However this had clearly been forbidden by her Communist bosses, who nevertheless expected her to keep in touch with us, thus placing her in the exceedingly awkward position of constantly having to engage in discussions with us but never to any purpose. This happened time and again during my stay in Switzerland. Of Ilse Benedikt nothing could be assumed with any certainty except that she would not betray us. Nor did she ever do so. But in accordance with her instructions she sabotaged everything that might have been conducive to co-operation between our group in Switzerland and Communist resistance groups in Austria. Hence we were compelled to seek our own contacts with Communists at home – with, for instance, the members of the group of Viktor Matejka, later City Counsellor in Vienna.

During the ensuing months Kurt Grimm and Hans Thalberg also succeeded in making contact with the refugee committees in London, New York, and Paris, the latter committee having been newly resurrected after the liberation of the French capital. Our relations with it, however, were not to assume a really positive nature until my first encounter with Ernst Lemberger. Then things really began to happen, and to happen fast.

But my first concern during these weeks was to prepare a plan of action that could be implemented simultaneously from our bases in Switzerland and Austria, whither I was anxious to return as soon as possible. For nights on end during that summer of 1944 we laboured away at the tactical and strategic details of this plan, now with Kurt Grimm in the Hotel Bellerive, now with Hans Thalberg in my room at the Evangelical Hostel and occasionally, by kind permission of Fritz Dickmann, in the latter's office at Basle. The main features of the plan I then drafted were later accepted and substantially put into effect both by our Swiss group and by the Vienna headquarters of 05, the military resistance organization already in existence. It was based on a number of considerations.

In order to intensify and effectually stimulate the activity of the various Austrian resistance groups, it would be necessary, first to combine the most important of them into a tightly-knit organization and, secondly, to establish close and permanent relations with the Allies. Contacts such as these were the only means of inducing the more vigorous activity essential to the success of Austrian underground operations. To that end, our resistance groups would have to be given a boost by the Allies in the shape of material aid (supplies of weapons, radio equipment etc) and psychological support (co-ordination and intensification of Allied propaganda to Austria in a form comprehensible to Austrians). And to achieve this it would in turn be necessary to increase the Allies' confidence, then minimal, in the seriousness of purpose of the Austrian resistance movement.

These goals could, I believed, best be furthered in my own sector by two main causes of action. The first was the creation of a smoothly functioning intelligence and courier service between Austria and German-occupied Italy on the one hand, and Austria and our 'station' in Switzerland on the other, this last being already in contact with the Allies and recognized by the Swiss authorities. The second was the early concentration of all known resistance groups under a unified command, and the formation in Vienna of a political counterpart to 05* – a committee capable of assuming responsibility for the struggle and drawn from all parties and groups having an active role in the resistance. It had already become apparent that the creation of such a committee was essential if we were to receive support from the Allies and, more important still, eventually gain their recognition.

As regards the first we found it would be vital to establish a secure and efficient courier service between Austria and Switzerland, using as many routes as possible, and then, proceeding systematically from West to East, set up intelligence and liaison posts at key points in northern Italy and Austria. In the summer of 1944 the particularly close watch kept by the ss on the Austro-Swiss border meant in effect that liaison could be maintained with northern Italy only via the Ticino and with South Tyrol only via the Engadine.

Detailed investigations now revealed that the most suitable crossing point was in the Chiasso and Cernobbio border zone, that is the most southerly point of Ticino, notably the Monte

*Oesterreich 45, the military resistance organization.

Bisbino district and the region south-west of Mendrisio. We discussed the matter exhaustively with the Swiss Army and reconnoitred every inch of the border areas. Finally I decided to concentrate on the route via Sagno where, with the permission of the Swiss, we set up a small base in the Hotel Zentral.

The actual frontier was crossed at Tre Croci, on the southeast slope of Monte Bisbino. From there one descended by precipitous smugglers' tracks to Cernobbio, in those days still a peaceful little village on Lake Como. There we set up a base in the house of a young Italian partisan called Pietro, an experienced guide who was also to serve us in that capacity. This route had the advantage of being short; on foot, if all went well, it took only about three hours to cover the distance between Sagno and Cernobbio or vice versa. Moreover, the inaccessibility of the frontier at this point meant that there were comparatively few guards. These advantages outweighed the disadvantage of the very close watch that was kept on the roads further down, both in Cernobbio itself and in the Como area generally. A 'filo', or electric bus, ran from Cernobbio to Como, whence there were two railway lines to Milan. On the Swiss side of the border it was barely half an hour's drive by car from Sagno to Lugano.

In the course of our subsequent activities we succeeded in organizing the frontier crossings and onward transport from Cernobbio to Milan via Como and vice-versa so well that it was possible to leave Zurich by the early train, reach Lugano later the same morning, travel by car to Sagno, arrive in Cernobbio by the late afternoon and get to Milan on the evening of the same day. That, of course, was when everything went smoothly. But since the frontier could be more easily patrolled by day, we tended increasingly to cross it under cover of darkness; indeed, so well did we come to know the paths and such was the experience of our partisan guides that this came to be regarded as the safest thing to do.

During the last crossings, however, in March and April, 1945, we were intercepted both in the daytime and at night by the ss and sometimes Fascist militiamen. There was usually some shooting and we occasionally suffered casualties, but we always got through in the end.

The passage to Cernobbio via Sagno and Tre Croci was, as

Swiss army sources were to confirm more than once after the war, the only illegal route from Switzerland into the German-occupied parts of Europe that was never completely disrupted and always functioned without a hitch. In due course it was also used by Allied couriers, both French and American, as well as papal messengers – usually Franciscan friars. Towards the end it was to serve as an escape route, not only for a number of Jews who had been in hiding in northern Italy, but also for relatives of resistance men under arrest or on the run and, last but not least, for Renata Faccincani, who, though imprisoned after the disruption of our Goldoni station in Milan, had succeeded in eluding her captors. Later fugitives from Milan were also to include Franz Otting and Nam Brauer. The fact that the dissolution of the Goldoni station in April 1945 took place wthout any loss was due solely to the smooth functioning of the escape route via Tre Croci.

We also evolved other ways of crossing the frontier. A number of our couriers went to Austria exclusively by the Drei-länderecke, at the junction of the Swiss, Vorarlberg and Liechtenstein borders. But the conditions there were extremely dangerous. Only on one occasion did I myself cross the frontier in the upper Montafon, where I encountered considerable difficulties and nearly got caught, but some of our other couriers succeeded in making this crossing at least seven or eight times. It was, however, impossible to take a sizable group across, nor could one remotely hope to stick to any kind of schedule, whereas when crossing into northern Italy via Lugano, Sagno, Tre Croci and Cernobbio one could safely make arrangements from the Zurich end to hold discussions in Milan on the evening of the day one had set out.

The fastest trip I ever made from Allied territory into the heart of Germany was when travelling in winter from Caserta via Annemasse in liberated France to Geneva, from there by rail through Switzerland via Zurich to Lugano, then by our courier's route, Tre Croci–Cernobbio to Milan, from Milan by leave train, albeit with frequent halts due to air-attacks, to Innsbruck and Munich, and from there by ordinary German express to Berlin – this meant I had travelled from Allied Headquarters outside Naples to Berlin, the capital of German-occupied Europe, in just under four days. Sometimes, however, it might take as much as a fortnight to get from Vienna to

Switzerland, particularly if the railways were paralysed by heavy bombing.

But to return to my draft. When it was more or less complete and had been accepted by all concerned, I thought the time had come to put out feelers towards the Allies so as to get at least some idea of how we stood before I returned to Austria. My first contact with the Americans was made through the mediation of Kurt Grimm and Emil Oprecht, a hospitable Swiss publisher who was to be of assistance to us on numerous occasions. In a private apartment in Zurich I met Gero von Gaevernitz, a German-American and member of the hush-hush American Mission in Berne. We discussed the possibility of co-operation between the Americans and the Austrian resistance movement. Having quickly summed up the situation, and wishing to verify what I had told him, Gaevernitz said he would be getting in touch with me again – as, indeed, he did only a few days later. We now resumed our discussion in Zurich, this time in the presence of Gerry van Arckel, an enormously tall young man from Washington. They told me they had checked my statements in so far as this was possible and were satisfied with the result. Gaevernitz then invited me to attend a conference in Berne.

My first trip to that city was necessarily surrounded by secrecy, for Switzerland, and Berne in particular, were then positively swarming with German agents. I therefore left the train at the last main-line station before Berne, caught a bus and then travelled into town by branch line. Once in Berne I went to a little café in the arcades in which I met a Swiss who was clearly in the confidence of the Americans. He led me to his apartment, where I found Gerry van Arckel, and he in turn, after dusk had fallen, took me to the Herrengasse, in which Allen Dulles had his headquarters. There I met for the first time a man who had already become a legendary figure and with whom, in the next few years, I was to become more closely acquainted.

My first impression of Allen Welsh Dulles was that of a somewhat delicate but wiry grey-haired man, broad featured, with a trim moustache and a lofty forehead. Behind his steel-rimmed glasses his clear, grey-blue eyes were alive with interest, and his expression as he looked at me was friendly and encouraging. Never remotely supposing that I was about to be

introduced to my future father-in-law, I immediately felt at
ease, for he was a man who inspired confidence. Dulles had
risen; with a smile he shook my hand: 'It's good to meet a
genuine Viennese,' he said in German, 'I once spent two years
in that city.'

Dulles was the US President's personal representative in all
matters relating to the Secret Service and to underground activities in Euorpe. He had come to Switzerland shortly before
America's entry into the war and had established in Berne a
firm base from which to conduct underground work in the occupied territories of Europe and inside the Third Reich.

I realized that this interview with Dulles would be of crucial
importance to my future operations and to Austria's immediate prospects of obtaining American support for her underground activities. Hence I was at pains to give him as clear
and rational an account as I could of the situation, and was impressed by the amount he already knew about events in the
Third Reich and Austria. I remained with him for three hours.
In those days my English was anything but good. Dulles could
speak a little German and Gero von Gaevernitz interpreted
when the meagre vocabularly we had in common no longer
sufficed. The interview went off very well. Dulles was most
affable and, on saying goodbye late that night, he told me that
he would do his utmost to help us, but first we must show that
we could produce results. He looked forward, he said, to seeing my report as soon as I got back from Austria. Contact
with the Herrengasse and the Americans now existed; it was
up to us to provide proof of our own existence.

I left the darkened Herrengasse and set off for the central
station, accompanied part of the way by Gero von Gaevernitz,
who, after proffering a few more words of advice, finally shook
my hand and told me to take care of myself. I felt a twinge of
anxiety. This, then, was the moment of truth when I should
have to leave the safety of the big ship and the company of
the passive majority whose fate is decided by others, to em-
bark in the small boat manned by the minority who have to
decide, and therefore act, for themselves. Was I up to it? Should
I succeed in carrying out the tasks I had set myself – return
to Austria, meet our friends there, build up 05's intelligence
service? Above all, should I succeed in paving the way for the

attainment of our chief objective, the setting up of a civil governing body in Vienna?

Would I manage to elude the Gestapo and return, flushed with success, to Switzerland to report to Allen Dulles that an 05 did in fact exist and here was I, little Fepolinski of the Osterleitengasse, to prove it? Or would I succumb to the blandishments of Waschlapski and elect to await the end of the war in the safety of the land of big, round Emmental cheeses? Mindful of the times in my distant childhood when, at lunchtime, father had admonished me never in any circumstances to fall into the traps insidiously set for me by Waschlapski, I decided to fight back. In the almost empty dining-car of the last train to Zurich Fepolinski and I together emptied a whole bottle of red wine, and together we pushed the protesting Waschlapski into his self-dug grave.

Your good health, Fepolinski, and here's to our trip to Vienna.

11

Monika Calling Steamboat

'Leave train 202 is running about two hours late. It won't be leaving until about 22.00 hours, so I'd make myself comfortable until then if I were you.'

With these words the German sergeant in the movement control office at Milan station handed me a voucher for an evening meal at the Wehrmacht canteen. His manner was affable, for I was, after all, a fellow soldier and his equal in rank. He took a brief look at my pass, turned to the last page but one of my paybook, which contained the entry authorizing my leave, and returned me the documents. 'Have a good time,' he said.

He was addressing Sergeant Hans Steinhauser, bachelor, born 24 August 1919 in Lans in the Tyrol, RC, student, son of the late Ernst Steinhauser formerly a merchant in Innsbruck, and of Erna Steinhauser, née Nowak, now domiciled in Heidelberg at No. 191 Zehringerstrasse. At the end of September 1941 the aforementioned Hans Steinhauser had joined No. 4 Machine Gun Depot Company of the 133rd Infantry Regiment. Some months later, on completion of his training, he had been posted to No. 2 Company of the 324th Infantry Regiment, with whom he served for a year in Russia. After a spell with HQ Seventh Army in Smolensk he was transferred to the Lehrregiment Kurfürst in Kamenz. The Lehrregiment Kurfürst was the training organization for the Abwehr, Admiral Canaris's battle school in which his commandos learnt their trade. From there Hans Steinhauser was moved to a unit whose Field Post Office Number, 42411A, identified it as the Abwehr's station in northern Italy. Finally, after 20 July 1944, he was transferred to Station Zeno, which was controlled by the Munich area headquarters of the Reich Central Security Office.

In the meantime he had been promoted to lance-corporal, to corporal and then to sergeant with effect from February 1944. He had been awarded the Iron Cross Class II, the War Service Cross Class II, the Infantry Assault Badge in Silver and, on 14 May 1944, the War Service Cross Class I. His paybook also revealed that he possessed his own pistol, namely a 7.65 mm. Steyr, and had made a statutory declaration to the effect that the said weapon was his private property.

One might further learn from his paybook that Sergeant Steinhauser had handed back gas mask No. 28 II 24243 on 15 January 1944 and received gas mask No. 626 II in exchange; likewise that his rifle, serial No. 13549, issued on 16 February 1942, had since been called in, as had his bayonet. Finally, besides the numerous remarks relating to items of clothing and equipment, various spells in hospital, promotions etc, there was also, and most important of all, the entry authorizing his five days' leave.

It was now September 1944 and he was at Milan Station waiting for leave train 202 to arrive from Genoa and take him on to Munich. His pass required him to report in the first instance to his headquarters in Munich, before proceeding on compassionate leave to Heidelberg, where his mother awaited him in the Zehringerstrasse.

When he sat down in the former first class waiting-room in Milan station, Hans Steinhauser had had two hours in which to familiarize himself with his new role. For up till a couple of hours ago, that is up till the time he had changed his clothes at No. 19 Via Goldoni, he had been an Italian lieutenant or, more specifically, Tenente Pietro de Lago, student, domiciled in Borgo di Buggiano at No. 11 Via Roma, son of Ernesto de Lago and of Paula, née Gasser. By virtue of Tessera di circulazione Nr. 278 of the Italian Army, which had been issued to him on 2 September 1944 by the Commando Militare Regionale della Lombarda, Tenente de Lago had been able to move about freely in his capacity as interpreter and liaison officer at the headquarters of the Milan Military District. Moreover this pass had also been countersigned by the Provincial Headquarters of the Italian Army and by the German liaison staff with the Milan Military District on behalf of SS-Obersturmführer Kechelberg.

Today, 6 September 1944, marked my third trip from Switzerland to northern Italy, and on this occasion Austria was also to be included in the itinerary. The first two trips had been aimed at establishing communications between Lugano, Como and Milan, and everything had gone according to plan. Having by now made five crossings of the Italo-Swiss border either inwards or outwards by the steep tracks over Monte Bisbino, I felt satisfied that our helpers on the route, namely the partisans operating in the border area between Cernobbio and Sagno, were of first class quality and that we should certainly get on well with them.

In addition I had correspondingly enlarged the range of our operations from the Via Goldoni. Renata Faccincani had virtually taken charge there, assisted by Franz Otting, who in the meantime had been transferred to Monza. However, the distance between the two towns was negligible. Also in the group were a couple of young Italian friends of the Faccincanis, Carlo Piazza and Mario Vimercati, the first a student, the other a business man. Both were unsparing in the help they gave. On my first two trips I had done everything to ensure that all information deriving from what we regarded as safe or reliable sources in northern Italy should find its way to us. Intelligence posts had already been set up in Trieste, Verona, Brescia, Milan, Alessandria and Turin.

Now, for the first time, I was to continue my journey in German uniform with false papers, having assumed the exalted rank of sergeant in the Wehrmacht. My two years' experience of the army were to be of incalculable help to me in this role. I knew how one was supposed to conduct oneself, whom one was expected to salute, when it was in order to raise hell and how to set about it, when to turn a blind eye, what subjects of conversation were acceptable in trains and railway waiting-rooms. Above all I knew that the man least likely to be harassed by the countless patrols was a sergeant of *Portepeeträger*, a name dating back to the days when he wore a sword knot and sword, for privates were accorded scant respect and junior NCOs little more. However, there was always the danger that you might suddenly be let in for something that took you to a destination quite different from the one you had planned to go to.

Officers, on the other hand, belonged to a world of their own, a world, moreover, of which I had had little personal experience. Besides, they were very carefully watched, especially those as young as I was. A sergeant had several advantages. To a private or a junior NCO he was a much more imposing person than a young officer. To an officer he was someone deserving of respect; he bore considerable responsibilities and was in any case probably more experienced than a second-lieutenant. Irrespective of his unit, he was a man upon whom an officer had to be able to place complete reliance.

Such people were therefore usually left undisturbed. Most important of all, however, was the fact that the majority of the Wehrmacht patrols were commanded by a sergeant and, as everybody knows, it is rare for dog to eat dog. So if, in the course of his duties, the leader of a patrol had occasion to accost a sergeant, he would be greeted by the latter with great cordiality, often to the extent of being invited to come and have a drink. The patrol leader would examine the other's papers, but few if any questions would be asked. There was, after all, no knowing whether he might not himself be going on leave within the next few weeks and their positions be reversed.

However it was not enough merely to have the correct rank or to know how to conduct oneself, what to talk about, and whom one should or should not salute. Equally important was the need to be completely au fait with one's past history and the units one had previously served in. Hence it was not surprising that the first entry I had made in Sergeant Steinhauser's paybook was the name of a training unit with which I was familiar, namely the Machine Gun Depot Company of the 133rd Infantry Regiment, a regiment traditionally associated with Linz, whose barracks in the town had long been affectionately referred to by the locals as the 'Bug House'. I had been quartered there for a month and hence there was little I did not know about the place. It wasn't, of course, always possible to acquire a really detailed knowledge of one's previous units. For example, I knew very little about the Lehr-regiment Kurfürst, which was the depot formation to which Sergeant Steinhauser now belonged.

In order to remedy this defect, an experienced Swiss intelligence officer in Basle treated me to a four-hour lecture on the Kurfürst, its barracks, its commanders, its chief personalities and much else. He also told me how transfers were effected from regiment to Abwehr units in the field. Thanks to our friends in Milan I was able to learn in good time that the Abwehr station there had been taken over lock, stock and barrel some fourteen days after 20 July by the Reich Central Security Office, in other words it was now controlled by the department responsible to Heinrich Himmler, the Reichsführer-ss.

From now on the Abwehr was simply a tool of the SD, or Security Service, and the ss, though this had many advantages so far as I was concerned. Up till the end of the war, over ninety per cent of the military patrols were formed by the Wehrmacht and not by the ss. Anyone possessing papers issued by the Reich Central Security Office, that is by the all-powerful and much feared SD, was best left alone. At no time in my career, thank heavens, did I ever run into an SS patrol. One drawback, of course, was that my blood-group had not been tattooed on my arm, this being the identification mark of an ss man, though I could explain that away by saying that I had originally belonged to the Wehrmacht and had only recently been transferred. However the members of some Abwehr units were, to their despair, compulsorily tattooed in the autumn of 1944 and thus identified with the ss. As a result many of them were later sentenced to long terms of imprisonment in France or Russia, even though they themselves were in no way National Socialists.

The leave train finally arrived from Genoa at 11 pm and pulled out again after midnight. The delay had been caused by American bombers which had hit Alessandria station and cut the important rail link between Genoa and Milan for several hours. Like all trains at that time it was very full. But here again there was an advantage in being a sergeant, for as a *Portepeeträger* I was able to find a seat in an 'officers only' compartment whose sole occupant was a captain. 'By all means,' he mumbled sleepily on my asking whether I might join him. 'Go ahead.' I took a corner seat and we rattled onwards to Verona. In Brescia the compartment filled up on our being joined by a lieutenant and two senior NCOs. It was, of course, in pitch darkness, for down here, like everywhere else in German-occupied Europe, the lights had long since gone out and the blackout was strictly observed.

At four in the morning we reached Verona where, for some curious reason, the train was taken out of service instead of carrying us on to Innsbruck. Three and a half hours later came an announcement that a relief had arrived. The new train was relatively empty. We passed through Rovereto and Trento, and it was not until we were about to enter Bolzano that our hitherto peaceful journey was interrupted by an air-raid warning and everyone was ordered out of the carriages. After an hour's delay we carried on. By the early afternoon we were climbing smoothly up the Eisack valley and here, once again, was the Tyrolese architecture I knew so well, the castles on the mountain slopes, the feeling of home.

We were approaching Sterzing and getting ready for the frontier check on the Brenner when we came to an abrupt halt at Freienfeld alongside a large, newly constructed Wehrmacht marshalling yard where trains were being shunted or were standing in sidings to allow others to pass. Our own train was switched to a siding at the edge of the yard and in the lee of a hill from whose crest an old Tyrolese castle looked down on us. Again the air-raid warning sounded, the sixth that day. For those sitting in the train it was probably the hundredth, if not the thousandth, that year. Most of us remained where we were, for it was improbable that any attention would be paid to this relatively insignificant target in South Tyrol. The bombers would surely continue on over the Brenner to Munich, Augsburg, Stuttgart or, perhaps, Innsbruck.

For some inexplicable reason I had a sense of foreboding. There were still six or so soldiers in my compartment, two of whom, from the 362nd Division, had been having a long conversation with me. The division, which was operating somewhere in the central Apennines, was one I knew well and they had been giving me their unprintable comments on the situation south of Bologna. By now we could hear the sound of distant aircraft engines and I stood up.

'Right, men, get cracking. I reckon it'll start any minute. Everyone out.'

'You all there, sarge? What's going to start? Trying to scare us, that's what you're doing.'

However that might be, a sergeant was a man to be obeyed
and they therefore came along with me. The sound of flak
was already audible in the distance and my vague sense of foreboding had grown more acute. I raced up the hill towards the
castle together with my party, which had now increased to
about twenty men. The sound of aircraft engines was getting
louder. 'Faster,' I yelled, 'faster. They're not usually as low as
that.'

Aircraft heading for targets beyond the Brenner usually flew
no lower than about 12,000 feet; these were flying at 5,000
feet or less and they were losing height. Glancing back as we
climbed, we could see the beginnings of a mass exodus from
the carriages below. Then came the whistle of falling bombs.
By now I was just beneath the castle walls and, seeing a gateway, hurled myself inside accompanied by my two friends
from the 362nd and six or seven others. Not everyone had got
so far and already the raid was beginning.

Ten minutes later the marshalling yard was a blazing
shambles. Sixty bombers had chosen to attack this of all targets and had totally destroyed it. When they turned away after
their third and final run, we hurried back down the hill. All
that was left of our carriage was a wheel or two and some bits
of wood and metal. The locomotives were still on fire. The
whole place was strewn with casualties and it took us nearly
eight hours to single out the living from the dead. In a situation such as this the Wehrmacht was extraordinarily efficient,
for rescue teams were on the spot within twenty minutes.
Severe cases were removed to the hospital in Brixen, while
those with minor injuries were attended to in a nearby convalescent home.

Darkness had fallen by the time I put the last of the wounded
aboard a truck bound for the Brenner. On my asking the driver
whether he would take me too, he readily agreed. My briefcase was the only item of luggage I had brought with me when
escaping from the bombardment; my pack had been left in the
train. Fortunately the briefcase contained everything of importance, above all my papers and my spare pistol, so now I
was travelling light. I was still shaking all over and was to do
so for many hours to come; it had certainly been a very narrow squeak. The people in our truck were being taken to an
emergency dressing-station in Matrei on the North Tyrol side

of the Brenner, since the convalescent home could not accept any more casualties. This was a tremendous stroke of luck so far as I was concerned, for our passengers and we, as their attendants, were excused all formalities on arrival at the frontier.

Late that night, after we had delivered our wounded at Matrei, I went to the station and there managed to join a goods train bound for Innsbruck. We reached the city's Westbahnhof at 2 am, whereupon I climbed down from my waggon, which was loaded with Italian scrap iron, walked to the main station, applied for a billeting warrant and spent the rest of the night at the Grauer Bär. I then got up, washed, shaved carefully, reported to movement control that I had lost my kit during the raid on Freienfeld, was handed a form authorizing me to draw Wehrmacht-issue underclothing, socks etc, collected them, bought an ersatz cardboard suitcase at a little shop in the arcades next to the 'Goldenes Dachl', packed it with the above items, deposited the suitcase in the left-luggage office at the station and boarded a tram for Saggen, a residential suburb at the foot of the Karwendel Mountains. There, at No. 9, Erzherzog-Eugen-Strasse, lived the family of Professor Richard Heuberger, who was a fairly close relation of mine. Uncle Richard had lost his sight in the First World War but, despite his blindness, he was a very highly thought of professor of geography at Innsbruck University. He was a good friend, and much liked by my father, while his wife had been one of our favourites when we were small. They had three children, Helmut, Wolfgang and Gertrud.

I went there with some trepidation. Though I had shaken off the feeling of unease that had come over me after the raid on Freienfeld, it now returned, brought on by uncertainty as to what the Heubergers might say when I walked in at their door. They were kind and affectionate, it is true, but they had also been convinced National Socialists, though we knew that they had become bitterly disillusioned after the *Anschluss*. My father, who had visited them several times on his trips to Innsbruck, had told us that Hitler's betrayal of South Tyrol had been a severe blow to them. But how far did their disillusionment go and what sort of a reception would I get? However, I had made up my mind that everything depended on No. 9 Erzherzog-Eugen-Strasse, for what I needed was a secure base

in Innsbruck. All my friends of Freikorps days had left, most
of them gone to the war, if they were not already dead. There
was no one in Innsbruck I knew at all well. My only recourse
was the Heubergers and that was why I was standing on their
doorstep. The door opened, they let me in, noting with undoubted surprise but nevertheless without comment that I had
suddenly become a sergeant, gave me a delicious breakfast and
ushered me into the drawing-room. Frau Heuberger went off
to fetch Uncle Richard from the university, leaving me alone
with Helmut, their younger son, who, both in age and personality, was closer to me than any of the others. I kept little
back from him, though naturally I mentioned no names, this
having by now become the most vital and sacrosanct of rules.
We sat and talked until Uncle Richard arrived, followed by
Gertrud his daughter. By the evening the whole situation had
been clarified; nothing could have been more sincere than the
conviction with which the Heubergers, or rather those of
them who were present, unhesitatingly offered me their co-
operation. So great was their disenchantment with National
Socialism that they were only too ready to do everything they
could to help; indeed Helmut was to become one of our most
active assistants in North Tyrol. He would, he said, be willing
to establish contact with various groups pending my return
from Vienna in a week's time. He himself knew of several
people who would probably co-operate, provided they were
told exactly what it was they had to do.

Two days later I set off again on a relatively peaceful journey
to Vienna, having simply exchanged my original pass to
Munich for a spare which I had kept handy and filled in on a
typewriter supplied by courtesy of Uncle Richard's department at the university. The new pass entitled me to spend six
days in Vienna, where I arrived by troop train late in the afternoon.

I took a tram from the station to the Schottentor and then
proceeded on foot to the German *Kommandantur* in the
Universitätsstrasse. I told them who I was, showed my pass
and was directed to an hotel, or rather an inn of the better
sort, in the Fasangasse in the 3rd District. With its stables in
the courtyard, the place was reminiscent of a period long since
past and for me it was an ideal base. I had my own room, I had

ration cards, my pass had been stamped, and six peaceful days in Vienna lay ahead.

But now it was time for me to pick up the threads again, quickly but cautiously. I decided to set off at once for the Grand Hotel, where I knew that our dear cousin Nedica worked. I had already reached the vestibule and spotted Neda at the reception desk when it suddenly struck me that I had better get out of sight. For she would certainly utter a joyful shriek when she saw me and the last thing I wanted was to attract attention. So I went to a call box near the Opera, telephoned the Grand Hotel, asked for Nedica, told her for heaven's sake to keep her voice down, it being Fepolinski who was speaking, instructed her to say not a word to anyone and to meet me in the bar in ten minutes' time. 'Certainly, sir,' she said briskly. 'Thank you, it will be a pleasure.' Then she rang off.

Ten minutes later we were sitting face to face. The tears were running down her cheeks, for she had thought me long since dead. She, like my parents, Otto and others, had heard nothing from me for six months. My mother had written despairing letters to Lidi Mitteis, my godfather's wife, complaining about the absence of news. In August my parents had finally been notified that I was missing, nothing more. Early in September my father had learnt from a senior officer at the headquarters of the 17th Military District that a number of officers and other ranks had been tried by field general court-martial in Bologna and that my name had been on the list of accused. Moreover in my case the death penalty had been called for but, in view of my absence, sentence had been postponed. Such was the situation in September 1944. Neither they nor, of course, Nedica knew anything more. Otto was in charge of a small party of POWs in the neighbourhood of Berlin and both my parents were back in the Osterleitengasse. My father had had to leave Holland a year previously, as Seyss-Inquart had been unable to keep him there any longer.

Neda was overjoyed at finding me still alive and apparently none the worse for wear. She intended to go and tell my parents the news as soon as she came off duty at 5 pm, but would telephone them first. I asked her to pass on a message that I would meet them after dark in the Ungargasse, where I would be waiting from seven o'clock onwards on the railway embankment opposite my Aunt Amalie's house.

Thinking it unwise to spend too long in the Grand Hotel, I said goodbye to Neda after arranging to meet her on the following day. I then left the Inner City as quickly as possible in order to lessen the risk of bumping into an acquaintance. During my various visits in the months that followed I generally managed to avoid such unwanted encounters by keeping away from the Inner City in the daytime and if possible arranging my meetings at specific places on the outskirts. Once, comparatively early on, when I was in a great hurry, I did in fact make the mistake of entering the Inner City by the Kärntnerstrasse in the early afternoon. A moment later I was spotted by Wolfgang Müller-Hartburg, friend of my Schotten school-days.

'Hello, Fritz,' he yelled while some distance away, 'what are you doing here? I had no idea you were in Vienna.'

I assumed a look of astonishment. 'Stand to attention, can't you?' I snarled in my best North German drill sergeant's manner. 'What is all this anyway? You've made a mistake.'

Poor Müller-Hartburg looked abashed. 'But Fritz . . .' he said.

'Don't you give me any more of your Fritzes. And didn't anyone teach you how to salute? You're a disgrace to your uniform.'

Müller-Hartburg stood rigidly to attention. 'I'm awfully sorry, sergeant,' he said, 'but you look very like a friend of mine. Please excuse me, sergeant.'

I left him standing bewildered in the Kärntnerstrasse. Later on he told me he had been unable to make head or tail of the affair. Had he run into a ghost or had he, perhaps, had too much to drink? But neither explanation would do. That sergeant had surely been Fritz Molden and none other. Or had he?

Another time I was travelling by tram to Döbling in the blackout and, as a natural precaution, had chosen to ride on the platform, where it was particularly dark. At one of the stops I was joined by a girl whom I recognized as Hella Rohne. We had been good friends during my student days back in 1941.

'Fritz, Fritz, how marvellous to see you again,' she cried, flinging her arms round my neck.

There was nothing for it but to stick to my part. 'It's very kind of you to hug me, miss,' I said, 'but I'm afraid you've got me mixed up with someone else. I'm not Fritz, unfortunately.'

Hella, who knew me very well though she hadn't seen me for a couple of years, shook her head. 'I really can't believe it,' she answered. 'Excuse me, aren't you Fritz Molden?'

'No, my name's Steinhauser, I'm sorry to say.' By now Hella was getting embarrassed so I decided to put an end to this gruesome pantomime. 'Sorry, because I'd have liked to make the acquaintance of a pretty girl like you. What a shame I'm not Fritz.' At the next stop I got out, leaving Hella speechless.

I took the precaution of warning my family about the incident and a few days later, after I had left Vienna, Hella telephoned my mother and enquired whether she might drop in and see her. When they met she asked if I had been in Vienna recently. To this my mother replied: 'But don't you know, my dear, that my son is missing?' It went against all her instincts to mislead so nice a girl in this way, but there was no alternative. On learning that I was missing presumed killed, Hella made profuse apologies before sadly taking her leave. Unfortunately I have never seen her since and therefore cannot say whether she subsequently discovered that it had indeed been Fritz she had spoken to on the tram.

But to go back to my first day in Vienna. That evening my mother came to meet me on her own, for my father had been at his office when Neda telephoned. Sensing what it was all about, she had at once set off for the Grand Hotel and from there proceeded to our rendezvous.

Together we strolled through the gathering dusk and the first stars had long since appeared when we finally sat down on a bench in the Stadtpark close by the Ring. She told me she had always suspected I was alive and also that she knew beyond all doubt that we should survive the war. She raised no objection to my plans and was convinced that my father and Otto would be prepared to go along with them; she even asked whether she couldn't do something herself.

When I assured her that it was quite enough that she should care for the three of us and bear the consequences of everything I was doing and might ultimately do, she turned round and faced me.

'Don't worry about me, Feppchen,' she said. 'For "unsevered is the navel-cord, the pulse unstilled". Don't forget I come of border stock. Back in the days of Johann Preradović, our ancestor, in the days of the Turkish invasions and the Thirty Years' War, mothers and wives never sat at home. In those days the border families had to fight on the old Imperial military frontier. And, when the Turks were attacking from all sides, the women were expected to take up arms and fight alongside the men. I'm not a warlike person, Feppchen, quite the contrary, and nothing hurts and distresses me more than these frightful strife-ridden times in which we live. But we cannot do other than combat evil when it threatens to engulf us, and we must try and preserve our integrity, even at times when to do so might be dangerous. For man does not live by bread alone. I'm very glad, Feppchen, that you've decided to do what you have got to do. Whatever may happen to us because of it, we shall see the thing through together; we shall see it through as a family, so don't have any qualms on my account.'

We got up and walked along the Ring to the tram stop in the Schwarzenbergplatz. In the shadow of one of the large trees beside the thoroughfare she embraced me, described the sign of the Cross three times on my forehead and said gaily: 'Au revoir Fepolinski, we shall meet again soon.' The tram arrived and she was gone.

A busy time lay ahead. The following evening I was reunited with my father, who had been told the whole story by my mother and had already drafted a rough plan. As we walked through the Prater in the darkness, we talked at length about ways and means of bringing the various resistance groups together. I also spent two long nights with the military leaders of the resistance, preparing the ground for a co-ordinated effort on the part of the various groups, some of which were duplicating each other's activities. Indeed progress was such that it was possible for me to memorize the essentials of a report I would later submit on the organization known as '05'. Memorizing this was necessary, because it contained the names of several hundred persons and military units and must under no circumstances fall into German hands.

At that time, 05's activities were based on resistance cells in German military units in Vienna and Lower Austria. The disruption of these cells after the assassination attempt of 20

July meant that they had to be built up again, a task ably performed by Major Szokoll, one of the leaders of the military resistance. It also involved restoring and expanding the links between the military units and the various civilian resistance groups in such a way as to provide the basis for a sound organization.

At the end of my 'six days' leave' in Vienna, I returned to Milan and the Via Goldoni, where I found Renata full of enthusiasm over a visit she had had from a Frau Nam Brauer, someone I had been expecting ever since my first conference in Vienna. As a girl Nam Brauer had lived in Berlin, where she had joined in the cosmopolitan social life of the 'roaring twenties'. Consistently anti-Nazi ever since 1933, she had worked with Canaris and been closely connected with various participants in the 20 July plot. In the early part of 1944 she had been obliged to leave Berlin and had joined Marogna-Redwitz in Vienna, from where, with Colonel Lahousen's help, she was subsequently transferred to the Abwehr's (after the 20 July, the Reich Central Security Office's) 'Station Zeno' in Milan. I was, of course, delighted, for what better could we want than to have a reliable collaborator in the heart of the Milan Abwehr? That same evening I went to call on Nam Brauer in the Albergo Milano, where she was living. I found an elegant and extremely entertaining woman, full of witty and original ideas and speaking the language of a Germany about which my generation knew only from hearsay – the Germany of the pre-Hitler period. Nam was entirely fearless and at once declared herself ready to attempt things that would have been too hazardous for anyone else; for instance she would, if possible, obtain the Abwehr's minutes for us and would even try and get hold of their code. True, the cipher used by the Abwehr for signals traffic was changed regularly at this time, but the possession of one code would make it possible to decipher the others. It would, we thought, be a truly splendid haul, for we were then unaware that the Abwehr's codes had long since been broken by the Allies. At all events, Nam brought me the code next day. Unable to make any use of it myself, I eventually presented it to my Swiss friends, who were delighted at being thus promptly provided with so rare a tit-bit.

On 30 September I set off for Switzerland again. It was already dark when I reached the frontier at Tre Croci. After I had scrambled through the barbed wire, it was no more than a few paces to the top of the ridge, from which I could see brightly-lit Switzerland spread out below me – Lake Lugano, Mendrisio, beyond it Lugano and, in the far distance, the loom of Bellinzona's lights. But behind me to the south all was darkness, black as sin – occupied Europe, plunged into the shadow of deepest night.

My first journey to occupied Austria and Vienna was the prelude to many others. Between September 1944 and the beginning of May 1945 I visited Vienna seven times and Innsbruck twelve. I became a very seasoned traveller and, after a while, these journeys became almost a matter of routine.

Yet somewhere at the back of my mind was always the fear of being caught, a fear which, strange to say, did not grow less with experience but rather tended to increase. There were various techniques you acquired: for instance, before embarking on a mission you always had to memorize your curriculum vitae, a different one for every trip. You got someone to wake you repeatedly when you were fast asleep, until you were able to reply correctly when suddenly confronted with catch questions. Again, if you were lucky enough to have a bedroom to yourself, you always locked the door lest someone came in, gave you a shake and received the wrong, or rather the right, answer to the question, 'Are you Lance-Corporal Molden?' But if they had to bang on the door because it was locked, you would have, say, five seconds in which to wake up and collect yourself. Moreover, in restaurants and such-like places, you would never sit with your back to the door, for if you faced it and kept your eyes skinned you could take rapid evasive action. I have never, since that time, been able entirely to shake off these habits and still hate sitting with my back to the door in a restaurant. Nor, for a long time, could I sleep properly unless I had locked my bedroom door, though I have now succeeded in overcoming this habit, at any rate in my own house.

During my absence our communications centre in Zurich had been doing very well under the direction of Hans Thalberg. Permission had been obtained from the Swiss authorities to go to internment camps and seek out Austrian volunteers, contacts were being established across the frontier with Vorarlberg, and we had acquired several new recruits. Two were Austrian students, Herwig Wallnöfer and Louis Mittermayer, who had volunteered as couriers and whose services were soon to be of vital importance, especially during the last months of the war, when the north Italian route was seldom practicable because of the repeated closure of the Brenner Pass. A third acquisition was a teacher from Upper Austria, Lieutenant Hans Berthold. All these men were experienced mountaineers and hence willing and able to tackle the difficult routes into Vorarlberg via Lichtenstein and the mountainous Swiss frontier.

In October I again visited Berne. Allen Dulles, who was suffering from an attack of gout at the time, received me sitting down, in his hand the inevitable pipe. He had already seen an appreciation of my reports and, skilled as he was in separating the wheat from the chaff, had evidently decided that I was worthy of his confidence. So my first major excursion had paid off, for only with Dulles's help could we gain access to the appropriate Allied agencies, while our only hope of recognition and military aid lay in his sponsorship. During my two days' stay in Berne I had some three hours of conversation with A.W.D., as he was generally known, and spent the rest of the time with Gerry van Arckel and Gero von Gaevernitz. We made plans for parachute operations and considered the necessity of my doing some parachute training with a view to making a jump myself.

At the beginning of November I came back from my second trip to Vienna, where 05 was now in a position to receive Allied liaison officers, similar arrangements having also been made at Salzburg and Innsbruck. In addition we had settled on three districts to which officers were to be sent for the training of partisans. The first was the Ötztal, into which Fred Mayer was later parachuted, the second, the Kematener Alm near Innsbruck, to which Joe Franckenstein (under the cover name Horneck) and Karl Nováček were to be assigned as training officers, and the third, Carinthia, where Rudolf Charles von Ripper was to operate in a similar capacity.

In Basle Dr Dickmann introduced me to two French officers who had applied through Swiss intermediaries for permission to go with us to Austria. One, Lieutenant Foussé, was a member of the French Secret Service. The other, Capitaine de Rellier, had volunteered for a mission in Austria which involved contacting underground groups among French

POWs there and, at the same time, liaising with the Austrian resistance.

Now I attached particular importance to co-operation between Austrian resistance groups and the French Army, for only thus, it seemed to me, could sufficient confidence be engendered for France to accord us the recognition to which we aspired. I therefore agreed without hesitation to take both officers to Austria with me.

The trip was something of an adventure because de Rellier couldn't speak a word of German, while Foussé knew only just enough to make himself understood. I, for my part, spoke barely two dozen words of French so that English was our only medium of communication. This was later to produce the incongruous situation whereby three men dressed in German uniform conversed together in English in German-occupied territory. We now began our preparations for the trip. With the help of our Swiss friends we overcame the language difficulty by forging paybooks and special passes for de Rellier and Foussé. According to these documents, they were natives of Lorraine who, having volunteered for the Wehrmacht, had been drafted to an SS Walloon Regiment, then transferred to the Lehrregiment Kurfürst to be trained for the Abwehr and, in due course, assigned to Station Zeno in Milan, my own theoretical unit.

Next, we ran through the basic principles of German military drill in the Hotel National in Basle. As regular officers, both men were well-versed in military matters, but they still had much to learn about the niceties of saluting in the German armed forces. Nor was it easy to convince them that, since 20 July, the raising of the right arm in the Hitler salute had been made obligatory throughout the army. But once they had finally cottoned on, there was no denying that their execution of it was uncommonly smart. We then betook ourselves outdoors where, in the private park of a man closely associated with the Swiss Secret Service, we spent two days practising the goose-step and other such things.

Everything was just about ready, including documents and the appropriate uniforms, when all of a sudden an obstacle presented itself, an obstacle of unimaginable size. For one day the two officers, after a return trip to France, reappeared at the frontier with a delivery van which, with the utmost difficulty, Fritz Dickmann succeeded in smuggling into Switzerland. Its contents, we now discovered, was a large box about five foot long and four foot deep in which was a vast, antiquated French radio set. Since the two men had been trained on this apparatus and could use no other, they insisted upon taking it with them to Austria. And so anxious was I to enlist the friendship of this pair with a view to obtaining the help of the French army for far more important ventures later on, that I agreed with a heavy heart to do as they wished. But quite clearly we should never be able to smuggle that box unnoticed through all the check-points and across the many frontiers that lay between us and our destination.

I racked my brains and, out of sheer desperation, ultimately conceived an idea which evoked a broad grin from Dickmann, who took it to be a good joke. But in the event that good joke was to get us safely through to Innsbruck. What I had thought up was this: The box should be left as it was, but to each of its four sides a large white label should be affixed bearing the legend: 'Fragile. Do not drop. Captured enemy signals equipment for delivery to HQ, 17th (Vienna) Military District by order of C in C, Army Group C South-West.' Each of the labels would then be impressed with a good facsimile of the C in C's stamp. To the German military mind, the message was unequivocal: the object in question had to be accompanied to its destination, HQ, 17th (Vienna) Military District by a sergeant – with, in this case, the two volunteers from Lorraine as porters.

So we set off and all went well as far as Sagno, when our partisans appeared and caught sight of our burden. After some argument we opened the box, distributed the contents over three carrying frames and in this way managed quite easily to convey the whole lot to Cernobbio during the night. In the morning we repacked the box and with considerable difficulty found a wood-fuelled taxi to take us to Monza, where Franz Otting was able to procure a Wehrmacht vehicle for us. In this we and our enormous radio set made our way to the central station in Milan; I put the thing in the German left-luggage office and, to make doubly sure, obtained an extra receipt from the sergeant on duty, telling him I would collect it early next morning for onward transport to Germany. For it seemed altogether too much of a risk to take the box to the Via

Goldoni, where the two Frenchmen and I were spending the night. That evening Nam Brauer and Franz Otting both dropped in and we had an international conversation, the brunt of which, to my relief, I no longer had to bear since Renata, Nam and Franz all spoke fluent French.

The next day we continued our journey quite normally by leave train, and all would have gone well had it not been for those confounded American bombers which again came to queer our pitch. Some twenty kilometres south of Brixen, not far from Klausen station, our train suddenly came to a halt because of an air raid warning and we had to leave it in a hurry and make for the nearest tunnel, of which there are large numbers on the Brenner section of the line. I reached it in the nick of time, closely followed by my two French volunteers, sweating and exhausted with the effort of carrying their precious box, which must have weighed forty kilograms at the very least. Then the bombers arrived, dropped their loads and cut the line. The Brenner road was only two kilometres away, but to lug a heavy and awkwardly shaped box two kilometres is no laughing matter. Being a sergeant I naturally couldn't lend a hand, but I lavished a torrent of advice – in German, of course – on my two Frenchmen who could do nothing in return but nod their heads and say: 'All right, sarge.'

It took us three-quarters of an hour to reach the road. We were not alone; practically everyone else from the train was there trying to thumb a lift. But finally we succeeded in getting a truck to take us as far as Brixen. There we again waited in the hope of being picked up. Suddenly an enormous German motor-car – I think it was a twelve cylinder Horch – with the flag of an ss general on its bonnet stopped in front of us. 'Dear God!' I thought, 'this is it!'

The ss general wound down the window and beckoned me across. I came to attention and stated my business: 'Sergeant Steiner, sir, and two men, proceeding to HQ, 17th (Vienna) Military District with captured signals equipment.' 'What unit d'you belong to?' the ss general asked. 'Station Zeno, Milan, Sir.' The ss general beamed. 'And how's my old friend Werner?' he asked. Lieutenant-Colonel Werner was in the best of health, I told him, and had been called to Turin two days previously – this I had learnt from Nam Brauer – to make a report. 'Ah yes, of course,' remarked the ss general, 'so Wolff's up in Turin again, eh? Well, what am I going to do about you, I wonder? You won't fit into this car with that great box!'

But fit in we did, although the boot wouldn't close and had to be fastened down with two leather straps. The Frenchmen were ordered to sit in front with the driver while I was allowed to continue the journey in the back along with the ss general. It transpired that the great man who had picked me up was the commander of the ss Security Group Brenner, in other words he was responsible for security, not only on the Brenner but along the whole Italo-Swiss border between Reschen and Sondrio. Delighted though I was to make the acquaintance of a man who meant so much to me, my blood ran cold at the thought of what might happen should it occur to him to inquire about the other officers at Station Zeno or, worse still, ring up his dear old pal Werner.

Again we were lucky, for at Gossensass there was another air raid warning. We instantly drove into a huge tunnel converted into an air raid shelter and now crowded with ss equipment and ss vehicles, not to mention ss officers and other ranks. There the general, having treated us to a plain but hearty meal, expressed his regret at being unable to take us any further himself; however, to ensure the safe and timely arrival of the captured signals equipment he would, he said, see to it that we were transported onward without delay. Sending for an aide, he ordered him to get hold of a vehicle for us and, five minutes later, a truck appeared complete with ss driver. To our already faultless movement order our patron now added an endorsement directing the ss guards on the Brenner Pass not only to allow us through without let or hindrance, but to do all they could to promote our progress. In addition he gave us a chit for the ss patrol at Innsbruck station.

We thanked him profusely and, having promised to pass on his regards to Lieutenant-Colonel Werner, took our departure. About twenty minutes later we reached the frontier at the Brenner, where everyone was subjected to the most careful check; not us, however, who were waved on with the cheery words: 'Have a good trip, mate, and mind you remember your wavelengths.' Having arrived safely at Innsbruck Station we tried to thank our friends of the Waffen-ss, who, however, insisted first on carrying our captured radio set into the main waiting-room and then on standing us a glass of beer, needless to say in the canteen used by the SS patrols.

When we at last succeeded in getting rid of them the relief was indescribable. Once again we had been watched over by a guardian angel of no mean stature. And as for the two Frenchmen, they could hardly get over their astonishment at having been conveyed almost all the way to the frontier in the car of the SS general responsible for its security.

Three hours later the equipment had found its way to Professor Heuberger's department at Innsbruck University. This had the great advantage of being quite close to the laboratories of the Department of Physics where morse was regularly practised. In this way our apparatus remained undetected right up to the end of the war and became one of our most important transmitters in that region. While I went on to Vienna, the two Frenchmen remained at Innsbruck, from where they intended to get in touch with the underground movement in French POW camps. It was arranged that they should meet me at Salzburg on my return journey.

While considerable progress had been made in Vienna since my last trip, it had become ever more apparent that 05, being a purely military organization, could not represent the Austrian underground movement vis-à-vis the outside world. Hence there was an urgent need for a political instrument which might also, at a later date, constitute the nucleus of an underground government. On 12 December 1944, therefore, after complex political negotiations, we formed the POEN (Provisional Austrian National Committee), consisting of seven members including Major Alfons Stillfried, Dr Josef Ezdorf and my father, Ernst Molden. Conservatives, Liberals, Monarchists and Christian Socials were all represented and were shortly to be joined by members of the Communist, but not as yet the Social Democratic, Party.

At this stage the task of the POEN was above all that of paving the way politically for the military operations of 05 and ensuring effective collaboration with the Allies abroad. While I was to be primarily responsible for building up relations with the latter, our communications centre in Switzerland was now made the official representative body of the POEN vis-à-vis the western countries.

On the day after this glorious achievement, the formation

of the POEN, I lay contentedly in bed in my hotel room trying to think up a call signal to precede the transmission of coded messages to Austria by the BBC and 'The Voice of America', thus alerting resistance groups to the fact that what followed was of concern to them. But my mind remained a blank. As it happened, I had arranged to meet someone round about mid-day at a point beside the Danube Canal where the steamboats, then used as ambulance ships, unloaded the wounded for on-ward transport to hospital. As I stood there waiting I happened to glance up and saw Monika Krünes – Monika of the black plaits whose sharp teeth had once drawn blood from my nurse-maid Erna's thumb – passing by in the street above, all unsus-pecting that her old friend of kindergarten days was there, a few steps below her. And, as she went by, the call signal came to me: 'Monika calling steamboat.' To this both the Allies and the Vienna underground movement agreed and up till May 1945, all coded messages were preceded by the words: 'Monika calling steamboat' – the free world calling 05. Monika, to whom I told this story after the war, remembered having sometimes heard the signal though she had never, of course, known what it meant, and still less that it had any association with herself.

12

Tyros in the Underground

On 26 December 1944, St Stephen's day – in Vienna, a festival second only to Christmas but in Switzerland, that stronghold of Protestantism, just another working day – we had all forgathered in Dr Grimm's apartment in the Hotel Bellerive. Besides Dr Grimm and myself, there were Hans Thalberg and various other loyal friends, who had arrived all agog to hear the latest news from Austria. The sun was shining and everyone was jubilant, for the Provisional Austrian National Committee had at last been founded. What better Christmas present could one wish for in the year 1944?

Kurt Grimm was also the bearer of good tidings. Within the next few days, it seemed, I was to proceed to Berne for consultations. Having discussed the matter among themselves, the Allies had more or less agreed to recognize our resistance group. While the discussions would initially be conducted by the Americans, they would also be attended by a British representative, Geoffrey Lindlar, and, later, by the French. This piece of news was almost as welcome and unexpected to me as my own report on the founding of the POEN in Vienna had been to Dr Grimm.

Two days later I travelled to Berne where, after the usual manoeuvres designed to shake off possible German agents, I made my way to Allen Dulles's office in the Herrengasse. There, besides Gerry van Arckel, I found Gero Gaevernitz, an Englishman, Edge Leslie, and a couple of high-ranking American soldiers who had evidently come to Switzerland via the recently liberated Annemasse in order to take part in our discussions. I made my report while the gentlemen took notes and marked up what seemed relevant on enormous maps.

After dinner that evening, a small group of us discussed matters of principle. Dulles informed me that the Americans had decided to accord provisional recognition to the POEN and 05, but this would be quite unofficial and would in no way preempt decisions made in political quarters. Nevertheless, we would now be regarded as partners and, so far as internal communications were concerned, treated as allies and provided with liaison officers, military aid, expert advice and so forth.

He then went on to give me a detailed account of the Allied proposals for the occupation of post-war Europe. Like nearly everyone else, whether in the Allied, the German or the Swiss camp, he believed that the Nazis would make a last stand in the 'Alpine redoubt'. In fact, though no one knew it at the time, this existed only on paper, having been worked out by, amongst others, Franz Hofer, Gauleiter of the Tyrol, South Tyrol, Trentino and Vorarlberg, and Karl Rainer, Gauleiter of Carinthia, whose dominion extended from the Adriatic coast to Trieste. At all events, the general belief in its actuality explains the interest shown by the Allies in the possibility of Austria's contributing to her own liberation, an interest which grew with every week that went by. It also explains the determination of the German authorities, and notably the Security Service, to suppress all resistance operations and every attempt to set up an opposition government in an area they looked upon as their last bastion. Hence, as early as the autumn of 1944, they embarked on a mopping-up operation in that part of Austria.

After all the others had gone, Allen Dulles and I spent a quiet half hour in his library, during which he explained with his usual patience and kindness that there was no prospect whatever of a split between the Russians and the Western Allies who, as he said, would stick together until they had completely done away with 'Hitler and his henchmen'. He also pointed out that policy was not determined solely by the Americans; the British, with centuries of diplomacy behind them, also had a significant contribution to make. Together, the Americans and British would do everything in their power to ensure that democratic elections were held in the countries of the Danubian area and eastern Europe, notably Poland,

Roumania, Bulgaria, Yugoslavia, Hungary and Czecho-slovakia. However, he qualified this remark with the words 'We shall not wage a third world war in order to determine what government comes to power in Sofia or Bucharest.' At this time, I should add, neither the British nor the Americans had anticipated the rapid advance of the Russians in the early months of the following year, being still under the impression that the three Allied armies would meet on the Oder.

However, he cheered me up by saying that the United States and Great Britain would never assent to the accession of non-democracies or Soviet-dominated governments in Austria or Italy. On this point they were not prepared to budge an inch. The things Allen Dulles told me that evening at his fireside were of crucial importance to our deliberations and plans in the months to come.

Dulles rounded off the evening by appointing me – in the names of Field Marshal Alexander, then Allied Commander-in-Chief in southern Europe, and General Mark Clark, com-manding the US Fifth Army in Italy – Austrian Underground Forces liaison officer with Allied Forces Headquarters in Caserta. Suddenly it dawned on me that this was really rather a solemn occasion. Anglo-Saxons, however, and members of the Dulles family in particular, are not in the habit of an-nouncing when such an occasion has arrived. But, feeling a slight nudge from Gerry van Arckel, I stood up; Dulles shook me by the hand and said: 'You are the first Austrian to be accredited as liaison officer at Allied Headquarters. I'm sure we shall work happily together.'

I spent that night in the Herrengasse, a bed having been rigged up for me in one of the rooms there. Early next morn-ing we at once embarked on detailed discussions. The two officers from Allied Headquarters in Caserta, a palace on the outskirts of Naples, asked innumerable questions. Poring over maps, we spent the whole of that day discussing questions of supply, liaison, etc. I was told that I was expected sometime during the next ten days at General Eisenhower's headquarters in Paris. This was a lucky coincidence since I had already received from Capitaine de Rellier an invitation to visit HQ French 1st Army at Besançon as a prelude to discussions with the French government in Paris. It was therefore decided that I should go to Besançon on 2 January. I was also informed that,

in accordance with oss practice, I would henceforward be referred to in inter-Allied signals and reports as 'K28' and,
finally, that as liaison officer I would hold the rank of Lieutenant-Colonel and be entitled to the corresponding rights and
'facilities' among the Allies. To be promoted straight from
Lance-Corporal in the German army to Lieutenant-Colonel at
Allied HQ, and this at the ripe age of twenty, seemed to me a
somewhat sudden rise in the world, and I might have fallen
prey to megalomania had it not been for the thought that, in
my principal haunts, namely German occupied territory, the
privileges of an American Lieutenant-Colonel would avail me
little or nothing.

So I set off at the beginning of January and crossed the
frontier at Basle-Burgfelden, equipped with a pass from the
cantonal authorities in Zurich in which I figured as a refugee
and student, resident in Zurich; I also possessed an impressive
red, white and blue *ordre de mission* issued by the French 1st
Army. At the frontier I was met by a lieutenant in a car wearing
the French colours who drove me, first to Montbéliard and
then to Besançon. There I remained for two days, engaged
in talks with the Deuxième Bureau of the French 1st Army on
the subject of co-operation between the POEN and/or 05 on the
one hand and French Intelligence in northern Italy and Austria
on the other. Another topic was the despatch of French liaison
officers and parachutists to support the operations of the
Austrian resistance. On the second day I met a number of
young French officers who had volunteered for liaison duties
in Austria.

I was also presented to General de Lattre de Tassigny and
other high-ranking soldiers, who seemed to me very grand and
aloof and altogether a bit reminiscent of First World War
officers, perhaps because of the old-fashioned képis they wore. I
then left for Paris where I met Capitaine de Rellier, in fact the
Duc de Roquemorel, who had been with us in Austria. He put
his apartment at my disposal and secured me an entrée, no only
to his exclusive clubs, but also to General de Gaulle's office
and to the Quai d'Orsay, where I met the Foreign Minister.

For me, my travels in France and my stay in Paris proved
an interesting experience. For it was barely two years since I
had left the capital, then still under German occupation. The
country seemed worse off materially than it had been at that

time; there was not much to eat in the restaurants, which were also colder because of the fuel shortage, but otherwise everything was much as before.

During this particular visit, in January 1945, I arranged to meet a member of the us Headquarters staff at the Hôtel Claridge in the Champs Elysées, which had once housed my sometime superior officer, Riki Posch-Pastor. I had frequently called in on him there, finding him as often as not in the bar with some pretty girl or other. On this occasion I again made for the bar, ordered a drink and, while waiting for my American, observed with interest the busy comings and goings in the large entrance hall. Little had changed except the colour of the uniform – Allied khaki instead of German field grey.

Suddenly I was tapped on the shoulder by the hotel porter, who beckoned me over to his desk. Then he whispered in German: 'For goodness sake, Molden, whatever are you doing here? Better get out quick or they'll come and arrest you and, before you say knife, shoot you for a spy!' He had remembered me, even down to my name, and had wanted to warn me. Greatly touched, I tried to explain matters to him, but all in vain. 'This is no time for fooling about,' he replied. 'Go and give yourself up to the police – it's the only thing to do. After all, you weren't a Nazi; you'll be all right.'

He was an Alsatian, a nice, friendly chap who had always treated me considerately, even in 1943. He now suggested I should hide in the little cubby-hole behind the porter's desk until the arrival of a police official, a regular customer, to whom he would hand me over. 'Then you won't be shot,' he said, 'but put in a pow camp.' In desperation I showed him every pass I had got but entirely failed to impress him. Luckily, just at that moment, my American turned up with Guy de Roquemorel, the sight of whose uniform at long last convinced the good porter. Greatly relieved, he lost no time in producing a bottle of champagne, then almost unobtainable in Paris.

I also met other friends made during my earlier stay in the capital, amongst them Jean Menier, who was still living in his luxurious apartment. He told me that the Germans had left without many alarums and excursions. Indeed, Paris, it seemed, had been little affected by the change-over, though collaborators were being given a pretty rough time.

On this occasion I stayed in Paris for ten days – not, however, as before at the Wagram, now occupied by American officers, but at an hotel on the Left Bank. My first negotiations were conducted with my hosts the French, several hours of each day being spent at the Quai d'Orsay in discussion with M de Chauvel, Directeur Général aux Affaires Etrangères, and at French Army Headquarters with Général Manuel of the Deuxième Bureau. My object was to induce the French government to lose no time in according at least de facto recognition to the POEN as the representative body of Austrian underground movement. Once this had been achieved we hoped that the Americans, who had already adopted a positive attitude towards us, could be persuaded to follow suit, and that the combined influence of the French and Americans might then help to modify the extreme scepticism with which we were regarded by the British. We also hoped that positive relations might eventually be established with the Russians. With this in view, I called in at the Russian military mission in Paris, where I was very courteously received by a Counsellor named Kozurev.

My talks with the French were altogether satisfactory. M de Chauvel made an official statement in which he asked me to convey to my Austrian colleagues the strong feelings of sympathy with which his country viewed Austria's heroic struggle for liberation. His government, he went on, had expressly declared its readiness to help in the restoration of a free and independent Austria, the more so since the Austrian question was seen as quite distinct from the German. He also assured me of his government's appreciation of Austrian resistance activities, about which they were kept fully informed by their observers and liaison officers, and which they would do everything in their power to support.

I was also handed this statement in writing and, of course, immediately sent it to Zurich, whence it was forwarded to Vienna. It was an important, indeed almost historic, occasion because it could be interpreted as a first step towards de facto recognition.

The question of material aid for 05 was also discussed. In fact, such aid could hardly be more than a token, for the French Army was now almost wholly dependent on American subsidies, while the country's economic position after four years of occupation seemed well-nigh hopeless. But the French were genuinely anxious to co-operate with us and did all they could in the months that followed to supply us with radio equipment, arms and the like. They also provided liaison officers and made every effort to back us up politically during our negotiations with the Americans and British in Paris, London and Washington.

We discussed at length the possibility of forming an Austrian Legion in France consisting of émigrés and perhaps also prisoners of war. The French government agreed in principle that such a legion should be set up within the framework and under the aegis of the French Army. At the time I was not aware that, before many weeks were out, Ernst Lemberger, or Commandant Jean Lambert as he was then called, the highest ranking Austrian officer in the French Army, would be playing so important and vital a role in the POEN and 05. His appearance on the scene was to bring about a radical change in the situation.

At the Quai d'Orsay it was also agreed that, in addition to the broadcasts already being made to Germany and the German forces, transmissions to Austria should begin forthwith, as, indeed, happened. In course of time the contents of the broadcasts came to be largely determined by us, despite the fact that some of the editors were Austrian communists who evinced considerable skill in substituting signals they had received from Moscow for the information supplied by us.

My final task in Paris was to hold discussions with representatives of Allied Supreme Headquarters, these being conducted on the American side by Colonel Vanderstrike, Dr Lorenz Eitner (a native of Vienna), James Thomas and a number of other staff officers. Our discussions were primarily concerned with questions of material aid for the active resistance in the Austrian mountains. After a certain amount of bargaining it was agreed that three American Scout Liaison Officers should be sent to Austria as an advance party, Lieutenant Fred Mayer being selected for the Tyrol, Captain Rudolph Charles von Ripper for Carinthia. Captain Jack Taylor had already departed with his Dupont team from Bari for Vienna two months before. Contact with his radio soon lost, and Taylor and his man were arrested by the Gestapo.

These three were entrusted with the task of maintaining communications with the branches of 05 operating in their respective areas, and with the agencies of the POEN. The radio sets they were to take with them would serve to guide the aircraft making the drops that had been agreed during my previous talks in Paris. It was decided that Carinthia and the Tyrol should each receive five hundred machine pistols, five hundred pistols, twenty dismantled machine-guns, three tons of plastic explosives, sabotage material and ammunition, as well as two more transportable radio sets.

The three liaison officers had been carefully selected and given a most thorough vetting, as had the two others, Lieutenant Horneck and Karl Nováček, who were next on the list. Nováček was an Austrian who, immediately after his capture by the Americans in 1942, had let it be known that he was a socialist and, after retraining, had been accepted by the US Army. What Nováček's true name was, I never knew. Joe Horneck, however, was really called Josef von Franckenstein. He came of an old Tyrolese family, and up till 1938 his uncle, Georg von Franckenstein, had been Austrian Ambassador in London. Novacek, Horneck and Ripper were of my own choosing, whereas Fred Mayer and, of course, Jack Taylor had been selected long before my arrival in Paris.

Mayer and Ripper, who were the first to be dropped into Austria, put up an excellent performance there. After the dissolution of the Dupont team, a new Liaison Officer had to be chosen for Vienna who was to be Ernst Lemberger, who did not, after all, jump, but travelled to Vienna in my company. As leader of the Ötztal partisans, Mayer was arrested by the Gestapo in April 1945 and taken to Reichenau concentration camp near Innsbruck. After a successful escape he took an active part in the liberation of the Tyrol.

Rudi Ripper had completed his mission in Carinthia and was on his way back when he ran into a German patrol at Spittal station near the Millstätter See. After an exchange of shots he was able to board a moving train and escape into the Lienz Dolomites. Thence he made his way through German-occupied territory to the Po, across which he swam, eventually reaching the Allied lines south of Bologna. He was a most unusual man. His grandfather had been a high-ranking Austrian officer, his father an admiral in the Imperial Navy, while he himself was a young modern artist of the type considered 'degenerate' in the Third Reich.

His career as an artist had been cut short relatively early. A student at the Berlin Academy of Art in 1932, his first commission had come from the Social Democratic Party. This was an anti-Nazi poster, extremely acidulous and witty, which made fun of Hitler and the National Socialists. It was put up on 25 January 1933, and five days later Hitler came to power. Ripper was one of the first hundred people to be confined in Oranienburg concentration camp, from which, on the representations of the Austrian government, he was ultimately released and deported to Austria.

In 1936 he went to Spain and joined the Republican air force as an air-gunner, was shot down, taken prisoner by the Falangists and ultimately succeeded in escaping to France. From there he went to the United States and, on the outbreak of war, at once volunteered for service in the forces. He parachuted into the Aleutians and, at a later stage, was put ashore in North Africa, where he served as an oss agent with the Arab underground. He then fought in the Italian campaign and between Sicily and Rome managed to add another four or five wounds to his already large collection. Never have I seen so many scars on one man's body. Ripper was pleasant enough if he liked you; if he didn't, it was better to keep out of his way. Joe Franckenstein was a man of similar breed. Warm and affectionate at heart, and a fervent patriot who read poetry and quoted Rilke, he was, besides, a ferocious fighter who began his day by carolling 'Heimatschutz! Let's do 'em, get yer knives out quick. Stick 'em in and twist 'em round, cor, lads, what a kick!'

The discussions at the American Embassy laid the foundations for all further developments in the two main areas in which 05's partisans were operating, namely the Tyrol on the one hand and Carinthia and South Styria on the other. A third centre of militant Austrian resistance during the crucial months leading up to the spring of 1945 was the Salzkammergut, and in particular the Höllengebirge, where a number of men whose underground career had begun in England were actively at work. One of these, a Social Democrat by the name of Albrecht Gaiswinkler, had parachuted into the Höllengebirge under the auspices of the British army in the autumn of 1944 and succeeded in setting up a first-rate resistance network that functioned throughout the Ausseer Land. Thanks to his timely intervention this and neighbouring areas, including the shores of the Traunsee, were protected against the levy en masse being conducted in that region by the Third Reich. He also prevented the destruction of irreplaceable works of art hidden in the Ausseer salt mines, and saved the lives of countless people. But unfortunately there was no communication between Gaiswinkler's group and 05 until the final weeks of the war, by which time there could be no question of any real co-operation.

One of the great tragedies of the Austrian resistance was that the amalgamation of the various groups and the co-ordination of their activities was achieved, if at all, when it was already too late. For this the Allies were partly to blame. Until May 1945 the British, who were in the closest touch with Gaiswinkler, were careful not to breathe a word about the existence of his group. They allowed us to go on dropping men who were picked up and executed by the SS simply because they were not aware of the safe zones that had already been established there by Gaiswinkler and his friends. This state of affairs was due to rivalry between the various secret services, notably the British on the one hand and the French and Americans on the other, and was to be not a little troublesome to us all through the final year of the war. Nor did the British invariably pursue this business with their customary regard for fair play.

During my stay in Paris, I made another good friend – Martin Herz. At one of my many sessions with the Americans I caught sight of a young major and was struck by his clean-cut features and air of intelligence. Looking alert and interested, he sat there saying little and only occasionally interposing a question. Afterwards he and I went for a stroll during which he questioned me closely about Austria, and so well did he seem to know the country that I suspected he might even be Austrian by birth. However, in those days one didn't inquire too closely into people's names and antecedents, especially in my particular branch. I have often seen Martin since – the first time, a few days after the end of the war when he suddenly turned up at Innsbruck and summoned those who had played a leading part in the resistance to a meeting at the printing works of the University Press. In response to our pleas he persuaded the American governor to sanction the publication of a newspaper, the *Tiroler Tageszeitung*, which is still in existence today. Josef Moser, one of the leaders of the Tyrolese resistance, was appointed its first editor.

I flew to Caserta in a US Air Force c47. Spring was already in the air when we landed on the badly damaged airfield at Naples. Several jeeps were there to meet us, for I had not been alone on my trip from Paris; also aboard the aircraft were half a dozen American generals, one or two civilians and a Catholic prelate. As I left the plane, I was at once approached by four or five American officers who had evidently seen my photograph, for one of them said: 'You must be Jerry Wieser.' I nodded and they introduced themselves – Colonel Howard Chapin, Lieutenant-Commander Alfred Ulmer, Captain Jim Hudson and Lieutenant Fred Harris.

The oss units which came under Allied Forces Headquarters in Caserta were known as the 2677th Regiment, of which Detachment A was responsible for Austria. Its chief was Colonel Chapin, with Ulmer as his second-in-command. They greeted me as though I was an old friend, straightaway calling me by my Christian name, and asking me to do the same by them. With my central European background, it took me a little while to get used to this. For the first time I found myself in immediate contact with the US Army, from whose vast headquarters in the royal palace of Caserta more than ten thousand officers, NCOs and officials were engaged in directing the Italian campaign.

In January 1945 Austria was the only territory within AFHQ's sphere of responsibility which still had to be conquered in its entirety and where no Allied troops had as yet set foot. Inevitably, in the circumstances, Austrian affairs were much to the fore, and of this I immediately became aware. After a frugal supper in the mess of the oss, whose HQ occupied one wing of the great palace, Howard Chapin took me to see the commander of the American Fifth Army, the renowned General Mark Clark.

He received me in a large but simply furnished office. Though lightly built, he was so tall that although I can hardly be described as small, I had to look up at him. Shaking my hand, he assured me that he had already heard something of me from Allen Dulles, and congratulated me on having successfully got back from occupied Vienna. He then went on to inquire about conditions there, also showing especial interest in information about the German and Russian armies then fighting in Hungary. Having told him what I knew, I went on to repeat in all innocence a story brought back from the front by wounded Germans, namely that, on occupying the Hungarian town of Miskolc, the Russians had raped almost every woman they could lay hands on. At this, General Mark Clark rose abruptly. 'That's enough,' he snapped. 'If Allen Dulles had not assured me of your integrity, I'd have you placed under arrest. But I would ask you never again to refer in my presence to the lying tales about our Soviet Allies put about by German propaganda.'

Howard Chapin and Al Ulmer accompanied me back to my quarters. This, my first encounter with General Clark, had gone badly awry. Much perturbed, I apologized to Chapin, assuring him that I had had the information about the rape of the Miskolc women from a wounded Austrian officer who had been captured and had subsequently escaped. The man was anything but a Nazi, and I had had no reason to doubt his word.

Chapin reassured me, saying that he had himself heard similar reports and was afraid they might be true. He went on to explain that, in the us Army, such things were regarded as German propaganda simply because no one could believe they were true. Besides, the Russians were friends and allies, and hence, by definition, beyond reproach. I had evidently trodden in a hornet's nest and, since it was far from my intention to disseminate anti-Soviet propaganda in Caserta, I decided to steer clear of the subject in future. When I next saw General Clark after my return from a trip to Vienna some weeks later, he reverted to the incident, and made some sort of apology for his brusque behaviour. I, too, said I was sorry if my bad English had given rise to a misunderstanding, and in this way my difference with the General was settled. Thereafter, our relationship was invariably pleasant, not to say amicable. Indeed, at a later date he was actually to recommend me for one of the highest American military awards. But by then, of course, his experiences in Vienna had radically changed his opinion of the Russians and the behaviour of their troops.

As for myself, while deploring the rape of the Hungarian women by the Russian soldiery, I realized as a Central European that it was also inevitable. From time immemorial wild, warlike hordes – whether Magyar, Turk or Russian – had tended, when victorious or after a long period of abstinence, to run amok and rape indiscriminately the women of the losing side if not of their allies, a case in point being Yugoslavia. Hence it did not seem to me an indication of any particular turpitude on the part of the Russians, but rather of the state to which the Red Army had been reduced after four years of severe fighting. As an American puritan, on the other hand, the General was bound to take a somewhat different view. The very idea of rape was abhorrent to him and, in January 1945, he dismissed as absurd any suggestion that Allied soldiers could have been guilty of such a crime.

In 1946, however, when Austria had become a bone of contention and the weekly meetings of the Allied Council in Vienna seldom went off without a fracas between General Clark and his opposite number, the Russian High Commissioner for Austria, the situation changed drastically. Being now in possession of all the reports from American missions in eastern Europe, the general had learned not only about the conduct of the Russian troops, but also about the way the Soviet leaders were handling the political post-war problems of Hitler's victims in that area. The comrade-in-arms had become an arch enemy and a 'cold warrior'.

Howard Chapin and his OSS colleagues in the Austrian Section at Caserta had been sent all my previous reports by Allen Dulles and had studied them down to the last comma. They knew almost as much about Vienna as I did, though none of them had seen the city except on the map. True, their headquarters boasted a number of former Austrians who had, of course, known it very well, but their Vienna was the city of the days before 1938 and had long ceased to exit.

Both Chapin and Ulmer made the most of my first short stay at Caserta to pick my brains about Austria and Austrian morale. I, young 'K28', was trusted by them because vouched for by Allen Dulles, to whom they all referred simply as A.W.D. To them I was 'Jerry', for such was the name that figured in my American travel documents and other necessary credentials. We were soon on the most cordial terms and felt complete confidence in one another. Never in my military career had I met anyone so disarmingly ingenuous. Nor, for that matter, had I met any young Americans of this success-and-progress-orientated generation, who epitomized, not only the victorious US army in Europe, but the United States as a great world power.

It was an optimistic, positive-thinking, active and, for all that, altogether moral, generation of young men and women who clearly believed that happiness and success were theirs by right. They were convinced that the American era had dawned and would bring peace and happiness to all mankind. I, at the age of twenty, was profoundly impressed by this philosophy and those who professed it; the young Americans with whom I came in contact were a thoroughly decent, intelligent, healthy and high-spirited lot.

Their country seemed to have reached the apogee of technical and scientific achievement and yet not to have forgotten its humanitarian mission as a leading world power. What struck me above all in 1945 was the unlimited freedom Americans seemed to enjoy – freedom in every sense of the term. They were politically free but also, and in the best sense, free human beings, democrats who believed in the success and the moral worth of a parliamentary form of governmnet and a democratic way of life, both for individuals and for whole nations.

I was impressed by all this, none of which I had experienced in Germany or – in so far as I, a mere boy, had been able to judge – in the authoritarian Austria of Dollfuss and Schuschnigg. Small wonder, then, that on first coming into contact with American citizens, their manners and their political mores, I became a devotee of the American way of life. To me, the United States seemed the home of liberty, the home of progress and of an optimistic philosophy of life which I wanted to share and to see established in my own country.

In later years, when I paid longer visits to America, I came to know a good many of its less pleasing aspects, likewise discovering that the consequences of excessive liberty may be of a very negative kind. But at the time, more than three decades ago, when I became acquainted with the America of 1945, first at Caserta, then in US Army camps in Europe and, finally, in that country itself, I thought, as many millions of Europeans in the nineteenth century had thought before me, that I had discovered a paradise on earth. And in this I was not alone.

During this first stay in Caserta Howard Chapin and Al Ulmer took me on a kind of conducted tour of American headquarters in the area, including that of the 15th Air Force, whose bombing operations over South Germany and Austria were carried out from Caserta and from Bari, its main base. It was now that I made my first attempt to persuade them to discontinue the indisciminate bombing of Vienna and other Austrian cities. I tried – on this occasion in vain – to make the us Air Force commanders understand how negative was the psychological effect of such operations on the inhabitants of the places concerned. Several weeks later I was asked to make a further attempt to get this policy reversed and, with considerable difficulty, succeeded in doing so.

Much of my time was taken up with discussions on the need for deliveries of arms to our 05 units in the Tyrol, Carinthia and Vienna, the urgency of which I impressed upon the Americans. I was also asked to vet a number of radio operators and instructors for 05 units who were to be infiltrated into Austria. These were to be sent out in the wake of Freddy Mayer, Rudi Ripper, Joe Franckenstein and Karl Nováček, whom we had already selected in Paris.

This pleasant spell in Caserta went by all too quickly and soon I was flying northwards, away from the early spring of southern Italy, to land on a snow-covered airstrip near Annemasse, the closest an American aircraft could approach to Switzerland. I was taken by jeep to the frontier, across which I was safely shepherded by an emissary from my Swiss friends in Berne. Then I climbed into a florist's van and, thus camouflaged, reached Geneva, whence I set off almost at once for Zurich, on board one of the now familiar light alloy carriages of the Swiss Federal Railways.

The next few days were taken up with discussions in the course of which we attempted to assess the implications of the talks I had had in Paris and Caserta, and also considered the somewhat tricky question of finance. For, like the conduct of war generally, clandestine operations cost a great deal of money. In Austria itself this presented no particular problem, for in the winter of 1945 cash for resistance purposes was more easily come by than anything else. Large numbers of loyal

Austrians had liquid assets which they put at our disposal, but these accounted for only a small part of the means available to 05 and the POEN. The largest sums came from people who, not so long before, had thrown in their lot with the National Socialist rulers and now, having seen the writing on the wall, wanted to insure against the confiscation of their factories or other property. More money was forthcoming from such quarters than the leaders of the resistance movement knew what to do with.

In the Tyrol, for instance, there was a certain manufacturer, the owner of a large textile mill, whose name was almost a household word. As early as the summer of 1944, he approached an anti-Nazi acquaintance – let us call him X – and, greatly to the latter's alarm, offered him, in ready cash, a million marks for the resistance movement. Now, not only had Herr X never heard of any resistance movement but, being timid by nature and blessed with a large family, wanted to have nothing to do with any such thing. He therefore indignantly rejected the offer, and there was nothing for the mill-owner to do but take himself off together with his suitcaseful of notes. Eventually this story reached the ears of Dr Höflinger, one of our people in the Tyrol, who passed it on to me when I was next in Innsbruck. We decided to waste no time in laying our hands on the cash, and Höflinger successfully persuaded Herr X to overcome his timidity and arrange a rendezvous between his wealthy friend and ourselves. This took place in romantic circumstances, on a bright moonlit night on the Hungerburg. Höflinger, masked and in a slouch hat, as in a melodrama, took the textile manufacturer's money and handed him a receipt signed, not with his own name, but with three crosses. Since this did not altogether allay the donor's fears for his safety on the collapse of the Thousand Year Reich, Höflinger agreed to divulge his own identity after the liberation of Innsbruck. As, indeed, he did, in addition giving the man a proper receipt signed with his own name.

The same sort of thing was happening all over Austria so that the resistance was never short of money, if constantly in need of arms, ammunition and equipment. The situation in Switzerland and, later on, in France and England, was almost exactly the reverse, our funds being drawn, not from worried

National Socialists, but almost exclusively from Austrians living in northern Italy or Switzerland, whose contributions were relatively meagre. Dr Kurt Grimm, the treasurer of the resistance movement's Swiss committee, must often have dipped into his own pocket to help us surmount the constantly recurring crises in our finances.

Even so, our friends in the Swiss army often had to come to our rescue at the last moment. While we gladly accepted anything they could give us in the way of documents, weapons and equipment, we were not so happy about the sums of money which, particularly in the early days, they several times placed at our disposal, for money was something about which we were rather more touchy than, say, machine pistols or explosives. This is readily understandable, considering our circumstances at the time. For we had decided once and for all not to be financially dependent on anyone, not even the neutral Swiss.

The Americans repeatedly offered us substantial sums but we did not wish to accept subsidies even from them. Eventually a fund was set up into which all donations from whatever source were placed. Its permanent trustees, Kurt Grimm and Anton Linder, were solely responsible for deciding to what use the money should be put. I myself, I am thankful to say, was never concerned with the financial side, but I still remember vividly the impotent despair of Grimm, Linder and Thalberg in the face of their depleted exchequer. Yet somehow we always managed, and funds just lasted out till the end of the war, which in the event came more quickly than anyone had anticipated. In this way we all successfully avoided being 'on the payroll' – even in the most honourable sense – of an Allied power.

Not that this was of much benefit to me personally, for Moscow's communist propaganda, parroted by Prague, East Berlin and, finally, the Vienna Communist Party rag, the *Volksstimme*, for years persisted in maintaining that, during and after the war, I had acted as an American agent and a highly paid one at that.

13

Master Plan

It was in late January, at the old-fashioned Hotel National in Basle, that I first met Dr Ernst Lemberger, a short, slight, dark-haired, youngish man who did not then wear a moustache. I knew that, as Commandant Jean Lambert, he had served with great distinction in the French army and the maquis. Not only had he been awarded the highest French war decoration, he had also been sent to Paris by the French resistance of the Région du Midi to inform General de Gaulle of that region's liberation.

Lemberger was a member of a Viennese Social Democratic family; his mother, then still in Vienna, had been a district councillor and, for many years, an official of the Social Democratic Party. He had studied law in the Austrian capital and had emigrated to France after the *Anschluss*. He then joined the French army and, soon after the capitulation in 1940, had gone underground. Before long he became an officer in the resistance forces, ending up with the rank of commandant, equivalent to major.

Ernst Lemberger was a fervent Austrian patriot and a liberal Social Democrat of the best kind. We were very soon on good terms and, in the course of the journeys we made together to and from Vienna, we engaged in long political discussions about the future of Austria after the liberation. It was through Ernst Lemberger that I first became acquainted with the Social Democratic approach to many important issues. Since he was a peculiarly tolerant man, arguing with him was not only easy but also exceptionally rewarding. From him I learnt much that enriched my political view of the world. True, I did not, to his chagrin, become a Social Democrat, but it is to him I

owe many of the best ideas, originally the stock-in-trade of
Austrian and western Social Democracy, which I have incor-
porated into my own political credo.

In Basle, however, we had no time for politico-philosophical
discussion. This time we were concerned with more down-to-
earth matters, with our master-plan to unite all political resistance groups within the POEN. Lemberger was anxious that we
should both go to Austria as soon as possible in view of the
urgent need to bring about a merger between 05 on the one
hand and the Social Democratic and Revolutionary Socialist
resistance groups on the other. He had been given plenary
powers by the Social Democratic émigré groups in London,
Paris and New York and, what was even more important, enjoyed the full confidence of his friends in the party. Moreover
Lemberger was, of course, an officer in the Allied forces and had
been empowered by the Allied Commission for Austria, a body
which had been set up in London in the early months of 1944, to
proceed to Vienna and there find out to what extent 05 and
the POEN were to be taken seriously, and whether they could
be regarded as partners by the Allies. To me, therefore, Ernst
Lemberger came as something of a godsend, while to him I
represented a vital link with the active resistance in the
Austrian underground.

Here, then, were two men, each of whom was indispensable
to the other. We lost no time in preparing our trip to Vienna,
for which we set off after Lemberger, now Private Nowotny,
had been fitted out with a German uniform and supplied with
the necessary documents. We arrived after a six-day journey,
broken at Milan, Bolzano, Innsbruck, Salzburg and Linz, in
each of which we laid the foundations for co-operation between
existing 05 groups and Lemberger's Social Democratic friends.

In February 1945, after five years and five months of war,
Vienna presented a sorry spectacle. What remained of the city
was covered in a thick pall of dust – dust from the ever-in-
creasing number of bombed buildings, from the streets and
squares which no one now bothered to sweep, and from the
partially excavated fire-fighting reservoirs. Since the autumn
of 1944 all attempts to maintain the illusion that the capital
was functioning normally had been abandoned. There were no
more plays or operas, for the singers and actors had now been

conscripted into the armaments industry. Public services functioned only at intervals, and air-raid warnings, now become a daily routine, paralysed the life of the city and its inhabitants.

The daily tragedy of the air-raids began first thing each morning with the preliminary alert, the notes of a cuckoo, broadcast by Vienna radio. Then came the first announcement, 'Enemy bomber formations approaching Carinthia and Styria', which left a glimmer of hope, for there was still a chance that the American bombers from southern Italy might attack Graz or the industrial region of Upper Styria, or even alter course for Hungary to support the Russian offensive there. The old country saying, 'Pray spare our house, St Florian, and burn our neighbour's cottage down', gained fresh currency in a form applicable to the US Air Force. But all hope was dispelled by the announcement, twenty minutes later, that enemy aircraft were passing above Steinamanger, whereupon people would begin to take cover. At first their progress was orderly as they made their way, loaded, perhaps, with ready-packed emergency bags, to one of the 'safe' air raid shelters; only with the sounding of the full alert – the familiar intermittent blasts from countless sirens – would the general sauve-qui-peut begin as people jostled outside the entrance to cellars, the doors of which were protected by sandbags against blast and splinters.

Already one could hear the drone coming closer and closer, of anything up to eight hundred Flying Fortresses of the 15th Air Force from Bari. As the drone gradually increased to a roar that heralded death and destruction, the German flak would open up. Vienna's anti-aircraft defences were comparatively good thanks to the timely building of flak towers. Several thousand anti-aircraft guns had been brought in to prevent the city – the 'pearl' of Hitler's erstwhile dreams – from being reduced to rubble and ashes. No doubt these strong defences were attributable not so much to any excessive sympathy felt by the German High Command for the city of Vienna as to the fact that, after the heavy air attacks on the west and north of Germany, the armaments industry had been increasingly transferred to the then still safe area around Vienna. The Messerschmitt aircraft works, for instance, had been evacuated to Wiener Neustadt.

However, since the conquest of southern Italy by the Americans and British, Austria had also come within the range of Allied bombers and now, in the late winter of 1944–45, there were virtually no German fighters left to intercept them. Nevertheless, they suffered heavy casualties when attacking Vienna and, on some days, forty or fifty might fall victim to heavy flak. In one respect this heavy barrage worked to Vienna's disadvantage, for it diverted many of the pilots from their allotted targets in the industrial areas and marshalling yards; instead they found it simpler to release their bomb loads over residential districts or the Inner City.

But the severe physical and nervous strain of spending many anxious hours almost daily in shelters from which people might, and increasingly did, emerge only to find their homes in ruins, was compounded by what, after five and a half years of war, was coming to be their main problem, namely the shortage of essential foodstuffs. Up till then the authorities had succeeded in providing the actual amounts laid down in the ration books. But now that the transport system was rapidly collapsing and the principal sources of supply in the east had ceased to be available, more and more provisions had to be drawn from the stockpiles in the large warehouses beside the Danube Canal so that the quantities distributed, and consequently the rations, dwindled correspondingly. Now, as hostilities neared their end, the territories at the heart of the Thousand Year Reich began to bear the full brunt of the war. A last minute attempt was made to build an 'Eastern Wall' in the Burgenland but it never got beyond a few trenches and fieldworks. The front drew ever closer; Budapest had fallen and the Russians had already reached western Hungary.

At the end of February Vienna gave the impression of being almost a front line city. Those who had been wounded in the last big battle between the Danube and Lake Balaton were taken, not to casualty clearing stations, but straight back to Vienna, where many of the as yet intact hotels had been turned into emergency hospitals. The two senior classes of the Viennese secondary schools had been conscripted into the Volkssturm and put to digging trenches in the eastern outskirts of the city. The Reich Defence Commissioner, Baldur von Schirach, began to issue bombastic proclamations in which his 'Viennese boys and girls' were told they must prepare to fight to the death for Greater Germany on the soil of the German city of Vienna. What neither Schirach nor 'his boys' could have known, as they laboured away at machine-gun emplacements in Favoriten, was that six weeks later Soviet troops, having circumvented their pathetic little defensive positions, would enter the burning and sorely wounded city from the west.

The only commodity that was always on tap in the Vienna of that time was the political joke. The more hopeless the situation grew, the less seriously the Viennese appeared to take it; indeed, political humour seemed to be the only bright spot in the all-pervading gloom. Here, for instance, is one of the innumerable 'Bobby' jokes then rife.

Meeting Bobby in civilian clothes, his friend Rudi, a war-weary conscript, asks enviously: 'Haven't you been called up, then?'

'Called up? What, me? I'm in a reserved occupation, see? I'm working on a miracle weapon.'

'What sort of miracle weapon?'

'It's a secret, really,' says Bobby. 'But seeing as you're an old pal . . .' and proceeds to explain that it's a new invention requiring only German raw materials. Nothing could be simpler, he says. 'All you have to do is fell some great big oaks, two hundred years old, hollow out the trunks, fill them with high explosive – made in Germany, of course – and chuck them into the North Sea on the ebb tide, when they'll simply float across to England and, before you can say knife, perfidious Albion, not to mention that old liar Churchill, will be blown to smithereens.'

Rudi, overcome with admiration, asks excitedly: 'And where do you come in, Bobby?'

'Me?' says Bobby. 'I'm the one that plants the acorns.'

Or again there is the story of the soldier returning from leave who goes to the Ostbahnhof to catch a train back to the front. 'No train today,' a railway official tells him, adding helpfully, 'but just round the corner you can get a 71 tram. Take it all the way to the terminus, and you'll find the Eastern Front a couple of streets further on.' A few weeks later this joke was to become bitter reality.

Through his prolonged absence from Vienna Lemberger had lost touch with his Social Democratic acquaintances in the city, but thanks to his mother was able to pick up the threads again on the very day of his return there. He thereupon engaged in detailed discussions with a number of Socialist party functionaries. In the Vienna of those days there was a distinction between Social Democrats and Revolutionary Socialists which to me, as an outsider, was not altogether evident. All I knew was that some of the Socialists with whom I was acquainted – usually the younger and more radical ones – described themselves as Revolutionary Socialists, while others continued to call themselves 'Social Democrats' as of old. This obviously meant that it was far more difficult for Ernst Lemberger to achieve the unity he desired – indeed, on more than one occasion he told me as much after discussion with representatives of both groups.

I myself was investigating the collapse and complete disintegration of the Frederiksen group's intelligence apparatus, which, at the time of my previous visit, had been functioning with admirable efficiency. Harald Frederiksen had been arrested at the beginning of February in consequence of a statement extorted under severe torture from a Croatian lieutenant belonging to the Croatian training brigade stationed at Stockerau; this officer had also been closely linked with Harald since November and had brought us a number of Croatian recruits. Harald had, in fact, once introduced him to Neda and myself without, however, mentioning my name. Nevertheless, the lieutenant would seem somehow to have discovered my real identity. After his arrest at the end of January, in its turn due to statements made by imprisoned compatriots, he had unfortunately begun to 'sing' very freely. Though himself a man of integrity, he could not withstand the interrogation methods of the Viennese Gestapo, who excelled in this field, nor was it by any means the first time that a brave and decent man had begun to talk after several nights of torture in the Morzinplatz. But his revelations were to involve us in serious losses.

By the end of February, Harald Frederiksen would, in the normal course of things, have faced trial in a People's Court and almost certain execution. He was saved, however, by the fact of his being a US citizen, from which the chiefs of the Viennese secret police had concluded, quite erroneously, that he was a prominent member of OSS. He was held on remand and never subjected to torture, but instead was visited in his cell by a string of Gestapo valiants in the hope that he might later secure privileges for them if not avert their own executions.

However, the fact that the Croat had mentioned my name under interrogation was to have the most dire consequences. A few days after Ernst Lemberger and I had left Vienna my mother was arrested by the Gestapo, who took her, first to the Morzinplatz, and then to the remand prison in the Elisabeth-Promenade. There she was incarcerated two floors above my father, whose arrest, a couple of days after Lemberger's and my departure, had come about as a result of the disruption of the POEN executive committee. In Milan, Renata Faccincani, her mother and Mario Vimercati were also arrested by the ss, this being the first time the Goldoni station had been 'blown'. However, Nam Brauer immediately transferred its functions to her quarters at the Hotel Milano.

On 23 February I, of course, knew nothing about the dreadful storm that was gathering over the two families, one in the Osterleitengasse, the other in the Via Marconi. Needless to say, I had suspected that something might happen when I learnt that the Croatian lieutenant had been arrested in January, and had said as much to Nedica, who, however, decided to remain at the Grand Hotel, arguing that the arrested man had seen too many people there during recent months to single her out. We knew that Harald wouldn't talk. But to be on the safe side we redisposed what remained of our information channels, on which occasion I discovered to my horror that Alfons Stummer, the intelligence group's second in command, had either been arrested or had gone to earth, for he and his associates had disappeared without trace. They had, as I later heard, managed to clear out in the nick of time, just before the Gestapo struck. Stummer was to remain in hiding in the Waldviertal until the end of the war.

In view of this disaster, I made tentative efforts to establish another intelligence network, in collaboration notably with Dr Karl Rudolf and his group. Being of a religious nature, his institute still afforded reasonably good camouflage; indeed, the fact that nearly all our activists there were either portly clerics or middle-aged women from the archiepiscopal office in the Stephansplatz seemed virtually to preclude any immediate action on the part of the Gestapo, who already had enough on their hands at this particular time. In the circumstances, therefore, it seemed to me expedient to transfer our resistance movement's information channels to this quarter. I talked the matter over with Dr Rudolf, who personally authorized me to make use of his institute for this purpose.

Meanwhile Ernst Lemberger had so far succeeded in marshalling his divergent Revolutionary and Democratic Socialists that, on 25 February, he and I were able to discuss matters with Dr Adolf Schärf, who held the somewhat macabre post of counsel for the defence at the National Socialist people's court in the Palace of Justice. Schärf was a quiet, deliberate man who weighed his every word, and seemed to me more like a senior civil servant than a politician, though before very long he was destined to be leader of the Socialist Party, Vice Chancellor and, ultimately, Federal President. It was only during adjournments that he was able to come down into the hall and talk to us in circumstances that were not a little eerie. For 'Private Nowotny' and 'Sergeant Steindler' might very well have themselves been standing in one of the courtrooms, facing summary conviction on at least a dozen counts, each of which carried the death penalty. Oddly enough, neither of us felt any fear that morning, but conversed easily with Dr Schärf, who listened attentively to what I had to say about the POEN and 05. Then, with dignified gestures all the more august for his black lawyer's gown, he declared that he and his party friends had decided to collaborate with the POEN. To begin with, Frau Louise Lemberger and he would join the Executive Committee, which was known, from the number of its members, as the 'Committee of Eleven'. It was further agreed that Dr Schärf should meet my father and Ezdorf for a preliminary discussion, which, in fact, took place next day. It was, however, to remain without a sequel, for both Ezdorf and my father were arrested shortly afterwards. Dr Schärf subsequently kept in touch with Heinrich Otto Spitz until the latter was shot by the SS in the early days of April, just before the liberation.

We had now implemented the first part of our master-plan by bringing together the Socialists and the POEN. That same afternoon we set about realizing the second part. In Spitz's beautiful house beside the Danube Canal in Heiligenstadt, Dr Lemberger and I were received by all the members of the Executive Committee who were able to attend, namely Wilhelm Spitz, Ernst Molden, Josef Ezdorf, Hans Becker and Major

Alfons Stillfried. The Communist, Matejka, was also there but remained in an adjoining room, since for security reasons he refused to meet face to face any of those present with whom he was not already acquainted. He therefore spoke to us only via Becker and Spitz, whom he knew, a procedure which did not exactly expedite matters.

Everyone expressed the greatest satisfaction on being told by Dr Lemberger that Schärf, as representative of the Social Democratic Party, had decided to join the POEN and, together with Bertha Lemberger, become a member of the Committee of Eleven. At last we had attained the great objective upon which we had set our sights so many months before. The Austrian resistance movement and its representative body, the POEN, now embraced all the more important political groups.

Lemberger and I were overjoyed, for this step was of the utmost importance in obtaining what we had been hoping and striving for – recognition by the Allies of the POEN as a provisional government. But over and above that, it was also an historic occasion. For the first time since 1933 and – if one probes a little way beneath the immediate surface of things – perhaps for the first time since the early days of the First Republic twenty-five years before that, Social Democrats, Christian Socialists, Monarchists, Liberals and Communists had been brought together in a joint Austrian organization for the purpose of collaborating at the highest political level. It was an achievement which only a few months previously had seemed to us unattainable.

The Executive Committee proceeded to nominate the POEN's official representatives – Dr Kurt Grimm and Karl Linder for Switzerland, Dr Lemberger for Paris, Franz Novy and Dr Franz Schneider for London, Hans Sailer and Dr Martin Fuchs for the United States. In addition, Dr Lemberger and I were empowered to represent the interests of 05 and the POEN vis-à-vis the various Allied political and military organizations, notably Allied headquarters in Caserta and Paris.

On top of that we were both urged to enter into negotiations at the earliest possible opportunity with representatives of the Soviet Union so that a POEN delegation could be sent to Moscow without delay. In view of the advance of the Red Army towards the frontiers of Austria, special emphasis was placed on the importance of political contacts with the Russians. We were instructed to make these contacts through the Soviet Mission at Allied HQ in Paris.

The conference was resumed that evening in Döbling at Alfons Stillfried's house in the Saarplatz, though its composition was not quite the same; there were now military representatives present, for the questions under discussion were primarily those of military aid for 05. The latter was represented not only by Dr Hans Becker and Jörg Unterrainer, but also by Major Karl Biedermann, commanding the military police patrols in Vienna, and Lieutenant Wolfgang Igler. Igler was deputizing for Major Karl Szokoll, chief of the military resistance organization and also head of the department responsible for organization at the headquarters of the Vienna Military District.

A number of important things happened during this conference, which continued long into the night. For a start, Lemberger and I were for the first time provided with lists, set out according to location and unit respectively, of the civilian groups and Wehrmacht cells belonging to the Austrian resistance movement; also, an appreciation of 05's overall role and its proposed organization in the Federal Länder of Vienna, Lower Austria, Styria, Carinthia, Salzburg, the Tyrol and Vorarlberg. The proposals for two of the Länder, Upper Austria and the Burgenland, were not forthcoming at this time. The document ran to many pages and was eventually transported in our packs – in code, of course – to Switzerland and, finally, to Allied headquarters.

Next, we were given, for submission to the Allied bomber commands, a detailed list of military objectives in Austria, accompanied by a request from the leaders of 05 and the POEN that the senseless bombing of Austrian towns, in particular the Inner City of Vienna, be discontinued. On 26 February we ourselves had experienced one of the heaviest air-raids on the capital. It was the day on which a large part of the Inner City went up in flames. The Rathaus and the Burgtheater were hit, and the Palais Liechtenstein was largely destroyed. Thus we had seen with our own eyes how pointless and strategically inept it was to attack the wrong targets while leaving the right ones, those of military importance, unscathed.

While we were deeply engrossed in discussion in Major Stillfried's studio there was an exchange of shots in the Saarplatz outside which was to have momentous consequences. An armed

05 squad (members of a Wehrmacht patrol) had been posted in
the gardens of the Saarplatz to protect our conference and frustrate any action by the Gestapo. In fact, the latter had been informed – by whom we never discovered – that something was
afoot there. More than that they obviously did not know and
their information must have come from a person who was aware
only of the watch being kept by the 05 picket. In due course the
police turned up but, having failed to detect our people in the
darkness of the gardens, decided it was a false alarm and went
away again.

However, it would seem that the Gestapo either did not believe the report made by the police or had arranged an additional foray of their own. Whatever the case, it was not long
before a patrol vehicle – clearly belonging to the Security Service – arrived in the Saarplatz and began sweeping the gardens
with its searchlight, which was promptly shot out by the 05 men.
Their fire was returned and there would appear to have been
casualties among the security police, while one 05 man was also
injured. At all events, the exchange of shots led to the immediate evacuation of the Saarplatz by the Security Service. We
had heard the shooting but did not learn what it was about until
the 05 squad commander, wearing Wehrmacht uniform, came
into Stillfried's house to make his report to Major Biedermann.
The meeting at once broke up – we had in any case concluded
our business – and in small groups we made our way through
blacked-out Döbling to our various hideouts. About ten minutes after everyone had left the police arrived in force, complete
with searchlights, but found nothing except a few empty cart-
ridge cases. Nor did a search of the houses in the square produce
any clue. They also drew a blank at Stillfried's house, almost the
last they entered, finding there only a middle-aged couple who
had been rudely awakened from their sleep.

Unfortunately, however, the whole affair was rumbled within
forty-eight hours, but even today I don't know how this happened – whether as a result of the shooting in the Saarplatz or
of the Croat's revelations. At all events, from 2 March onwards
there was a wave of arrests affecting nearly all the leading men
in the POEN but not, at this juncture, the military resistance,
namely 05. Virtually every member of the POEN's Executive
Committee was arrested, notably my father, Josef Ezdorf,
Alfons Stillfried and Hans Becker.

Lemberger and I left Vienna early next morning by the Wehrmacht leave train. Fearing that patrols might be on the prowl after the events of the preceding night in the Saarplatz, we took a tram as far as Hütteldorf and waited for the train there. When it came in it was already crowded to capacity and we had to force our way on, together with our packs, which were bulging not so much with personal possessions as with documents, lists, records – in short, the fruits of our week's stay in Vienna. At last we managed to find a seat in one of the overcrowded compartments. With some difficulty we stowed away our luggage and sat down among the somnolent troops. The train set off again. Barely ten minutes had passed when the door of our compartment flew open and a corporal appeared, accompanied by a lance-corporal, each with a metal gorget-plate, or 'dog label', about his neck.

'Wehrmacht patrol,' the corporal shouted, 'show your pay-books, passes and movement orders.'

Everyone began fishing in their pockets for their paybooks etc. which the two NCOs then proceeded to examine. I was disagreeably struck by the fact that the corporal devoted far more attention to my paybook than to anyone else's. Moreover, before returning the documents and passing on to the next compartment, he also jotted down something on a pad. I looked at Lemberger out of the corner of my eye and he nodded imperceptibly; so he, too, had noticed. I decided that, whatever happened, we must leave the train at the next stop, St Pölten, and in a low voice conveyed as much to my companion, who agreed. But we were not to be given the opportunity.

A quarter of an hour later, just as the train was puffing slowly up the gradient between Pressbaum and Rekawinkel, the compartment door again flew open and the corporal of the Wehrmacht patrol reappeared. Pointing at me he said:

'Can I have another look at your paybook, sergeant?'

I handed it to him without a word. He looked at it, then at my pass, and asked: 'That man next to you, Private Nowotny, does he belong to the same outfit?'

'Yes.'

'Then I must ask you both to come and see our officer in the last coach.'

I looked at Lemberger. Then I got up, slowly and deliberately took down my pack, buckled on my belt and holster and left the compartment, preceded by the corporal and lance-corporal and followed by Lemberger. I was thinking hard. This was bound to end badly; somebody must have tipped them off; we were wanted men, or at least I was. Maybe I had dragged poor Lemberger into it as well by saying yes when asked if he belonged to the same outfit. There was only one chance, I told myself; the train was going very slowly – we should have to try and jump out of the moving train.

In the vestibule between two coaches, I told Lemberger in a whisper what I proposed to do. He nodded. The next coach was the last but one on the train, so the attempt would have to be made from there. I therefore paused for a moment, then stepped across to the nearest door and was about to open it when, with a noise like thunder, the train entered a tunnel. This put paid to my plan of escape, for inside the tunnel the line began to run downhill and the train was rapidly gathering speed. To jump would have been suicide, apart from which we should have to wait until we were out in the open again.

The corporal was growing impatient. 'It's further down, sergeant,' he said. As I trudged along behind him I put my hand in the pocket of my greatcoat, felt for my spare pistol and slipped the safety catch. If it came to the point, I wasn't going to sell my life too cheaply. At last we reached the compartment of the officer in command of the train, an elderly captain of Austrian origin. I stood to attention and saluted.

He looked up: 'Stand easy, sergeant,' he said, 'and take a seat. Let's have a look at your paybook.'

I sat down and handed him my paybook and pass; he examined first one, then the other.

'Tell me, Sergeant Steindler,' he said, 'that man out there who's travelling with you, does he belong to the same unit?'

'Yes, sir. Station Zeno, Munich Area HQ, Reich Central Security Office. We've been to Vienna on duty and are on our way back to Milan.'

The captain looked at me. 'I'm sorry, sergeant,' he said, 'but I shall have to ask you to check the front coaches, otherwise we shan't get the job done before Salzburg. The train's too full as it is and we're short of men. I expect you're used to this sort of thing, being in the Security Service. Lucky the corporal took a good look at your papers. Hope you don't mind – it's a beastly job.'

I stood up and came to attention. 'Not at all, sir. Glad to oblige.'

Little did the good man know how genuinely glad I was. Lemberger, rather pale, had remained standing in the corridor. He smiled at me.

'Nowotny,' I barked, 'wipe that smile off your face. You're in for a surprise.'

We looked most impressive as, each adorned with a nice big gorget-plate, we set off up the corridor. Before the train had reached Salzburg, we had been able to glean in a few hours more information about troop movements in what remained of the Greater German Reich than even the best spy could have done in as many months. Not wanting to make ourselves unduly conspicuous, we took no names but made copious notes. If ever I had a sense of being a round peg in a round hole, it was now. Nor could the worthy captain possibly have picked on a finer pair of wolves to tend his flock.

After being handsomely entertained in the provost canteen at Salzburg station we were handed over to another patrol due to leave for Innsbruck on the next express, with the request that we, as colleagues, be allowed to travel in comfort in their reserved compartment. In this way we got to Innsbruck with no questions asked, and thence to Switzerland by way of Milan, where I learned of Renata's recent arrest.

Lemberger's performance had been first-rate, and all the more admirable for the fact that he had never before worn German uniform and thus had no idea how a soldier should comport himself in German-occupied territory. A good comrade at all times, he was upright and brave and had a never-failing sense of humour. During that journey we came to know each other very well, and the friendship begun then between the young Social Democrat and the still younger Liberal Conservative has endured for over thirty years.

Our return to Switzerland was followed by prolonged discussions with the representatives of the POEN in that country. We were concerned not only with making the most of the new situation produced by the entry of Socialists into the POEN, but also with exploiting its possibilities vis-à-vis the Western Allies. It was decided that Lemberger and I should at once carry out the Committee's mandate and contact the Russians in Paris, after which Lemberger would go on to London and, having informed the Foreign Office of developments in the POEN, sound them out about the possibility of according that body provisional recognition. I, for my part, was to fly to Caserta in the hope of inducing the 15th Air Force to comply with the Committee's urgent plea that they discontinue their heavy raids on non-military targets in Austria.

In order that work in the field for which I had hitherto been responsible should proceed without interruption, I increasingly handed it over to others. Thus, so far as Switzerland was concerned, I delegated my responsibilities to Hans Thalberg and Mundi Treu, while our couriers and chief agents, Wallnöfer, Mittermaier and Lieutenant Berthold, whose services were proving invaluable, took charge not only of the organization of missions and courier trips direct from Switzerland to Austria, but also of liaison with, and supplies to, resistance and partisan groups in the Vorarlberg and the Tyrol. Liaison with the POEN in Vienna was made the province of Dr Staretz, who had accompanied me there on my last trip, and the reconstruction of our intelligence post in Milan was entrusted to Franz Otting and Nam Brauer. This released Lemberger and myself for the conduct of negotiations with the Allies in the political as well as the military field.

On 10 March we both called upon the Soviet Mission in Paris. The place was positively swarming with Russian officers and functionaries. I had already called there in January, on my first visit to Paris, when I had spoken at length to a Counsellor by the name of Kotsurev and informed him of developments in the Austrian resistance and the POEN. On that occasion Kotsurev had refrained from expressing a personal opinion, but had merely taken copious notes, which he recorded in an intriguing Russian shorthand on a large pad. In the end it had been agreed that I should call again on my next visit to Paris, Kotsurev having promised that what I had told him would be conveyed forthwith to the proper quarter in Moscow.

The first thing Lemberger and I discovered was that Kotsurev had vanished, apparently without trace. However, another, no less reticent, Russian diplomat, who knew about my first visit, arranged for us to come again on 25 March. I was not in Paris on that date and Lemberger therefore went to see the Russians on his own. He was received by a sizeable group of officers headed by General Susloparov, Chief of the Soviet Military

Mission to General Eisenhower's headquarters. Lemberger was able to place before them all our more important requests, namely that the POEN be represented in Moscow, that a Russian liaison officer be despatched with a minimum of delay to 05 headquarters in Vienna in order to co-ordinate the plans of the Red Army and the resistance movement for the liberation of the city, and that an 05 liaison officer be similarly attached to the headquarters of the Red Army's 3rd Ukrainian Front in the Austro-Hungarian border zone. Finally, he conveyed to them the POEN's wish to be recognized by the Soviet Government as the provisional government of Austria, thus laying the foundations for close collaboration with the Soviet Army in the administration of Austrian territory and the work of reconstruction after the country's liberation. Lemberger also handed over to the Russians all the reports we had brought with us from Vienna on the military situation in Austria and the composition of the POEN and 05.

There were now signs that the Russians were warming to us after all, for they responded with great interest and affability to Lemberger's proposals. They expressed a wish to be supplied with detailed information about the background of leading members of the POEN. At the same time, however, General Susloparov plainly showed surprise at the failure of the POEN and 05 to get in touch with the Russians any earlier. At this, Lemberger pointed out that the Provisional Austrian National Committee had not been formally constituted until 18 December and that early the following month its first official representative and liaison officer, Herr Wieser (myself), had called at the Mission, where he had spoken to a M Kotsurev. Furthermore, Herr Wieser and Dr Lemberger, the duly appointed and accredited representatives of the POEN, as finally constituted in February to comprise all democratic groups from Communists to Conservatives, had only very recently come to call upon the Soviet authorities.

The Russians promised to convey all this information to Moscow forthwith. They showed a particular interest in our military reports and seemed anxious that there should be no delay in establishing communications between 05 representatives and the Soviet troops advancing on Vienna. They suggested that this should be done either by radio or by couriers dropped by parachute. The next day Lemberger had another interview with General Susloparov, whose attitude had grown perceptibly more friendly. The Soviet Union, he said, had decided to send a liaison officer to Vienna immediately. He asked for addresses and passwords that would enable contact to be made with 05 headquarters.

On 30 March Lemberger and I again went to see the Russians. I had just arrived from Zurich, where we had received via Caserta signals from Vienna giving us the latest reports on the situation in the Vienna defence zone and, above all, fairly precise details of Major Szokoll's plans for the liberation of the city. The messages also contained an urgent request that we get in touch with the Russians and make arrangements for the establishment of a direct link between 05 and the units of the Red Army then approaching Vienna, and went on to stress that, while every step would be taken to ensure that the city would be handed over smoothly and, in all likelihood, peacefully, within forty-eight hours of such a link being established, no time must be lost if the plan was to be successfully carried out.

All this I reported to General Susloparov and the members of his staff. We gave them the frequency of our radio set in Vienna and also the code used by our operators in communicating with SO and SI (OSS's Secret Operations and Secret Intelligence sections) in Caserta. We further agreed – and the message was transmitted through Caserta the same evening – that 05 should, for its part, attempt to get an accredited representative through the battle lines to the Red Army. Three days later, on 2 April, a signal from Lieutenant Igler confirmed that this would be done and, in effect, Sergeant Ferdinand Käs gallantly made his way through the German lines and reached Marshal Tolbukhin's headquarters.

Igler also reported that two SS Panzer Divisions were being moved up to reinforce the front south-west of Vienna and were expected to arrive in two days' time. This vital signal began and ended with the words 'Hasi to Wenzel', Hasi being Igler's code name and Wenzel mine. We had agreed to use them only in cases of extreme urgency so as to preclude any possibility of our being misled by a fake German signal. For the codes used by the Allies and their supporters in the underground were frequently broken by the Germans, who turned them to their own account.

Lieutenant Igler's important message, which we retransmitted to Moscow within a matter of hours, marked the end of radio contact between 05 in Vienna and the outside world. I was later to learn that on 3 April the radio set had suffered irreparable damage when the car in which it was being moved – as was regularly done to avoid detection by the Germans – drove into a bomb crater. For their better concealment, the reserve sets had been kept in the building previously occupied by the Austrian War Ministry which later housed the headquarters of the 17th (Vienna) Military District. But as it happened this was now the arena for the last tragic confrontation between the leaders of the resistance movement and the ss. Hence the radio sets were no longer available for use. Between Vienna, embattled and in flames, between the men of 05 who were making their last stand there – between these and the outside world, a pall of silence had fallen.

On 12 March, while Lemberger was negotiating with the Russians in Paris, I had flown down to Caserta and Bari. My first meeting was with the commander of the American 15th Air Force, General Cabell, and our subject of discussion the cessation of air raids on non-military objectives in Vienna and other Austrian cities. The argument was somewhat heated and hard words were exchanged. Several Allied representatives, notably a British brigadier, took the view that, since all Austrians were Nazis anyway, it would do no harm to drop a few bombs on them. I produced our documents on the bombing of civil objectives in Vienna, Innsbruck and Salzburg, and tried to convince Cabell and his colleagues that this type of attack achieved the very reverse of what was intended.

The next day Colonel Chapin, my friend and mentor in Caserta, handed me a copy of an order which Cabell had issued to all pilots of the 15th Air Force instructing them to avoid civil targets in Austria. Cabell also ordered the issue of fresh maps indicating the targets suitable for attack. I don't know what effect if any was produced by this order. It was issued on about 14 March and a signal from our intelligence centre in Vienna, then still functioning admirably, did at any rate confirm that, after 20 March, the bombers appeared to be concentrating on road and rail junctions and industrial objectives. I was not to have a chance of verifying this in person, however.

Aside from the good intentions or otherwise of the Allied air commanders, the bombing techniques in use at the time made it difficult to restrict raids to non-military targets. Operations over Germany had accustomed American pilots to saturation bombing, nor did they worry unduly about the possibility of hitting an old church, say, or a hospital or palace; it was no concern of theirs and, after all, terror bombing was part of psychological warfare. True, they had been forbidden to employ the same tactics over Austria, but how many American bomber pilots could really say for certain whether or not they were flying over Austrian territory?

From Caserta I went straight on to Bari to do a shortened course in parachute jumping, only to discover that I was in no way cut out for that sport. It was not simply that I was frightened all the time I was in the air, but I never really learnt how to roll so as not to hurt myself on landing. Nevertheless, after seven practice jumps and five days' training, my instructor, a hefty captain from Oakland, said everything was okay and I could go ahead and do an operational jump. As, indeed, I very shortly did – for the first and only time.

It was arranged that, in the course of the next few days, I should be flown northwards in a specially converted four-engined bomber. This aircraft was to accompany one of the bomber formations bound for a night raid on Munich. Above the Trentino our machine would leave the rest of the formation and proceed independently to the neighbourhood of Cles, where two Italian partisan leaders would be dropped. It would then fly on to the Tyrol, thereby sparing me the usual circuitous journey via France, Switzerland and Northern Italy which at this time took at least a week. oss in Caserta had arranged with Freddy Mayer, an American lieutenant who operated in the Ötztal and possessed a radio set, to have a reception party waiting for me in a side valley of the Ötztal.

The first hitch came when weather conditions kept the aircraft grounded in Bari for a day longer than originally planned. Though the wireless operator in the Ötzstal was informed of this delay, the fact somehow failed to percolate through to the worthy Ötztal partisans. At all events, twenty-four hours later than estimated and shortly after nightfall, I climbed into the big, four-engined aircraft and greeted my two travelling companions, the Italian partisans, whereupon we took off through dense cloud and in very windy conditions. We flew at a height of about 10,000 feet in fairly close formation and over Bologna ran into flak. One aircraft was hit, caught fire and turned back. We ourselves came through unscathed and flew on, but I had an uncomfortable feeling in the pit of my stomach.

Somewhere in the region of Verona our machine left the others and headed north-west. It then circled the mountains of western Trentino, that is roughly the area between Mezzolombardo and Arco. Below us two signal rockets rose into the air and my Italian friends took their departure. Everything seemed to be going according to plan. The aircraft resumed a northerly course and in twenty minutes' time reached the Central Alps, which, unfortunately, were obscured by a fairly dense layer of cloud. The pilot, who was obviously in a hurry to get back, consulted his maps and made two runs over the dropping zone. Not a sign of rockets. Suddenly he spotted a fire approximately in the area where the reception party was supposed to be waiting; we peered down but could see practically nothing, being unable to come in any lower owing to the mountainous nature of the terrain. The pilot flew two more circuits and then told me that either I must jump now or he would have to take me back to Bari.

I plumped for the first alternative, although I didn't care for the idea. The crew shook my hand, then one of them gave me the usual shove from behind and I was out. The parachute duly opened; a stiffish wind was blowing from the north-west, and I went floating down into nothingness through the black night. There was no sign of the fire we had spotted from the aircraft. Nothing surprising about that, however, for in this region mountain ridges alternated with deep, precipitous valleys, besides which I had probably been blown some way off course. But if not surprising it was none the less disagreeable. There was absolutely no knowing where I would eventually land. Luckily the dense cloud had begun to disperse and it was no longer as dark as it had been just after my jump, though the moon hadn't come through properly. Seeing a steepish slope rising towards me, I rolled myself up like a snail in its shell as I had been taught to do and awaited my fate. I came down with quite a bump on my hip and was dragged along for several yards before finding the automatic parachute release. I then became aware of a sharp pain in my left ankle – a sprain, presumably, for later my foot swelled up like a balloon and for two days I couldn't put any weight on it. Otherwise I was unhurt. I tried to get my bearings, but unfortunately the clouds had closed in again; it was pitch dark and there wasn't a light to be seen anywhere. Nor, since it was mid-winter, could I judge where I was by the temperature. However, there was not much snow. The slope on which I lay was strewn with boulders and, so far as I could see, there were no trees, though a soughing noise in the distance indicated that I must be below the tree line.

I was beginning to shiver and wrapped myself up in the parachute, not that it made much difference to my body temperature, but it did at least serve to keep me dry. In this way I spent the night and, though almost frozen, kept going on chocolate and an occasional cigarette, being careful, as I lit up, to shield the flame so that no one should see it. Where, I wondered, could that confounded reception party be? At last dawn came, enabling me to look at my maps and eventually get my bearings. I now found that I was in the wrong valley. The pilot had been about twenty miles off course and had dropped me, not as intended in a side valley of the Ötztal near Sölden, but in a valley that leads up from Gries im Sellrain to the Lüsenzer Ferner.

I was sitting on a steep Alpine pasture; three or four hundred yards below me, on a level patch of ground, stood an Alpine hut, which as it was wintertime was not in use. Taking my parachute with me, I limped down to it. There were no tracks in the virgin snow around the place and it looked as though no one had been there for months. With some difficulty I managed to break open the door and set about making as habitable as possible the one room which, as always in such huts, did duty for kitchen, byre and bedroom. Having first ensured that the hut could not be seen from below, and thinking it improbable that, with such deep snow, anyone would come up far enough to see the smoke, I lit a fire. Then, after dealing with my ankle as best as I could, I took out the little radio set from my jumping pack and succeeded in tuning in to Beromünster and Munich. My cargo parachute, much to my chagrin, had got lost nor, in the absence of a reception party, was it ever recovered. At all events the smaller pack contained enough food to last a few days and also a first-aid kit including some pain-killers. Forty-eight hours later my ankle had recovered sufficiently for me to walk more or less normally. The weather had also improved, which didn't please me very much, but on the second day of my enforced stay at the head of the Sellrain valley, I nevertheless decided to leave at dusk. Though no one was likely to discover before spring came that I had been there, I cut up my parachute into small pieces and burnt it. Then I set off, but the deep snow made the going so bad that, by the time I came within sight of the familiar silhouette of Gries church, darkness had already fallen. Rather than risk a chance encounter, I decided to spend the night in a barn. Next morning, wearing German uniform and equipped with the necessary papers, I took a cautious look round and was greatly relieved to see German soldiers moving about in the village, which meant that I would not be particularly conspicuous. Presumably some inn had been turned into a convalescent home or the like. There was also a bus but, not wanting to try my luck too far, I decided not to take it. Instead, I set off along the Inntal road and, half an hour later, was given a lift into Kematen by a lorry. As I walked through this picturesque village it occurred to me that, with a bit more luck, I would have landed on the Kematener Alm, where some two dozen partisans were already operating. But one can't expect to have things all one's own way.

I reached Innsbruck in the afternoon and was able to hobble round and attend to the most urgent of my business, after which I looked up a doctor who belonged to 05. Though an ear, nose and throat specialist, Dr Stricker ascertained without difficulty that my still badly swollen ankle was merely sprained and not broken. He attended to me with touching solicitude and urged me to keep my foot up for a day or two. I couldn't spare the time, although the injury had put paid to my original plan of going straight on to Vienna for, lame as I was, it would have been madness to show my face in a city where I was already the subject of a hue and cry. However, I succeeded in finding a trustworthy courier to carry my message to the capital.

Whether I wanted to or not, I was forced to retrace my footsteps and, three days later, found myself back in Switzerland. It would after all have been easier and quicker to cover the distance between Caserta and Zurich by plane via Annemasse

and then in the comfort of the Swiss Federal Railways' express
from Geneva. For the apparent 'short cut' via Bari and Gries
had cost me eleven valuable days and a sprained ankle. At all
events, any desire I may have felt to make parachute jumps
had been satisfied once and for all.

The evening air was filled with the scent of spring as I walked
from Tre Croci on the frontier to the hamlet of Sagno and
watched the sun go down into the mists round the Monta Rosa
massif; I pondered on the 'master-plan' hammered out ten
weeks previously in Basle by Ernst Lemberger and myself. Our
first objective had been to bring together under one umbrella
all the various political parties and groups. Obviously this was
feasible only in Austria itself and under the pressure of Nazi
dictatorship and the war. All such attempts undertaken by
émigrés in the compartive security of Paris, London or New
York had always come to grief, fizzling out in endless arguments
about who was guilty of what, who was better than whom and,
last but not least, who was and was not capable of governing –
and all this to the inevitable accompaniment of mutual denun-
ciations to the governments of the host countries.

It was to achieve the necessary unification of the two big
traditional political camps, the 'blacks' and the 'reds', that Lemberger and I had together made our way to Vienna. And there,
on 25 February 1945, we had achieved our first objective.
Christian Socialists, Social Democrats, Monarchists, Liberals
and Communists, each of whom had hitherto been fighting
their own, and therefore a losing, battle, had at last joined
forces and achieved union in the POEN and 05.

What course would things take now? Some twenty miles east
of Vienna the battle was at its height, in the western part of our
country the false gods of the Third Reich were preparing to
make their last stand. Were my parents in prison, in a concentration camp? Were they, in fact, alive at all? Would Otto win
through and return to our midst? Would I ever again see all the
friends who had rallied round and followed me as though I
were the Pied Piper of Hamelin?

Would the second part of the 'master-plan' ever become
reality, our country ever be free in a world that was at peace?
And in that new world, would we young people at last be able
to live the kind of life we wanted to live?

I didn't know the answer to any of these questions of mine

but, as is the privilege of youth, I was full of hope and optimism. In the distance Monte Rosa was bathed in the light of a spectacular Alpine sunset. The friendly glow seemed to beckon me on and it was with a high heart that I reached the first houses of Sagno.

Not many days later I was reunited with my brother Otto. After the wave of arrests that followed the events in the Saarplatz, his escape from Germany had become a matter of the utmost urgency. To that end I had travelled to Berlin, where I had enlisted the help of Ulli Rüdt-Kollenberg, who, in the guise of his fiancée, had gone out to Rathenov and handed over the military documents and passes we had fabricated for him in the name of Sergeant Alfred Steiger. And now here he was on Zurich station, having succeeded in reaching Switzerland via Munich, Innsbruck and Nam Brauer's Station, now located in the Hotel Milano. I thought Otto looked well, and rejoiced to know that he was safe, if only for a few days. He at once decided to join us and was anxious to be sent into the Tyrol as soon as possible. But first we had to fatten him up a bit and give him a chance of acquainting himself with the details of what we were planning.

In early April an opportunity presented itself of assembling a small party to accompany me to Austria. This consisted of Otto, once more as Sergeant Alfred Steiger, the newly arrived Lieutenant Joe Franckenstein as Corporal Horneck and, lastly, his wireless operator and colleague as Lance-Corporal Karl Nováček. They were all to accompany me via Milan to Innsbruck, and then I was to go on to Salzburg and Linz. Owing to the state of hostilities, the POEN groups there, hitherto answerable to headquarters in Vienna, had now been left without leadership, and it was my intention to attach them to the Prinz Eugen Station run by Helmut Heuberger at Innsbruck, which would thus take over the POEN's executive function in western Austria. Having accomplished this mission, I was to return to Caserta via Tre Croci and Annemasse. Otto was to remain at Innsbruck, where he would be responsible for the expansion and organization of military resistance groups in the Tyrol, their co-ordination with existing partisan groups in the Ötztal, on the Kematener Alm, in the Paznauntal and in the Vorarlberg and, finally, for liaison with Lieutenant Berthold's military group. This was to enter Austria from Switzerland via the

Dreiländereck and attempt to set up a firm base in one of the Vorarlberg valleys, thus creating the first 'liberated zone' in western Austria.

I was anxious to get back to Caserta as soon as possible, for the battle was already raging outside Vienna and the Allied Supreme Command was confident that, by mid-April at the latest, it would be able to land its first 'liaison mission' on an airfield liberated by the Russians. I was to be attached to this mission as liaison officer and was determined to be one of the party on board the first aircraft to fly to Vienna in order to play my part in the liberation of the city and the formation of the first provisional government. However, things don't always turn out as one expects. I had again reckoned without my host, and half a year was to go by before Fepolinski and Waschlapski returned to the Osterleitengasse.

14

Last Act in the
Piazzale Loreto

On 8 April, my twenty-first birthday, I left Lugano for Milan ahead of Otto and the two Austro-Americans, who were to follow on next day. The decisive battle for the liberation of Vienna was then in progress and I was exceedingly anxious about my parents, both of whom had been arrested and taken to the remand prison in the Elisabeth-Promenade. The immediate cause of mother's arrest had been the Gestapo's discovery that I was still alive, and I could not but feel partially responsible – not a very agreeable thought, especially as I knew the kind of treatment the Gestapo were meting out to their prisoners during the final months of the war.

My anxiety about my parents had been considerably increased by one of the last signals to reach Caserta from Vienna at the beginning of April. From this I had learned that political prisoners were being removed from the Rossauer Lände prison – the Liesl – and marched off in the direction of Mauthausen concentration camp. Since my parents were amongst those prisoners, I could only fear the worst. At this juncture Otto and I were condemned to inaction, there being nothing we could do to help them. Our communications with Vienna had been cut and I could only hope and pray that my parents would survive.

On my arrival in Milan I avoided going to the Via Goldoni for fear of falling into the hands of the police and went instead to see Nam Brauer de Beaufort at the Grand Hotel Milano. Nam had been expecting me and we now proceeded to discuss the dramatic events of the past few months and their implications for the future.

Renata Faccincani, whom I had taken to Switzerland and

safety, refused to remain in Zurich, however, being intent on returning to Milan; in January, in defiance of all our remonstrations, she made her way back to Mussolini's crumbling Repubblica Sociale Italiana. Then, at the beginning of February, the Germans struck again. Late one evening when Renata was alone in the house in the Via Goldoni, the SS came and took her away. Before leaving, she had time to scribble 'San Vittore' – the name of a big prison in Milan – in lipstick on the looking-glass. Shortly afterwards, Siro, the old family retainer, came home, saw the message on the looking-glass and spent the whole night burning our secret papers and documents, which Renata had concealed behind her mother's bed. Barely had he finished when the SS returned and searched the house from attic to cellar but, thanks to his efforts, found nothing. On this occasion they also arrested Renata's mother and Mario Vimercati, who, however, were soon released. Meanwhile Renata was in a dire predicament. She was being subjected to a series of rigorous interrogations during which she was plied with questions about me. But her escape was eventually engineered by Mario, who bribed an interpreter for the considerable sum of 40,000 lire, after which she was conveyed across the Swiss border by Pietro, our partisan friend in Cernobbio. At last she realized that, if she were not to endanger everyone else, she must remain in safety and await developments.

All this was discussed while Nam had been feeding me one bar of chocolate after another. Calmly, as was her wont, she now came out with the bad news that the search was on for Franz Otting, with whom she had continued to run the Marconi Station. All military headquarters had received a teleprint from the Controller of SS and Police, Italian Theatre ordering his arrest. She herself had so far managed to elude suspicion but no one could tell how long this would last.

With no less imperturbability, she now opened the drawer of her desk and drew out a large poster. Couched in German and Italian, it stated quite unequivocally that Lance-Corporal Friedrich Molden, alias Pietro de Lago, alias Sergeant Hans Steinhauser etc, etc. was 'wanted for desertion and high treason as a ringleader' by the German authorities, who went on to enjoin caution on anyone who might challenge the wanted man since he was armed and likely to resist arrest. The price put on his head was 20,000 lire, a substantial sum in those days.

The poster, she told me, was already on display everywhere in Milan, and it would be unwise for me to spend much longer there. I was somewhat dismayed by this, knowing as I did that, on their arrival in Milan next day, Otto, Horneck and Nováček would make straight for our rendezvous, Nam's room in the Hotel Milano. But the building had, she told me, been under constant police surveillance for several days. There were a number of things that had to be done, and done quickly. First of all I looked for and found a messenger whom I despatched to Cernobbio to intercept Otto and his two companions and tell them on no account to go to the Hotel Milano, but to meet me instead at the central station at eight o'clock next morning.

Nam went out to look for Franz Otting; he had to be told that he was on the wanted list and must get ready to flee to Switzerland, also that arrangements had been made for him to spend the night at Lori Possanner's. I myself now left the hotel by the staff entrance and went into town to warn Mario Vimercati. Over the telephone we arranged to meet at seven o'clock that evening at the station of the Ferrovia Nord Milano, a privately-owned railway running from Milan to Como and a few other places in northern Italy. At this time railway stations, with their perpetual bustle, especially during the evening rush hour, were considered safe and inconspicuous meeting places.

In this instance, however, I could hardly have chosen a worse spot, for just then a search was in progress there. I was struck by the fact that, in the booking-hall in the front part of the station, a double line of Italian police and German MPs were checking all passengers on their way to the trains. From this it was clear that they were looking for a German, very possibly one in civilian dress. It was early evening and thousands of Milanese were returning to their homes in the suburbs. I hugged the wall and moved inconspicuously towards a side door that led from the booking-hall into a large waiting-room.

As I entered it, the first thing that caught my eye was my own likeness on the wanted poster, whereupon it suddenly dawned on me that the person they were looking for was me. I passed on into the next waiting-room, which was in semi-darkness, its windows being covered with blue paint on account of the blackout. There, amidst the throng of peasant women, children and chickens and the huge piles of luggage, I felt momentarily safe. But the respite could only be short-lived. From this waiting-room, a door led straight onto the platform and beside it stood an Italian ticket collector, past whom I, as a German sergeant, pushed my way. But beyond him stood an Italian policeman, who now demanded to see my pass.

'*Forze armate tedesche,*' I barked, '*commando della SS.*'

Taken aback, he let me pass but he was looking at me curiously and I lost no time in mingling with the crowd. Then I strode rapidly along beside the train and, near the far end of the platform, jumped into the fourth or fifth coach. As I did so, I heard the sound of a whistle; out of the corner of my eye I could see the policeman signalling towards the end of the platform. So he had recognized me after all.

Now I had to move fast. Climbing out on the other side of the train, I was alarmed to find myself on an empty line. From the end of the platform a German officer bellowed:

'Halt, you there! Halt!'

The hunt was on.

Two strides took me across to the train standing on the next track; I boarded it, ran the length of two coaches and jumped down on the far side. Third time lucky, I thought, for on the very next line another train was just beginning to pull out and, by running hard, I succeeded in catching it. As I jumped onto the step, two Italian workmen leaned out and hauled me into the overcrowded corridor. Shots rang out somewhere to the rear and several bullets raked the platform.

'*Poverino, tutto va bene,*' one of the Italians said.

I made it, for even if a military policeman had succeeded in boarding the last coach, he would not have been able to make his way up the train, into which people were packed like sardines, until we got to the next station. The Italian workmen had instinctively understood what was up. They told me that, just before the working-class suburb of Sesto San Giovanni – known as Piccolo Stalingrad because of its strong Communist sympathies – the train would have to slow down because the line had been damaged by bombing, and they advised me to jump out when we came to the goods station.

I did as they suggested, fell neatly into a bomb crater and, for the time being, was saved. It took me almost an hour to cross the huge marshalling-yard and the adjoining industrial area and find a tram-stop from which to travel back to Milan.

I telephoned Nam, who had some good news for me. She had succeeded in contacting Franz Otting and directing him to Lori Possanner's. There remained only the question of Otto, Horneck and Nováček. Once I had settled that, I should have to try and get through to Switzerland with Otting and Nam.

Nam didn't really want to go with us since she did not believe she was in any immediate danger. That night we had a prolonged discussion in a back room at Lori's during which I sought to persuade her that, within twenty-four hours at the outside, she would be no less at risk than any of us. It could not be very long before the trail would lead to her, and then not even the best of connections could save her. Finally she agreed to come, but only on one condition, namely that she be allowed to bring her luggage. All unsuspecting, I naturally said yes. The next day Nam turned up at Pietro's house in Cernobbio for our flight into Switzerland via Monte Bisbino. With her she had brought eight cabin trunks.

Prior to this I had gone to the central station in Milan to meet Otto and his two companions. In great haste I told him about the new situation that had arisen, the necessity we were in of getting Nam and Otting safely into Switzerland and the possible danger to himself of the search for me that was going on in Milan. After a moment's reflection we decided that Otto, Horneck and Nováček should go on to Innsbruck as planned. Otto also took charge of the radio set for Salzburg.

We shook hands, not at all sure whether we should ever see each other again. At this juncture Otto, Joe Horneck and I were pretty down in the mouth, but Karl Nováček cheered us up again. He was a typical Viennese, a real card who was always in good spirits and would keep up a running commentary in broad dialect on whatever happened to be going on. Nor did he let us down on this occasion.

'Blow me if you lads doesn't look like Hitler after Stalingrad,' he said. 'Why, it'll be a walk-over – you'll see. Only a couple of days, I tell yer, and the Ivans'll be in Vienna and the Yanks in Salzburg. An' a month from now, when we all of us meets at the Tivoli, we'll lay down comfortable-like under a tree and get ourselves pissed on Heuriger.' He nudged my shoulder amicably. 'So long, me old chum. Only a few weeks from now we'll be slapping each other on the back.' Those were the last words I heard Novaček speak, nor did I ever see him again. A month later I was standing at his graveside in the cemetery at Kematen.

I mingled with the morning crowd that was leaving Milan station and, an hour or two later, at Pietro's home in Cernobbio, met the rest of our little caravanserai consisting of Franz Otting, Nam Brauer de Beaufort and her eight cabin trunks. I don't know how Nam had got her boxes up to Cernobbio, but I know only too well how, with the sweat of our brows, we lugged them as far as the frontier, heaved them over the barbed wire fence and lifted Nam after them. Trunks and all, we were safely in Switzerland, and that was the end of the Goldoni Station.

A fortnight later I again went south via the St Gotthard, and this time Renata Faccincani went with me. Much had changed during those few days. The Americans and British had begun their long-awaited big push and had broken through the German defences on the northern slopes of the Apennines. Bologna had fallen. In Piedmont, Lombardy and Venetia an insurrection had broken out against Mussolini's tottering Salò Republic. In Milan, too, it was only a matter of days before the Fascist regime, now wholly dependent on German bayonets, was swept away.

So it behoved us to hurry if we were to get to our friends in time to save them. At my request some of them had worked with the Germans and also with the Fascist authorities in order to obtain information we could use for sabotage purposes. When Vienna was liberated they would be in grave danger of being arrested as 'collaborators', if not killed outright. Moreover, I was extremely anxious to anticipate the looters at the Milan headquarters of the Security Service and of the Abwehr, where I hoped to lay my hands on important documents including, perhaps, the mysterious 'Mob Plan' for the defence of the 'Alpine Redoubt'.

At Lugano station Renata and I were met by a Swiss acquaintance of ours, an officer of the Bellinzona Military District, who strongly advised us against crossing the frontier at Sagno since the Italian side of Monte Bisbino was the scene of a running battle between Fascist troops and groups of partisans, who had already gained control of part of the shores of Lake Como. He therefore drove us to Ponte Chiasso instead, and here we came to a temporary halt.

It was the evening of 26 April. The frontier was closed and the Swiss police had strict orders to allow no one across. On the Italian side, Carabinieri of the Repubblica Sociale were still on duty. Bursts of machine-gun fire could be heard coming from the houses on the outskirts of Chiasso, while not far away a huge cloud of smoke was rising above Como. Exhausted Swiss refugees from Milan told me about their ordeal. To get from Milan to Chiasso, a distance of less than fifty kilometres, had taken them the entire day. The main road, they said, was still under German control but partisans were already in action near Como.

As darkness fell, the southern horizon became dotted with lights and I suddenly realized that in Italy no one was bothering any more about the blackout. We were sitting in the dining-room of the frontier restaurant, the back windows of which looked out onto the Italian section of the road. Suddenly, from the check post outside the building, we heard a sound of shouting. A Swiss officer rushed into the room exclaiming: 'Mussolini's out there! He's trying to get into Switzerland!' We, of course, all wanted to go and have a look, but were asked by the Swiss police to stay where we were. So we went across to the windows, from which we watched, fascinated, this last manifestation of Fascism. Half a dozen men were standing in front of the barrier gesticulating excitedly as they harangued the Swiss officials. Behind them was a convoy consisting of several large, sombre motor cars and a truckload or two of Fascist militia. A Swiss customs officer intimated to me in a whisper that the second car contained Benito Mussolini and Clara Petacci, who were seeking asylum in Switzerland. Needless to say, we couldn't ascertain who the occupants of those cars really were – whether the dictator and his mistress or, maybe, his wife Rachele with her younger children. At all events, the vehicles in the convoy soon restarted their engines, reversed and drove off into the night in the direction from which they had come. It was an eerie moment and at the same time one of triumph for Renata and myself; within a matter of hours the picture had changed beyond recognition. The hunters of yesterday had become the hunted of today.

A large party of us sat up until late into the night, our numbers swollen by new arrivals, mostly Italians wanting to return home, but not allowed across the frontier. Soon the dining-room began to resemble an army encampment. Renata brought to our table a handsome-looking middle-aged man, Count Gaetano Sforza, brother of the Italian statesman. He asked whether we might be able to help him get to Milan. Since I intended to make use of my Allied papers to requisition a car in Chiasso or Como and get through early next morning, I told him we should be glad to give him a lift.

Some time later that night we learned that the Carabinieri had withdrawn from the Italian side of the frontier and that partisans of the Comitato di Liberazione Nazionale Alta Italia had taken over their duties. After snatching a few hours' sleep on benches in the restaurant, we succeeded, with the help of our Swiss Army friend, in getting permission to leave the country and, in the sunshine of a brilliant spring morning, we crossed the frontier legally for the first time in years.

With considerable zest, the Italian partisans applied the stamp of Allied HQ to my papers and in no time at all we found ourselves in possession of a magnificent Fiat, hitherto the property of the chief of the Italian frontier police in Chiasso. Not many minutes later, however, this car very nearly put a sudden end to our triumphal progress. For, as we drove at a spanking pace into Como, we were forced to pull up abruptly in front of a barricade, whereupon some wildlooking individuals, presumably partisans, began taking pot shots at us. They had recognized the car and assumed us to be fleeing Fascist police. Only just in time, Renata succeeded in rectifying this dreadful mistake. By a happy piece of foresight I had brought my American uniform along in my bag and this, together with an American flag improvised by Renata, was to be the saving of us more than once that day.

Our next stop was the Comitato di Liberazione in Como. We joined them in the consumption of large quantities of grappa and obtained an impressive *permesso*, this time adorned with an Italian stamp. Then we set off again at top speed, using minor roads that ran parallel to the autostrada so that all day we were able to observe the eerie spectacle of the German Wehrmacht in retreat.

Towards evening our stately Fiat, now almost at its last gasp, drew up outside the door of 19 Via Goldoni. With tears streaming down his face, old Siro rushed up to Renata, kissed her hands and then embraced me: 'Signorino! Signorino!' he exclaimed, 'So you're alive, too!' Suddenly, almost within minutes, all our friends had appeared, and everyone, including Mario and Carlo, was drinking everyone else's health. But I soon left the scene of festivity and drove to the headquarters of the German Security Service. The place was deserted except for a lone Italian policeman who saluted me as amiably as, no doubt, he had saluted the ss that very morning. I went up onto the first floor and through several offices before reaching that of the Controller of ss and Police. After trying for months, Nam Brauer had ultimately gained access to this man's office and had succeeded in obtaining all the details of the Security Service's filing system. Thus, despite the fact that I had never been there before, I knew exactly where to look for the documents I wanted. But I had arrived too late, the ss had had time to arrange for the removal of their papers, and the huge filing cabinets were empty. Twenty minutes later, in the similarly abandoned offices at Station Zeno, I was to have better luck. The Abwehr, which had so generously, if unwittingly, provided me with a disguise over the past few months, had again turned up trumps: we found the plans for which we were looking.

In Milan, one event succeeded another with bewildering rapidity, often with the most incongruous results. For instance, not only did I issue safe-conducts to those who had been our loyal helpers in time of danger, but was also instrumental in saving from lynch law no less a man than Marshal Graziani, Commander-in-Chief of Mussolini's army. I had happened to run into a swashbuckling American captain by the name of Laguardia, the only other oss officer besides myself to have succeeded in reaching Milan. The branch he belonged to was immediately evident from his uniform, which was as motley as my own. He begged me to help him frustrate the intentions of some five thousand partisans who proposed to deprive him of his proudest war trophy by hanging Graziani from the nearest tree. By keeping the partisans talking the pair of us managed to prevent them carrying out their revenge until the marshal could be taken into proper custody. Indeed, the commander of the Italian Liberation Army, General Cadorna, came in person to take him away.

With my breakfast next morning Siro brought the news that Mussolini and Clara Petacci had been strung up in the Piazzale Loretto. It was Sunday, 29 April 1945. After being refused asylum by the Swiss, the Duce and what remained of his suite had driven north along the shore of Lake Como in the hope of taking refuge in Valtellina until such time as he could honourably surrender to the Allies. But deserted by his Blackshirts, he was virtually alone. For a time he had enjoyed the protection of a Wehrmacht convoy which allowed him to travel in one of its trucks. But he had been discovered and taken prisoner by partisans. A day later he and his mistress, who had been following him, were shot and their corpses brought to Milan. Together with the bodies of various other executed Fascist leaders, they were strung up in the same square in which fifteen partisans had been executed in Mussolini's day.

Inexorably carried along to the Piazzale Loretto by a crowd several thousand strong, Renata and I eventually found ourselves beside the petrol station from whose cross-beams Mussolini and Petacci were suspended by the heels. Today I still recall with amazement the complete impassiveness with which I viewed this man who had so long been the object of my hostility. There he hung, ignominiously upside down – Benito Mussolini, Duce d'Italia, who had set out to create a second Roman empire. I was experiencing the last act of a dream of Shakespearian magnitude.

15

Euphoria and Disenchantment

Euphoria first set in at Quercinella. It was 2 May. The day before at Caserta I had run into difficulties and the world had seemed full of gloom. The Western Allies refused to recognize the Austrian government formed under Dr Karl Renner on 27 April, after the liberation of Vienna. As early as the 28th we, the representatives of the POEN abroad, had attempted to get in touch with that government and had finally succeeded in doing so by a circuitous route. But the Western Allies were not very happy about what seemed to them an ad hoc arrangement, believing – not, perhaps, without reason – that the Russians had set up the Renner government in order to present them with a *fait accompli*. The western powers did not wish to lay themselves open to surprises of this kind, having already experienced similar misadventures with allegedly democratic, but in fact communist-controlled, governments in Hungary, Roumania, Bulgaria and Poland. I had discussed the matter at considerable length in Caserta with John Erhardt, the new political adviser to the American High Commissioner, and Grey, the latter's deputy. The disscusions were also attended by General Flory, Clark's military deputy designate on the Allied Council for Occupied Austria. It was extremely difficult to convince these gentlemen that Renner and his government were preferable to no government at all. Erhardt seemed more prepared than anyone else to acknowledge that Renner was a reasonable man. Some of the other Americans, on the other hand, still remembered his pro-Hitler declaration of April 1938. I tried to make them understand that Renner had been under great pressure at that time and that his action had been prompted by the hope of keeping his friends in the Social Democratic Party out of Hitler's clutches.

The odds were against me, however, for, apart from anything else, it had already been agreed in London, where the Allied Commission for Austria had been sitting for over a year, that for the time being only local administrative bodies were to be set up in Austria, while the question of a central administration should be deferred until later. From the Austrian standpoint the matter necessarily looked somewhat different, for it was, of course, in our interest to have a central administration. Even to those of us who were in the West, it seemed that the majority in Renner's government was at least weighted in favour of western democracy, despite the fact that two of its important portfolios were held by Communists – a view I vainly endeavoured to put across. But the Americans appeared to be in no hurry at all to send a liaison mission to Vienna by air and, as my own chances of getting there dwindled, I felt correspondingly less inclined to spend any more time hanging about in Caserta.

On the afternoon of 2 May, having finally lost all patience, I went to Howard Chapin, head of oss for Austria, and suggested we investigate some other way of getting there. He looked at me in surprise and asked me to enlarge, whereupon I replied that it must surely be possible to get through northern Italy by jeep and enter Austria as it were by the back door. For the German armies south of the Brenner had, after all, already capitulated, even if they hadn't yet been disarmed.

What I had obviously forgotten, Chapin objected, was that the Wehrmacht had capitulated only in the area of Army Group South-West, but whether South Tyrol came under Army Group South-West, no one really knew. North of the Brenner, if not actually in Trento, the Germans were still in control, nor was there any means of telling how soon it would be possible to break down German resistance in the heartlands of the Alpine fortress, namely the Tyrol, the Vorarlberg, Salzburg, Carinthia and southern Bavaria. In an attempt to talk Chapin round I told him that, if he were to spend much longer sitting in Caserta, the American Seventh Army, whose armoured spearheads had already reached the neighbourhood of Garmisch-Partenkirchen and Mittelwald, would get to Innsbruck before the Fifth Army and thus steal a march on the oss units destined for Austria.

Though he thought it impossible to reach the Tyrol by road, Chapin was prepared to let me have a go. To speed up my journey as far as Quercinella, the advance headquarters of oss outside Leghorn, he arranged for me to be flown there, after which, he said, it would be up to me to convince Lieutenant Commander Alfred Ulmer, his deputy, that my bold scheme was not only practicable but sensible. As I went out after saying goodbye, Chapin remarked jovially, 'Good luck! See you in Vienna.'

It was at Quercinella, then, that euphoria first set in. I had managed to convince Al Ulmer of the feasibility of the proposed expedition to Innsbruck, and we had got together a smallish team that would just fit into a couple of jeeps. It consisted of Al Ulmer himself, Captain Jim Hudson, Lieutenant Al Harris, two staff sergeants as drivers and, of course, myself, the originator of the plan. Each jeep carried a light machine-gun and flew a large American flag fore and aft. We had stocked up with enough food to last us six days, and cigarettes and chocolate to distribute on the way, the latter destined mainly for children. Last but not least, I had also stowed in one of the jeeps a dozen or so small and medium-sized Austrian flags drawn from oss parachutists' store.

It was almost evening when we left, and by midnight we had reached the Po; there we had to spend two or three hours in a long file of vehicles before we were able to cross the pontoon bridge north of Ferrara built by the us Army only the day before. Then we drove on until, in the early hours of the morning, we reached the outskirts of Verona. This brought us to to a temporary halt because, by the terms of the armistice, the American Army was to occupy northern Italy in accordance with a carefully predetermined timetable, and as yet Verona did not form part of the occupied zone. We snatched a few hours' sleep and, circumventing the American check points on the main road to Verona, finally entered the town from the east, along the road leading from Venice via Padua and Verona to Brescia and Milan.

Verona was cramful of German soldiers, entire divisions being apparently held up there by the terms of the armistice prohibiting any further troop movements in a northerly direction, terms which Wehrmacht patrols were endeavouring to enforce. We and our jeeps, with the big American flags flying from radiators and roofs, were stared at in astonishment and nowhere did we experience any difficulty in getting through. My plan appeared to be working. So we drove through Rovereto to Trento, where we came upon a sizeable German HQ. Prompted by curiosity Ulmer decided to stop, whereupon we discovered it to be the headquarters of no less a person than the Chief of Staff of Army Group C. We spent some time there, chatting to half a dozen German generals, they in their field grey and we in our American khaki uniforms. It was for me an experience of quite a new kind.

Beyond Trento things became more difficult. The roads were jammed and it took us five hours to reach Salurn – a great moment for me. For at Salurn, German is spoken and Salurn is in the Tyrol – I was home! We decided to spend the night at a roadside inn. Like every other house along the highway from Italy to Germany, it was full to overflowing with German troops. We sought out the mayor of the little place – an Italian, as was only to be expected after twenty years of Fascist rule – and asked him to see that we were given rooms. Within five minutes an entire floor had been put at our disposal. Acting as interpreter, I thanked the mayor and asked him if food could be provided. He replied that the parish of Salurn would be only too happy to welcome us as their guests at dinner that night. I passed this on to Ulmer, who agreed. Barely half an hour later we sat down to a tremendous banquet, thanks to the efforts of the mayor.

At this juncture Waschlapski, who had for many months past been kicking against the pricks, succeeded in getting the better of me. For I suddenly realized that the worthy mayor – or, maybe, town clerk – did not speak a word of English, while Al Ulmer and his Americans knew virtually no Italian. And Waschlapski's chance came when the mayor asked the question I had long been waiting for – namely, what had brought us there.

With an innocent air I said: 'We belong to the American mission that has to determine the frontier at this point.'

The Italian official looked at me curiously. 'What frontier?' he said.

'The new frontier between Austria and Italy, of course.'

'New frontier? What new frontier?' he asked, utterly bemused.

'You know the Salurn Defile, just south of here?' I replied. 'That's where the linguistic boundary is, between Italian-speaking and German-speaking Tyrol, and where we intend to draw the new line.'

So great was the poor mayor's alarm that he almost fell off his chair. Needless to say he had taken me for an American and believed my every word. Nevertheless, he found this information difficult to credit.

'Are you sure,' he repeated, 'that the frontier will be drawn here?'

'I'll show you,' I said and led him down into the little square outside the inn where our jeeps were parked. The two staff sergeants were lounging about smoking and making presents of chewing-gum and chocolate to a crowd of round-eyed children who were gazing admiringly at them and their jeeps. From under the hood of one of the vehicles I took out some of the red, white and red flags I had tucked away at the last moment in Quercinella, and showed them to the mayor.

'You see? These are the flags with which we shall mark out the frontier tomorrow. Do you believe me now?'

Suddenly the mayor seemed exceedingly anxious to take his leave of us, nor did we see him again that night. Next morning we rose early, at about five o'clock, for we had a long and probably difficult journey ahead of us. The weather was glorious – blue sky and bright sunshine. As we were about to climb into our jeeps, the mayor appeared, wearing a dark suit and looking very down in the mouth. He had come to take his leave of me, the only one of the party who spoke Italian. But when I saw him standing dejectedly in his dark suit donned especially for the benefit of the American gentlemen, I could not help feeling sorry for him and decided not to let Waschlapski get away with his prank.

Taking the mayor on one side, I therefore told him we had thought the matter over and had decided it might be better to leave the frontier as it was for the time being, so there was no need for him to worry. Immediately his face lit up and, almost embracing me, he said that his wife had already begun to pack, for who could tell what might not have happened? They might have had to leave the place. It came to me then that even the best of jokes may have the most devastating effect. But all's well that ends well and his happiness had now been restored. We got into our jeeps and roared away, while the smiling mayor of Salurn, a small and steadily diminishing figure, stood waving after us.

We stopped at Bolzano, the centre of which, we noticed, had been largely destroyed, and then drove on past endless files of German troops towards Brixen and the Brenner. Every now and again a soldier would wave, but for the most part they completely ignored us, nor did we hear a single word of abuse. At Sterzing the Germans had set up a big road block manned by a large detachment of German military police. If only they knew, I thought, just who it was they were talking to, this chap in American uniform, if only they knew that he figured on their wanted list and that it was their duty to place him under arrest. But then I reflected that things were not at all what they used to be, nor would it now occur to the military police to arrest anyone or hand him over to his executioners.

This, we were told, was the point at which the jurisdiction of Army Group C South-West ended. Up on the Brenner there were German mountain troops and units, presumably belonging to the ss-Reichsführer Division which, being under the command of Army Group Kesselring, were not affected by the armistice. The military police, who belonged to Army Group South-West and had therefore ceased to regard themselves as belligerents, told us that they had heard gunfire that morning from the direction of the Brenner. Though a few trucks containing Italian officers and men had come down from the pass during the day, all traffic, it seemed, had now ceased. They had strict orders not to let anyone through, either from Italy into Germany or vice-versa. We therefore drove on through Gossensass and up the Brenner.

At the top of the pass all seemed quiet. A few civilians and customs men were standing around, but no German soldiers, armed or otherwise. Between the Brenner and Matrei all was quiet and nothing was to be seen except for one or two over-turned trucks and a couple of abandoned German tanks. It was Friday 4 May 1945, a glorious spring day of the kind one only gets in the Alps. Suddenly it dawned on me that I was at home again in a country that could once more be called by its proper name. As we were now entering Austria, I asked Al to pull up for a moment and fixed two red, white and red flags to each of the jeeps, and thus we drove down the Great Brenner Road flying both the American and the Austrian colours.

When we entered into the straight before Matrei I saw, flying proudly from the church tower alongside the Austrian flag, the red and white flag of the Tyrol. I gave Ulmer an exuberant punch on the arm and we drove on into Matrei. There we found policemen in German uniform but wearing red, white and red brassards. They came up to our jeep, saluted politely and addressed us in tortured English until told by me in German that there was no need for them to do so. Then, more fluently, they went on to say that the Nazis had been thrown out and that a Tyrolese Land government had once more been set up at Innsbruck – or as one of them put it, 'Austria has again been proclaimed there' – led by a man called Gruber. But they warned us to be careful, for further down at Schönberg there were still some German tanks belonging to the SS mountain warfare school at Fulpmes; the road to Innsbruck was blocked, no one could drive along it, and that was why we had encountered no traffic. We considered what we had better do. The two policemen advised us to take the old Brenner Road, a famous Roman road along which salt used to be conveyed from Hall in the Tyrol to Italy as much as two thousand years ago. At Matrei it branches off the main Brenner Road, skirts the flank of the Patscherkofel and takes one to Innsbruck via Patsch and Igls. We might try that route, they said, for there were no SS thereabouts. We thanked them profusely and left. It was about two in the afternoon.

Half an hour later we reached Innsbruck. In every street the houses were flying red, white and red flags and sometimes also white ones. In the Maria-Theresien-Strasse we encountered armed parties of resistance men wearing red, white and red brassards and, in the Landhaus, found many familiar faces. Everyone seemed to be there – Ötztal partisans and friends from 05 as well as a mass of strangers from inside and outside the city.

Excitedly they told me that two days ago the Nazis and Germans had been thrown out and that Karl Gruber and his men had taken over the Landhaus. I went upstairs to introduce myself to the new Land Governor, about whom I had heard so much, first as leader of a resistance group in Berlin and then as head of the Innsbruck activists. I was welcomed by a tall, fair-haired man with broad, honest features. He, for his part, had already heard of me and was not a little surprised to see me turn up all of a sudden in American uniform.

He was just then holding a council of war with the commanders of his military resistance groups and representatives of the civilian resistance. The senior officer of the Tyrolese arm of 05 was Major Werner Heine, a holder of the Knight's Cross. With him were the officers who, in the past few days, had led their men in repeated attacks on Innsbruck barracks, which they had finally captured; they had also taken prisoner the generals congregated on the Hungerburg. The civilians present at this conference included the POEN representative in the Innsbruck region. After introducing me to the people I did not know, Gruber invited me to join in the discussion.

'We can do with your services,' he said, adding with a laugh, 'we may have got rid of the SS and all but a few remnants of the German army, but instead we're now landed with the Americans, who seem to be under the illusion that they're in Stuttgart.'

He was obviously relieved to have at his side American officers who knew their way about in the Tyrol and would be able to clear up some of the many misunderstandings that had arisen through the arrival in the city of US troops in the form of the Seventh Army, whose original destination had been Stuttgart and who had not yet learnt to distinguish between Austrians and Württembergers.

Suddenly the door opened and in came an American officer in a colourful uniform largely of his own devising. It was Freddy Mayer, our liaison officer from the Ötztal. We greeted each other ecstatically, so delighted were we to find one another alive. Almost my first question was to ask whether he had seen Lieutenant Horneck. 'Joe?' Freddy replied. 'Why, sure. We were together in Reichenau concentration camp not far from here, and we also broke out together. He's down at the Dollinger Inn by the river and Helmut Heuberger'll be there too, I guess.'

I thanked him and hurried down into the street. There I found my American friends, sitting where I had left them in the two jeeps. They had a somewhat forlorn and abandoned air which cut me to the quick. After all, they had brought me to the Tyrol at the cost of enormous effort and at great risk to themselves, and then what did I go and do but leave them waiting a whole hour for me in their jeeps. I apologized repeatedly and profusely, until finally Al said with a grin: 'You don't have to go on apologizing, Jerry. After all, it's your country and you've just got it back. Forget about us; we're just extras here.' And so saying, he slapped me on the back.

They were typical young American officers, cheerful and full of enthusiasm. Full, too, of fellow-feeling for their no less youthful friend who was thrilled to death, as they say in the States if not in Vienna, at getting his country back. 'What shall we do now?' they said. 'Let's celebrate!' I told them that Joe was staying only a few blocks away. 'Come on!' Al shouted, 'we'll go find Joe!' And we jumped into the jeeps and drove hell for leather down the Maria-Theresien-Strasse and across the bridge to the Dollinger Inn. As we drew up with a screech of brakes we saw a figure on the balcony just above us. The next moment it was standing at our side for, on catching sight of us, Joe had simply jumped down onto the pavement. Not that he thought twice of it, being a trained parachutist – far better trained than I. So there he was, in our midst. We flung our arms round each other's shoulders, delirious with joy. Joe was still alive, we were still alive, everything was all right. I asked after Karl Nováček.

Joe looked me straight in the face. 'Karl was killed on the Kematener Alm on the day they came to get us,' he said. 'For half an hour we gave them as good as we got, but then our ammunition began to run out and I told the fellows – our partisan trainees – to run for it; we'd be able to hold off the ss for another ten minutes. They were fine fellows and at first refused to go, but eventually they did. We used up the rest of our ammunition and the ss kept coming on. Karl and I still had a couple of hand grenades; we threw them and then we too turned and ran. We were going well and had almost reached the top of the ridge, behind which we could have taken cover, when Karl was hit. They had opened up with a machine-gun and he must have stopped a whole burst. He dropped in his tracks. I turned back and knelt beside him but it was already too late. He died almost at once. His eyes were still open and his lips were moving, but he couldn't get a word out. I was still holding him when the first of the ss men arrived and grabbed me. Then they took me down to the Gestapo in Innsbruck and from there to Reichenau.'

Al Ulmer had fetched a bottle of whisky from the jeep and we drank to those of us who were still alive and to those who were alive no longer, notably Karl Novaček. Then we went upstairs with Joe and were given rooms, for the whole of the Dollinger had been placed at his disposal. Next he formally presented himself to Al as Resident Agent, 2677th oss Regiment, Dollinger Special Detachment, Innsbruck, and everyone burst out laughing. All of a sudden the tension was broken and a grand celebration began. Our sense of release spread to all those who came to join in the fun, amongst them Helmut Heuberger and, later that evening, Karl Gruber, the brand new regional governor. All that night we sat drinking together and exchanging dreams. Our sense of euphoria was tremendous. After seven years we had a country of our own once more; Austria had risen out of the ashes and we were no longer second, third or fourth rate human beings but just as good as the next man. Those, however, who had enslaved and spurned us throughout those seven years were vanished and gone – superannuated party members, supermen on the scrapheap.

All in all, it seemed scarcely conceivable, and months would go by before I could even begin to take everything in. Here I was at Innsbruck in Austria, sitting in the Dollinger with my friends, and we – they and I – were free men. We could go out into the street and look everyone in the eye, without having to show our papers or worry about saying Austria instead of Ostmark; nor would we ever again have to utter the words 'Heil Hitler'. Not having to say 'Heil Hitler', not having to raise one's arm in the grotesque German salute like a puppet on a string – the fact that all such indignities were a thing of the past was almost inconceivable.

And, when one looks back on it today, more than thirty years later, the whole thing seems no less inconceivable than it did then, only in the opposite sense. Today it seems inconceivable that there should ever have been a time when grown men marched about with their arms raised and greeted each other with the words 'Heil Hitler'. Nowadays such a thing is seen only in the cinema, perhaps in a Charlie Chaplin film.

But thirty-five years ago it was regarded as a matter of course, and everyone thought it perfectly normal. If, however, one views the matter in this light and reflects that, admittedly under different auspices, much the same thing is still happening today in East Berlin and Prague, in Tirana and Peking it may be easier to understand why the notion that the ghost had not been laid once and for all should have seemed even more inconceivable to us way back in May 1945.

The following day Joe and I drove out to Kematen and laid some flowers on the little mound of earth beneath which Nováček lay. On our way back we stopped at Igls and went to the aerial cableway which, as it turned out, was closed. In return, however, for a packet of Lucky Strike we induced the attendant to let us ride in solitary splendour to the top of the Patscherkofel. There we sat in the spring sunshine, looking down on Innsbruck and the surrounding mountains, their summits still clad in snow, and thought about the future.

'You know,' Joe said, 'what I'd like is a professorship at Vienna University.' He had read history at Innsbruck and taken his doctor's degree there before going as a teacher to America and, later, enlisting in the us army. Now he wished to come home. 'No difficulty about that,' I said. 'You'll be starting work in October.'

Joe Horneck did not start work, either in October or in November or, for that matter, at any other time. Even when he had long since resumed the name of Josef Franckenstein, of Hall in the Tyrol, D. Phil. of Innsbruck University, the professorship continued to elude him. Why? Joe was not a member of any party or association that might have given him a leg-up. He knew neither the Communist Minister of Education nor the member of the Austrian People's Party who succeeded him, nor did he know the Socialist Minister of the Interior – in fact, he knew absolutely no one. He was just another Austrian who, having spent seven years fighting for his homeland, sought to do what his studies had qualified him to do. Whereupon innumerable problems and difficulties arose. He was an American citizen, they told him; the process of renaturalization alone would take many years and 'who knows what might not happen in the meantime' – in short, they prevaricated so long that he gave up.

He went back to America, taught at various universities in

the Middle West and was eventually sent to Japan as cultural attaché by the State Department. On his return he again taught for a while, this time in California, before dying of a broken heart, a victim, one might almost say, of his own euphoria. Or, alternatively, a naive idiot. For if, in 1945 – preferably on 6 May when the first party offices reopened – he had instantly joined one of the big parties, if he had trotted obediently at the heels of some panjandrum, then everything would have turned out differently.

But why make an exception for the likes of him? Why, for that matter, did he leave the country? Out of self-importance, no doubt – or maybe this fellow Franckenstein is a Jew after all, or else there must have been something fishy about him. Respectable folk stayed put. And then back he comes in American uniform and gives himself airs – we'll soon show him where he gets off! Our sort don't carry on like that.

Even by the summer of 1945, it was not rare to hear such words, spoken behind the hand, it is true, and as often as not by men who were already well on their way to reoccupying those seats from which they had at some time been unceremoniously evicted.

Up on the Patscherkofel, carried away as we were by a feeling of euphoria, we, of course, knew nothing of all this. We saw a new, modern, democratic Austria arising out of the ruins of tyranny into the light of a new day, of another world. Up on our mountain top we were happy and full of plans, like thousands of others all over the country, from Vienna to Innsbruck. People old and young, people from the resistance, people home from the war, from POW camps, from prisons and concentration camps, all jubilant at having lived to see their country set free and at peace, and eager to build up everything anew. Many were more successful in the execution of their plans than Joe Horneck, who, beneath a tough and resolute exterior, concealed great sensitivity.

16

Home-Coming

The sense of euphoria engendered by the liberation had not yet died down before I was summoned to an interview with the new Regional Governor of the Tyrol, Karl Gruber, at the Innsbruck Landhaus. Only a few days before it had been occupied by his predecessor, Gauleiter Hofer, Reich Governor and Reich Defence Commissar of the Tyrol by the grace of the late Führer. It is no exaggeration to say that Gruber had captured the building in person. At the head of a group of resistance fighters he had sallied forth from his headquarters in the nearby Hotel Stadt München – ostensibly the temporary premises of a bombed-out Berlin electrical firm – and taken the Landhaus by storm. A few hours later he had been elected Land Governor by the executive committee of 05's Tyrolese arm. The Germans had withdrawn to the Lower Inn valley, but were still holding the Zirler Berg in anticipation of an attack by the armoured spearhead of the American Seventh Army, then at Scharnitz.

Karl Gruber and his comrades-in-arms will go down in history as the men who, several days before the arrival of the Allied armies, liberated the city of Innsbruck and the heartland of the Tyrol from the tyranny of the Third Reich, disarmed the German troops and set up an independent Austrian administration. Nothing then remained for the local American commander to do but give the new Tyrolese Land Government his blessing. This is what we had hoped would happen in Vienna and the other Austrian provinces, but Innsbruck was the only place where the operation was a hundred per cent successful.

My first job, which I owed almost entirely to my American

uniform, was that of head of the Security Department for the Tyrol and, as such, my most notable achievement was the capture of the former governor of Vienna, Baldur von Schirach. I later visited the man in his cell and, taking me for an American, he began a tear-jerking recital of the efforts he had made to save the Viennese Jews, whereupon I cut him short, remarking that in that case I was surprised never to have heard a word of all this while I was myself a prisoner in the concentration camps where those unfortunate people were incarcerated. At the end of the week I gladly resigned from this post in favour of a more experienced man, being entrusted instead with the task of organizing food supplies.

My new job entailed a fair amount of travelling, itself a major problem due to the almost total dislocation of communications at that time. Not only was it virtually impossible to get from Austria to Italy, Switzerland or Germany, it was also exceedingly difficult to travel from the Tyrol to Vienna or even to Salzburg. At the cost of a great deal of time and trouble you might, if you were lucky, obtain a rail permit. Then, having battled for a seat, you would be held up at Hochfilzen on the zonal demarcation line for some three or four hours until the French had worked their way through the train. The next check came at Leogang, this time carried out by the Americans and lasting anything up to three hours, after which the train was allowed to proceed, but only for a few kilometres, for at Saalfelden they had, for some incomprehensible reason, introduced another check, which also entailed the compulsory delousing of all passengers. Then, if you were lucky, you would get through to Salzburg, where you would be kept waiting a mere hour or two. And so it went on, with innumerable delays and frustrations until you came to the River Enns. Here the American check was relatively innocuous and lasted no more than one and a half hours but, as the train clanked slowly across the bridge and came to a halt on the other side, annoyance gave way to trepidation, for it was now the Russians' turn. All documents were minutely examined and every passenger's identity card checked to ensure that it had the correct number of stamps – eleven in all, three of them Russian. In the course of this examination, which might take anything up to five hours, perhaps ten per cent of the travellers would be ordered off the train because of some irregularity in their papers and, if they were unlucky, placed under arrest. Not a few of them ended up in Siberia.

So it could take as much as twenty-four hours to travel from Innsbruck to Vienna by the so-called Arlberg Express, which in any case was not brought into service until September 1945. Before that date travel of any kind was virtually impossible, especially if it meant crossing the demarcation lines between the various occupied zones. Nor, during the early days, was there any postal or telephone communications between those zones. Thus we in Innsbruck were unable to find out what had happened to our parents, or even whether they had survived. But towards the end of May a messenger did at last succeed in making his way to the Tyrol by a laborious cross-country trek which involved swimming the Enns to avoid the Russian check-point. On reaching Innsbruck he reported to Herr Gruber at the Landhaus and it was there that Otto and I were introduced to him. It was, for us, a momentous occasion. Not only was he the bearer of the first reliable information about our parents' survival, but he had actually brought us letters from them. Hitherto we had had good reason to fear that, like so many others, they had been shot during the death-march of the political prisoners from the Liesl to the infamous concentration camp in the quarries at Mauthausen. Now, however, we learnt that some five hundred prisoners had not been removed from the prison because of an outbreak of typhoid in their wing and the consequent fear on the part of the authorities that the infection might spread. Amongst those five hundred were my mother and father, who were to be released within a day of each other, on the 5 and 6 April respectively. They found the house in the Osterleitengasse badly damaged by bombs, but still inhabited by our eighty-three-year-old grandmother, who had remained there throughout and gallantly kept marauders at bay.

All this news increased my determination to get to Vienna at the earliest opportunity. But the matter was complicated by the fact that I was still a member of the American army, which would not be moving into Vienna until September. That was far too long to wait and I therefore decided to resign my commission. oss, by now removed from Innsbruck to Zell am See, staged a gigantic farewell party which went on for three whole days and nights and was attended by friends from places as

far afield as Paris, Rome and Caserta. To celebrate the occasion a prototype amphibious Porsche, evacuated by its
makers to the safety of Zell am See, was scuttled in the middle
of the lake. We danced on a floating pontoon and drank
champagne, two crates of which had been flown in from Paris
on the orders of the head of OSS Austria. In a long farewell
speech, my CO, Howard Chapin, revealed that General Mark
Clark had recommended me for the award of the Medal of
Freedom, a high honour accorded, I believe, to only two
other Austrians, one of them my comrade-in-arms Ernst Lemberger. I was deeply moved by all this and not a little depressed
at the thought of leaving so many good friends and colleagues.
All the same, I was glad to put aside the uniform of an army
which, however friendly, was nevertheless that of a foreign
power. For I was, when all was said and done, an Austrian,
not an American, and tasks of a different kind now awaited
me.

The reconstruction of the Tyrol had been proceeding apace
under the governorship of Dr Gruber, who had shown himself
fully capable of coping, first with the American, and then with
the French, occupying power. He now offered me the post of
secretary and personal assistant, which I readily accepted.
Shortly afterwards he was appointed Foreign Minister in Dr
Renner's provisional government and this enabled me to return to Vienna in the summer of 1945.

In fact I drove there with my brother Otto in an ancient car
that had been commandeered from a Tyrolese Nazi. We had
loaded the boot with food and other things calculated to make
life easier for our parents. On the advice of a friend we also
took the precaution of getting our documents stamped by a
species of Russian liaison officer who had recently installed
himself in the Landhaus in Linz. In this way we got through
all the various check-points without serious difficulty and, early
one afternoon, arrived in Vienna. The city looked shabbier
and more dilapidated and decayed than when I had last seen
it in February. There were few people about and even fewer
trams, while many of the roads were blocked with rubble or
pitted with craters. The place seemed to be in the grip of some
kind of paralysis and most of the shops were shut for there
was, as we soon discovered, little or nothing for them to sell.

As regards food, 'normal consumers' without money or contacts fared very badly. Their diet consisted mainly of peas and
beans, partly supplied by what was known as the 'Russian
Welfare', a Red Army organization that distributed food. Only
rye bread was obtainable and very little of that. There was
even a shortage of potatoes, hitherto plentiful. For months on
end there would be no butter or meat at all, and milk was
reserved for infants and nursing mothers. But in the black
market in the Resselpark you could get anything from bacon
to textiles and medicine, provided you were prepared to pay
the price. Barter was also practised – a piano, for instance,
might be taken in exchange for a pig. Supplies seemed to be
almost inexhaustible, a fact largely attributable to the looting
and wholesale theft that followed the precipitate flight from
Vienna of the Germans and the Austrian National Socialists.
Strangely enough, the perpetrators were the same people who,
as 'Nazi stalwarts', had once stripped the Jews of their belong-
ings but had in the meantime metamorphosed themselves into
Communists or 'resistance fighters'. They would often appear
on the doorsteps of politically incriminated persons in the
company of Russian soldiers who, if truth be told, were usually
somewhat better-behaved than their Austrian companions. In-
satiable though their appetite might be for watches and for
women, regardless of age, the 'Ivans' were, on the whole,
kindly disposed towards the hungry Viennese children, to whom
they liked to give food.

At last, leaving the shattered city behind us, we drove
along Döbling High Street, which looked much the same as
ever apart from a few gaps made by direct hits. But when
we turned into the Osterleitengasse we were shocked by the
appearance of our house. A bomb had demolished the upper part
of the roof and there was a gaping hole where our grandmother's
room used to be. The northern end of the building seemed to
be intact except for the windows, in which there was cardboard instead of glass. Suddenly one of these was thrown open,
we heard a cry and a moment later our parents appeared on
the doorstep. Flinging her arms round us as though she never
meant to let go again, mother kept repeating 'Otto, Fepolinski, Otto, Fepolinski!' But father, always averse to any display of emotion, turned his attention to our luggage with the

words: 'How about getting some of this stuff indoors? Otherwise the Russians'll snatch it away from under your noses.' Upstairs we embraced grandma and Nedica, who was now living in the Osterleitengasse. Then we sat down in the drawing-room and exchanged all our news.

It was only then that we noticed how small and frail our mother seemed to have become. Apart from her maltreatment by the Gestapo, she had had no proper food since May. But her dear face had not grown any older and was still the same kind, loving face that we had always known. Father, too, had lost weight and his hair had turned grey, for his time in prison and the months that followed had taken their toll. He had not been tortured like mother, but flogged so severely that his back was still raw. Towards evening he fetched up from a secret cache in the cellar two bottles of wine which he had been saving against our return. We drank to the better times in store and were happy and content because we were still alive, had come through the ordeal and, after seven years, were reunited in the Osterleitengasse, which, despite the many cracks in the walls and the absence of window-panes, was nevertheless habitable if not actually snug.

In her joy, my mother had almost forgotten about supper, but now proposed to warm up the potato 'stew' left over from lunch. Then she suddenly remembered the pile of food parcels we had brought with us. We all hurried into the kitchen to find that grandmama and Nedica had unpacked them and heaped up the contents on the kitchen table. Joyously my mother, cousin and grandmother set about preparing a meal fit to celebrate the return from the wars of two sons, one of whom, mindful of past admonitions, carefully kept his hands on top of the old, familiar dining-table.

And this brings us to the end of the tale of Fepolinski and Waschlapski's experiences, adventures and travels on the exploding star – an exploding star which, amongst so many other things, encompassed much of my mother's rich and rewarding philosophy of life. For in 1951, when she fell sick and died, Paula von Preradović was at work on a trilogy of novels based upon her own experiences and entitled *Pelagia on the Exploding Star*. It was to have been the account of a young woman's life amidst the confusion of a world in process of disintegration, change and ultimate reconstruction. The author did not live to bequeath Pelagia's story to future generations but, by and large, the tale of Fepolinski and Waschlapski, though told with far less grace and artistry, unfolded upon the same exploding star, and its protagonists were confronted by the same manifestations of a world in decay and in process of renewal. Now their adventurous journey was over – a journey across the magic rainbow of youth which ultimately led them back to their starting point, namely the drawing-room of the house in the Osterleitengasse. Like their predecessors, Little Hare Mandili and Jacob the Elephant, Fepolinski and Waschlapski should, perhaps, now be tidied away into one of the many small drawers in mother's old-fashioned writing table, to be taken out every now and again, dusted off and carefully replaced, so that the children of the Osterleitengasse need never go without a bedtime story. And, lying cosily in bed, clean and clad in white pyjamas, they will listen as mother recounts the tales of Yaromir the Monkey, Jacob the Elephant, Little Hare Mandili, and Fepolinski and Waschlapski from furthest Walachia.

Index